What is Marxism?

An Introduction to Marxist Theory

by Rob Sewell and Alan Woods

London

What Is Marxism?
An Introduction to Marxist Theory

What Is Marxism? by Rob Sewell and Alan Woods, supplemented by extracts of the works of Karl Marx, Frederick Engels, V I Lenin and Leon Trotsky.

Second edition published in July 2015. Copyright © Wellred Publications. All rights reserved.

Based on the first edition published in 2007. Extracts taken from *Marx and Engels' Collected Works*, *Lenin's Collected Works* and the Marxist Internet Archive.

Proofread by Adam Booth, Lee Singh Gill and Fred Weston.

Editing and layout by Wellred Books.

Cover design by Leonora Partington.

ISBN: 978 1 900 007 57 3

United Kingdom Distribution:

Wellred Books
PO Box 50525
London
E14 6WG

Email: books@wellredbooks.net

Wellred UK online Sales:
wellredbooks.net

United States Distribution:

Wellred Books
PO Box 1575
New York
NY 10013

Email: sales@wellredusa.com

Wellred U.S.A. online sales:
www.marxistbooks.com

Contents

Introduction

Preface to the First Edition

"Socialism, having become a science, demands the same treatment as any other science – it must be studied." (**Frederick Engels**)

We are repeatedly told, like some old gramophone record stuck in a groove, that Marxism is either irrelevant, or out-dated, or even dead. Yet, if that were true, why are so many books and articles churned out year-on-year attacking Marxism? Clearly the powers that be are rattled or indeed frightened by these "dead" ideas. This is because Marxism is far from dead. Marxism is, in fact, becoming more attractive in this epoch of instability, crisis, war and the ever-widening gulf between the classes. The old mole of revolution, to use Marx's phrase, is burrowing deep into the foundations of society.

In typical fashion, a recent critic, Niall Ferguson, Professor of Political and Financial History at Oxford, vents his spleen on Marxism by attacking Marx as a "washout" and a "class traitor", for siding with the working class instead of the bourgeoisie. Our learned Professor goes on to brand Marx as the advocate of a "socialist utopia [which] turned out to be a corrupt tyranny", presumably a reference to Stalinism, which had nothing in common with Marx or his teachings. Consumed with spite, he then goes on to criticise Marx's *Capital* as "long, verbose, abstruse" and ranking as one of the most "unreadable books of all time".

Another bourgeois critic, Dominic Lawson, recently peddled the old myth (yet again) that "Karl Marx's view was that we are all mere creatures of economic determinism. What we do and what we think have nothing to do with personal autonomy. We are simply cogs in a class-war machine." Such cheap misrepresentations and distortions are pumped out on a daily basis in an attempt to discredit Marxism. However, Marx was never a vulgar economic determinist, where every action is reduced to simple economics. This is a complete distortion.

As Engels explained:

> "According to the materialist conception of history the determining element in history is ultimately the production and reproduction in real life. More than this neither Marx nor I have ever asserted. If therefore somebody twists this into the statement that the economic element is the only determining one, he transforms it into a meaningless, abstract and absurd phrase."

Take note Mr. Lawson! Engels went on:

> "The economic situation is the basis, but the various elements of the superstructure – political forms of the class struggle and its consequences, constitutions established by the victorious class after a successful battle, etc – forms of law – and then even the reflexes of all these actual struggles in the brains of the combatants: political, legal, philosophical theories, religious ideas and their further development into systems of dogma – also exercise their influence upon the course of the historical struggles and in many cases preponderate in determining their form. There is an interaction of all these elements, in which, amid all the endless host of accidents (i.e. of things and events whose inner connection is so remote or so impossible to prove that we regard it as absent and can neglect it), the economic movement finally asserts itself as necessary." (*Engels to J. Bloch, 13 September 1890*).

Trotsky also answers this nonsense:

> "On the question as to how the economic 'base' determines the political, juridical, philosophical, artistic and so on 'superstructure' there is a rich Marxist literature. The opinion that economics presumably determines directly and immediately the creativeness of a composer or even the verdict of a judge, represents a hoary caracature of Marxism which the bourgeois professordom of all countries has circulated time out of end to mask their intellectual impotence." (*In Defence of Marxism*).

However, despite all the distortions and lies of our enemies, even these critics cannot help blurting out the truth once in a while. "Even so," says Professor Ferguson, "Marx's insights into capitalism can still illuminate... Marx got one thing right (!). Behind the bubbles and busts of the capitalist system there is a class struggle; and that class struggle is the key to modern politics." This is a bold admission from such a biased source. Normally, such ideas are strenously denied by all bourgeois apologists. Nevertheless, we should not get carried away, afterall, one swallow does not make a summer.

So what is this set of ideas that frightens the ruling class and its apologists so much? Put simply, Marxism, or Scientific Socialism, is the name given to the body of ideas first worked out by Karl Marx (1818-1883) and Friedrich Engels (1820-1895) more than 150 years ago. In essence, Marxism is a synthesis of the most advanced ideas at the time: English classical economics, German Hegelian philosophy and French socialism. In their totality, these ideas provide a fully worked-out theoretical basis for the struggle of the working class to attain a higher form of human society – socialism.

The component parts of Marxism fall under three main headings, corresponding broadly to philosophy, social history and economics – Dialectical Materialism, Historical Materialism and Marxist Economics. These are the famous "Three sources and three component parts of Marxism" of which Lenin wrote.

The present book comprises the *Education for Socialists* series and other material which was launched a few years ago to promote the study of Marxism. They were originally intended to assist the student of Marxism by providing a basic introduction to the subject matter, with suitable Marxist texts, that we hoped would whet the appetite for further reading and study. This material, aimed at the first-time reader, is suitable for individual study or as the basis of Marxist discussion groups.

While these introductory articles are illuminating and provide a good start to the subject, there is no substitute for proceeding from there to tackle the classic works of Marx, Engels, Lenin, Trotsky, Plekhanov and others. The newer reader should not be put off by the sometimes difficult and abstract ideas expressed in these writings. Whatever the initial difficulty, a certain perseverance will pay just rewards. Marxism is a science with its own terminology, and therefore makes heavy demands upon the beginner. However, every serious person knows that nothing is worthwhile if attained without a degree of struggle and sacrifice, and that applies to Marxism as well.

The theories of Marxism provide the thinking worker and student with a comprehensive understanding of the world in which we live. It is the duty of those who wish to learn, to conquer for themselves the main theories of Marx and Engels, as an essential prerequisite for the overthrow of capitalism and the establishment of a socialist society.

We recognise that there are real obstacles in the path of ordinary workers in their struggle to understand theory. Yet it was for the working class that Marx and Engels wrote, and not for "clever" academics. As Engels explained:

> "If these gentlemen only knew how Marx thought his best things were still not good enough for the workers and how he regarded it as a crime to offer the workers anything less than the best!"

"Every beginning is difficult" no matter what science we are talking about. To the class conscious worker and the student who is prepared to persevere, one promise can be made: once the initial effort is made to come to grips with unfamiliar and new ideas, the theories of Marxism will be found to be basically straight-forward and simple. It will open your eyes to a new world, where the irrational workings of class society become clear. Once the basic concepts of Marxism are conquered, it introduces us to a whole new outlook on politics, the class struggle, and, in fact, every aspect of life.

Above all, Marxism is a guide to action. It prepares theoretically us for the struggle for a new society. These ideas will become the property of millions as the scientific programme of socialism connects with the revolutionary movement of the masses. In the famous words of Marx, "Philosophers have interpreted the world; the point however is to change it."

Rob Sewell
September 2007

The Ideas of Karl Marx

Alan Woods

It is 130 years since the death of Karl Marx. But why should we commemorate a man who died in 1883? In the early 1960s the then Labour Prime Minister Harold Wilson declared that we must not look for solutions in Highgate cemetery. And who can disagree with that? In the aforementioned cemetery one can only find old bones and dust and a rather ugly stone monument.

However, when we speak of the relevance of Karl Marx today we refer not to cemeteries but to ideas – ideas that have withstood the test of time and have now emerged triumphant, as even some of the enemies of Marxism have been reluctantly forced to accept. The economic collapse of 2008 showed who was outdated, and it was certainly not Karl Marx.

For decades the economists never tired of repeating that Marx's predictions of an economic downturn were totally outdated. They were supposed to be ideas of the 19th century, and those who defended them were dismissed as hopeless dogmatists. But it now turns out that it is the ideas of the defenders of capitalism that must be consigned to the rubbish bin of history, while Marx has been completely vindicated.

Not so long ago, Gordon Brown confidently proclaimed "the end of boom and bust". After the crash of 2008 he was forced to eat his words. The crisis of the euro shows that the bourgeoisie has no idea how to solve the problems of Greece, Spain and Italy which in turn threaten the future of the European common currency and even the EU itself. This can easily be the catalyst for a new collapse on a world scale, which will be even deeper than the crisis of 2008.

Even some bourgeois economists are being forced to accept what is becoming increasingly evident: that capitalism contains within itself the seeds of its own destruction; that it is an anarchic and chaotic system characterised by periodic crises that throw people out of work and cause social and political instability.

The thing about the present crisis was that it was not supposed to happen. Until recently most of the bourgeois economists believed that the market, if left to itself, was capable of solving all the problems, magically balancing out supply and demand (the "efficient market hypothesis") so that there could never be a repetition of the crash of 1929 and the Great Depression.

Marx's prediction of a crisis of overproduction had been consigned to the dustbin of history. Those who still adhered to Marx's view that the capitalist system was riven with insoluble contradictions and contained within itself the seeds of its own destruction were looked upon as mere cranks. Had the fall of the Soviet Union not finally demonstrated the failure of communism? Had history not finally ended with the triumph of capitalism as the only possible socio-economic system?

But in the space of 20 years (not a long period in the annals of human society) the wheel of history has turned 180 degrees. Now the erstwhile critics of Marx and Marxism are singing a very different tune. All of a sudden, the economic theories of Karl Marx are being taken very seriously indeed. A growing number of economists are poring over the pages of Marx's writings, hoping to find an explanation for what has gone wrong.

Second thoughts

In July 2009, after the start of the recession The Economist held a seminar in London to discuss the question: What is wrong with Economics? This revealed that for a growing number of economists mainstream theory has no relevance. Nobel Prize winner Paul Krugman made an astonishing admission. He said "the last 30 years development in macroeconomic theory has, at best, been spectacularly useless or, at worst, directly harmful." This judgement is a fitting epitaph for the theories of bourgeois economics.

Now that events have knocked just a little sense into the heads of at least some bourgeois thinkers, we are seeing all kinds of articles that grudgingly recognise that Marx was right after all. Even the Vatican's official newspaper, L'Osservatore Romano, published an article in 2009 praising Marx's diagnosis of income inequality, which is quite an endorsement for the man who declared religion to be the opium of the people. Das Kapital is now a best seller in Germany. In Japan it has been published in a manga version.

George Magnus, a senior economic analyst at UBS bank, wrote an article with the intriguing title: *Give Karl Marx a Chance to Save the World Economy*. Switzerland-based UBS is a pillar of the financial establishment, with offices in more than 50 countries and over $2 trillion in assets. Yet in an essay for *Bloomberg View*, Magnus wrote that "today's global economy bears some uncanny resemblances to what Marx foresaw."

In his article he starts by describing policy makers "struggling to understand the barrage of financial panics, protests and other ills afflicting the world" and suggests that they would do well to study the works of "a long-dead economist, Karl Marx."

> "Consider, for example, Marx's prediction of how the inherent conflict between capital and labor would manifest itself. As he wrote in Das Kapital, companies' pursuit of profits and productivity would naturally lead them to need fewer and fewer workers, creating an 'industrial reserve army' of the poor and unemployed: 'Accumulation of wealth at one pole is, therefore, at the same time accumulation of misery'."

He continues:

> "The process he [Marx] describes is visible throughout the developed world, particularly in the U.S. Companies' efforts to cut costs and avoid hiring have boosted U.S. corporate profits as a share of total economic output to the highest level in more than six decades, while the unemployment rate stands at 9.1% and real wages are stagnant.

> "U.S. income inequality, meanwhile, is by some measures close to its highest level since the 1920s. Before 2008, the income disparity was obscured by factors such as easy credit, which allowed poor households to enjoy a more affluent lifestyle. Now the problem is coming home to roost."

The *Wall Street Journal* carried an interview with the well-known economist Dr. Nouriel Roubini, known to his fellow economists as "Dr. Doom" because of his prediction of the 2008 financial crisis. There is a video of this extraordinary interview, which deserves to be studied carefully because it shows the thinking of the most far-sighted strategists of capital.

Roubini argues that the chain of credit is broken, and that capitalism has entered into a vicious cycle where excess capacity (overproduction), falling consumer demand, high levels of debt all breed a lack of confidence in investors that in turn will be reflected in sharp falls on the stock exchange, falling asset prices and a collapse in the real economy.

Like all the other economists, Roubini has no real solution to the present crisis, except more monetary injections from central banks to avoid another meltdown. But he frankly admitted that monetary policy alone will not be enough, and business and governments are not helping. Europe and the United States are implementing austerity programs to try to fix their debt-ridden economies, when they should be introducing more monetary stimulus, he said. His conclusions could not be more pessimistic: "Karl Marx got it right, at some point capitalism can destroy itself," said Roubini. "We thought markets worked. They're not working." (My emphasis, AW.)

The phantom of Marxism is still haunting the bourgeoisie a hundred and thirty years after Marx's mortal remains were laid to rest. But what is Marxism? To deal properly with all aspects of Marxism in the space of one article is an impossible task. We therefore confine ourselves to a general, and therefore sketchy account in the hope that it will encourage the reader to study Marx's writings themselves. After all, nobody has ever expounded Marx's ideas better than Marx himself.

Broadly speaking, his ideas can be split into three distinct yet interconnected parts – what Lenin called the three sources and three component parts of Marxism. These generally go under the headings of Marxist economics, dialectical materialism and historical materialism. Each of these stands in a dialectical relation to each other and cannot be understood in isolation from one another. A good place to begin is the founding document of our movement that was written on the eve of the European Revolutions of 1848. It is one of the greatest and most influential works in history.

The Communist Manifesto

The immense majority of the books written one and a half centuries ago are today merely of historical interest. But what is most striking about the *Communist Manifesto* is the way in which it anticipates the most fundamental phenomena which occupy our attention on a world scale at the present time. It is really extraordinary to think that a book written in 1847 can present a picture of the world of the 21st century so vividly and truthfully. In point of fact, the *Manifesto* is even truer today than when it first appeared in 1848.

Let us consider one example. At the time when Marx and Engels were writing, the world of the big multinational companies was still the music of a very distant future. Despite this, they explained how free enterprise and competition would inevitably lead to the concentration of capital and the monopolisation of the productive forces. It is frankly comical to read the statements made by the defenders of the market concerning Marx's alleged mistake on this question, when in reality it was precisely one of his most brilliant and accurate predictions.

During the 1980s it became fashionable to claim that small is beautiful. This is not the place to enter into a discussion concerning the relative aesthetics of big, small or medium sizes, about which everyone is entitled to hold an opinion. But it is an absolutely indisputable fact that the process of concentration of capital foreseen by Marx has occurred, is occurring, and indeed has reached unprecedented levels in the course of the last ten years.

In the United States, where the process may be seen in a particularly clear form, the Fortune 500 corporations accounted for 73.5% of total GDP output in 2010. If these 500 companies formed an independent country, it would be the world's second largest economy, second only to the United States itself. In 2011, these 500 firms generated an all-time record of $824.5 billion in profits – a 16% jump from 2010. On a world scale, the 2000 biggest companies now account for $32 trillion in revenues, $2.4 trillion in profits, $138 trillion in assets and $38 trillion in market value, with profits rising an astonishing 67% between 2010 and 2011.

When Marx and Engels wrote the *Manifesto*, there was no empirical evidence for his claims. On the contrary, the capitalism of his time was based entirely on small businesses, the free market and competition. Today, the economy of the entire capitalist world is dominated by a handful of giant transnational monopolies such as Exxon and Walmart. These behemoths possess funds that far exceed the national budgets of many states. The predictions of the *Manifesto* have been realised even more clearly and completely than Marx himself could ever have dreamed of.

The defenders of capitalism cannot forgive Marx because, at a time when capitalism was in the stage of youthful vigour, he was able to foresee the causes of its senile degeneration. For decades they strenuously denied his prediction of the inevitable process of the concentration of capital and the displacement of small businesses by big monopolies.

The process of the centralisation and concentration of capital has reached proportions hitherto undreamed of. The number of take-overs has acquired the character of an epidemic in all the advanced industrialised nations. In many cases, such take-overs are intimately connected with all kinds of shady practices – insider dealing, falsification of share prices, and other types of fraud, larceny and swindling, as the scandal over the manipulation of the Libor interest rate by Barclays and other big banks has revealed. This concentration of capital does not signify a growth in production, but quite the contrary. In every case, the intention is not to invest in new plant and machinery but to close existing factories and offices and sack large numbers of workers in order to increase profit margins without increasing production. Just take the recent fusion of two big Swiss banks, immediately followed by the loss of 13,000 jobs.

Globalisation and inequality

Let us proceed to the next important prediction made by Marx. Already in 1847, Marx explained that the development of a global market renders "impossible all narrowness and national individualism. Every country – even the largest and most powerful – is now totally subordinate to the whole world economy, which decides the fate of peoples and nations." This brilliant theoretical anticipation shows, better than anything else, the immeasurable superiority of the Marxist method.

Globalisation is generally regarded as a recent phenomenon. Yet the creation of a single global market under capitalism was long ago predicted in the pages of the *Manifesto*. The crushing domination of the world market is now the most decisive fact of our epoch. The enormous intensification of the international division of labour since the Second World War has demonstrated the correctness of Marx's analysis in an almost laboratory fashion.

Despite this, strenuous efforts have been made to prove that Marx was wrong when he spoke of the concentration of capital and therefore the process of polarisation between the classes. These mental gymnastics corresponds to the dreams of the bourgeoisie to rediscover the lost golden age of free enterprise. Similarly, a decrepit old man longs in his senility for the lost days of his youth.

Unfortunately, there is not the slightest chance of capitalism recovering its youthful vigour. It has long ago entered its final phase: that of monopoly capitalism. The day of the small business, despite the nostalgia of the bourgeoisie, has been relegated to the past. In all countries the big monopolies, closely related to banking and enmeshed with the bourgeois state, dominate the life of society. The polarisation between the classes continues uninterrupted, and tends to accelerate.

Let us take the situation in the USA. The richest 400 families in the U.S. have as much wealth as the bottom 50% of the population. The six individual Wal-Mart heirs alone are "worth" more than the bottom 30% of Americans combined. The poorest 50% of Americans own just 2.5% of the country's wealth. The richest one% of the US population increased its share of the national income from 17.6% in 1978 to an astonishing 37.1% in 2011.

During the past 30 years the gap between the incomes of the rich and the poor has been steadily widening into a yawning abyss. In the industrialised West the average income of the richest 10% of the population is about nine times that of the poorest 10%. That is an enormous difference. And figures published by the OECD show that the disparity which began in the US and UK has spread to countries such as Denmark, Germany and Sweden, which have traditionally had low inequality.

The obscene wealth of the bankers is now a public scandal. But this phenomenon is not confined to the financial sector. In many cases, directors of large companies earn 200 times more than their lowest-paid workers. This excessive difference has already provoked growing resentment, which is turning to fury that spills over onto the streets in one country after another. The growing tension is reflected in strikes, general strikes, demonstrations and riots. It is reflected in elections by protest votes against governments and all the existing parties, as we saw recently in the Italian general election.

A Time magazine poll showed that 54% have a favourable view of the #Occupy movement, 79% think the gap between rich and poor has grown too large, 71% think CEOs of financial institutions should be prosecuted, 68% think the rich should pay more taxes, only 27% have a favourable view of the Tea Party movement (33% unfavourable). Of course, it is too early to speak of a revolution in the USA. But it is clear that the crisis of capitalism is producing a growing mood of criticism among broad layers of the population. There is a ferment and a questioning of capitalism that were not there before.

The scourge of unemployment

In the *Communist Manifesto* we read:

> "And here it becomes evident, that the bourgeoisie is unfit any longer to be the ruling class in society, and to impose its conditions of existence upon society as an over-riding law. It is unfit to rule because it is incompetent to assure an existence to its slave within his slavery, because it cannot help letting him sink into such a state, that it has to feed him, instead of being fed by him. Society can no longer live under this bourgeoisie."

The words of Marx and Engels quoted above have become literally true. There is a growing feeling among all sections of society that our lives are dominated by forces beyond our control. Society is gripped by a gnawing sense of fear and uncertainty. The mood of insecurity has become generalised to practically the whole of society.

The kind of mass unemployment we are now experiencing is far worse than anything Marx foresaw. Marx wrote of the reserve army of labour: that is to say, a pool of labour that can be used to keep down wages and acts as a reserve when the economy recovers from a slump. But the kind of unemployment we now see is not the reserve army of which Marx spoke, which, from a capitalist point of view played a useful role.

This is not the kind of cyclical unemployment which workers are well acquainted with from the past and which would rise in a recession only to disappear when the economy picked up again. It is permanent, structural, organic unemployment, which does not noticeably diminish even when there is a "boom". It is a dead weight that acts as a colossal drag on productive activity, a symptom that the system has reached a blind alley.

A decade before the crisis of 2008, according to the United Nations, world unemployment was approximately 120 millions. By 2009, the International Labour Organisation put the figure at 198 millions, and expects it to reach 202 million in 2013. However, even these figures, like all the official statistics of unemployment, represent a serious understatement of the real situation. If we include the enormous number of men and women who are compelled to work in all kinds of marginal "jobs", the real figure of world unemployment and underemployment would not be less than 1,000 million.

Despite all the talk of economic recovery, economic growth in Germany, the former economic powerhouse of Europe, has slowed down almost to zero, as has France. In Japan too the economy is grinding to a halt. Quite apart from the misery and suffering caused to millions of families, from an economic point of view, this represents a staggering loss of production and waste on a colossal scale. Contrary to the illusions of the labour leaders in the past, mass unemployment has returned and has spread all over the world like a cancer gnawing at the bowels of society.

The crisis of capitalism has its direst effects among the youth. Unemployment among young people is soaring everywhere. This is the reason for the mass student protests and riots in Britain, for the movement of the indignados in Spain, the occupations of the schools in Greece and also for the uprisings in Tunisia and Egypt, where about 75% of the youth are unemployed.

The number of unemployed in Europe is constantly increasing. The figure for Spain is nearly 27% while youth unemployment stands at an incredible 55%, while in Greece no fewer than 62% of the youth – two in every three – are jobless. A whole generation of young people is being sacrificed on the altar of Profit. Many who looked for salvation to higher education have found that this avenue is blocked. In Britain, where higher education used to be free, now young people find that in order to acquire the skills they need, they will have to go into debt.

At the other end of the age scale, workers approaching retirement find that they must work longer and pay more for lower pensions that will condemn many to poverty in old age. For young and old alike, the prospect facing most people today is a lifetime of insecurity. All the old bourgeois hypocrisy about morality and family values has been exposed as hollow. The epidemic of unemployment, homelessness, crushing debt and extreme social inequality that has turned a whole generation into pariahs has undermined the family and created a nightmare of systemic poverty, hopelessness, degradation and despair.

A crisis of overproduction

In Greek mythology there was a character called Procrustes who had a nasty habit of cutting off the legs, head and arms of his guests to make them fit into his infamous bed. Nowadays the capitalist system resembles the bed of Procrustes. The bourgeoisie is systematically destroying the means of production in order to make them fit into the narrow limits of the capitalist system. This economic vandalism resembles a policy of slash and burn on a vast scale.

George Soros likens it to the kind of smashing ball used to demolish tall buildings. But it is not only buildings that are being destroyed but whole economies and states. The slogan of the hour is austerity, cuts and falling living standards. In every country the bourgeoisie raises the same war cry: "We must cut public expenditure!" Every government in the capitalist world, whether right or "left" is in reality pursuing the same policy. This is not the result of the whims of individual politicians, of ignorance or bad faith (although there is plenty of this also) but a graphic expression of the blind alley in which the capitalist system finds itself.

This is an expression of the fact that the capitalist system is reaching its limits and is unable to develop the productive forces as it did in the past. Like Goethe's Sorcerer's Apprentice, it has conjured up forces it cannot control. But by slashing state expenditure, they are simultaneously reducing demand and cutting the whole market, just at a time when even the bourgeois economists admit that there is a serious problem of overproduction ("overcapacity") on a world scale. Let us take just one example, the automobile sector. This is fundamental because it also involves many other sectors, such as steel, plastic, chemicals and electronics.

The global excess capacity of the automobile industry is approximately 30%. This means that Ford, General Motors, Fiat, Renault, Toyota and all the others could close one third of their factories and lay off one third of their workers tomorrow, and they would still not be able to sell all the vehicles they produce at what they consider to be an acceptable rate of profit. A similar position exists in many other sectors. Unless and until this problem of excess capacity is resolved, there can be no real end to the present crisis.

The dilemma of the capitalists can be easily expressed. If Europe and the USA are not consuming, China cannot produce. If China is not producing at the same pace as before, countries like Brazil. Argentina and Australia cannot continue to export their raw materials. The whole world is inseparably interlinked. The crisis of the euro will affect the US economy, which is in a very fragile state, and what happens in the USA will have a decisive effect on the entire world economy. Thus, globalisation manifests itself as a global crisis of capitalism.

Alienation

With incredible foresight, the authors of the *Manifesto* anticipated the conditions which are now being experienced by the working class in all countries.

> "Owing to the extensive use of machinery and to division of labour, the work of the proletarians has lost all individual character, and, consequently, all charm for the workman. He becomes an appendage of the machine, and it is only the most simple, most monotonous, and most easily acquired knack, that is required of him. Hence, the cost of production of a workman is restricted, almost entirely, to the means of subsistence that he requires for his maintenance, and for the propagation of his race. But the price of a commodity, and therefore also of labour, is equal to the cost of production. In proportion, therefore, as the repulsiveness of the work increases, the wage decreases. Nay more, in proportion as the use of machinery and division of labour increases, in the same proportion the burden of toil also increases, whether by prolongation of the working hours, by increase of the work exacted in a given time or by increased speed of the machinery, etc."

Today the USA occupies the same position that Britain held in Marx's day – that of the most developed capitalist country. Thus, the general tendencies of capitalism are expressed there in their clearest form. Over the last 30 years, CEO pay in the USA has grown by 725%, while worker pay has risen by just 5.7%. These CEOs now make an average of 244 times more than their employees. The current federal minimum wage is $7.25 per hour. According to the Center for Economic Policy Research, if the minimum wage had kept up with worker productivity, it would have reached $21.72 in 2012. If inflation is taken into account, median wages for male American workers are actually lower today than they were in 1968. In this way, the present boom has been largely at the expense of the working class.

While millions are compelled to eke out a miserable existence of enforced inactivity, millions of others are forced to have two or even three jobs, and often work 60 hours or more per week with no overtime pay benefits. 85.8% of males and 66.5% of females work more than 40 hours per week. According to the International Labour Organisation, "Americans work 137 more hours per year than Japanese workers, 260 more hours per year than British workers, and 499 more hours per year than French workers."

Based on data from the US Bureau of Labor Statistics (BLS), the average productivity per American worker has risen 400% since 1950. In theory, this means that in order to achieve the same standard of living a worker should only have to work just one quarter of the average working week in 1950, or 11 hours per week. Either that, or the standard of living in theory should have risen by four times. On the contrary, the standard of living has decreased dramatically for the majority, while work-related stress, injuries and disease are increasing. This is reflected in an epidemic of depression, suicides, divorce, child and spousal abuse, mass shootings and other social ills.

The same situation exists in Britain, where under the Thatcher government 2.5 million jobs were destroyed in industry, and yet the same level of production has been maintained as in 1979. This has been achieved, not through the introduction of new machinery but through the over-exploitation of British workers. In 1995, Kenneth Calman, Director General of Health, warned that "the lost of life time employment has unleashed an epidemic of stress related illnesses."

The class struggle

Marx and Engels explained in the *Communist Manifesto* that a constant factor in all of recorded history is that social development takes place through the class struggle. Under capitalism this has been greatly simplified with the polarisation of society into two great antagonistic classes, the bourgeoisie and the proletariat. The tremendous development of industry and technology over the last 200 years has led to the increasing the concentration of economic power in a few hands.

"The history of all hitherto existing society is the history of class struggles," says the *Manifesto* in one of its most celebrated phrases. For a long time it seemed to many that this idea was outmoded. In the long period of capitalist expansion that followed the Second World War, with full employment in the advanced industrial economies, rising living standards and reforms (remember the Welfare State?), the class struggle did indeed seem to be a thing of the past.

Marx predicted that the development of capitalism would lead inexorably to the concentration of capital, an immense accumulation of wealth on the one hand and an equal accumulation of poverty, misery and unbearable toil at the other end of the social spectrum. For decades this idea was rubbished by the bourgeois economists and university sociologists who insisted that society was becoming ever more egalitarian, that everyone was now becoming middle class. Now all these illusions have been dispelled.

The argument, so beloved of bourgeois sociologists, that the working class has ceased to exist has been stood on its head. In the last period important layers of the working population who previously considered themselves to be middle class have been proletarianised. Teachers, civil servants, bank employees and so on have been drawn into the ranks of the working class and the labour movement, where they make up some of the most militant sections.

The old arguments that everybody can advance and we are all middle class have been falsified by events. In Britain, the US and many other developed countries over the past 20 or 30 years, the opposite has been happening. Middle-class people used to think life unfolded in an orderly progression of stages in which each is a step up from the last. That is no longer the case.

Job security has ceased to exist, the trades and professions of the past have largely disappeared and life-long careers are barely memories. The ladder has been kicked away and for most people a middle-class existence is no longer even an aspiration. A dwindling minority can count on a pension on which they could comfortably live, and few have significant savings. More and more people live from day to day, with little idea of what the future may bring.

If people have any wealth, it is in their houses, but with the contraction of the economy house prices have fallen in many countries and may be stagnant for years. The idea of a property-owning democracy has been exposed as a mirage. Far from being an asset to help fund a comfortable retirement, home ownership has become a heavy burden. Mortgages must be paid, whether you are in work or not. Many are trapped in negative equity, with huge debts that can never be paid. There is a growing generation of what can only be described as debt slaves.

This is a devastating condemnation of the capitalist system. However, this process of proletarianisation means that the social reserves of reaction have been sharply reduced as a big section of white collar workers moves closer to the traditional working class. In the recent mass mobilisations, sections that in the past would never have dreamt of striking or even joining a union, such as teachers and civil servants, were in the front line of the class struggle.

Idealism or materialism?

The idealist method sets out from what people think and say about themselves. But Marx explained that ideas do not fall from the sky, but reflect more or less accurately, objective situations, social pressures and contradictions beyond the control of men and women. But history does not unfold as a result of free will or conscious desires of the "great man", kings, politicians or philosophers. On the contrary, the progress of society depends on the development of the productive forces, which is not the product of conscious planning, but develops behind the backs of men and women.

For the first time Marx placed socialism on a firm theoretical basis. A scientific understanding of history cannot be based on the distorted images of reality floating like pale and fantastic ghosts in the minds of men and women, but on real social relations. That means beginning with a clarification of the relationship between social and political forms and the mode of production at a given stage of history. This is precisely what is called the historical materialist method of analysis.

Some people will feel irritated by this theory which seems to deprive humankind of the role of protagonists in the historical process. In the same way, the Church and its philosophical apologists were deeply offended by the claims of Galileo that the Sun, not the Earth, was at the centre of the Universe. Later, the same people attacked Darwin for suggesting that humans were not the special creation of God, but the product of natural selection.

Actually, Marxism does not at all deny the importance of the subjective factor in history, the conscious role of humankind in the development of society. Men and women make history, but do not do it entirely in accord with their free will and conscious intentions. In Marx's words:"History does nothing", it "possesses no immense wealth", it "wages no battles". It is man, real, living man who does all that, who possesses and fights; "history" is not, as it were, a person apart, using man as a means to achieve its own aims; history is nothing but the activity of man pursuing his aims." (Marx and Engels, *The Holy Family, Chapter VI*)

All that Marxism does is to explain the role of the individual as part of a given society, subject to certain objective laws and, ultimately, as the representative of the interests of a particular class. Ideas have no independent existence, nor own historical development. "Life is not determined by consciousness," Marx writes in *The German Ideology*, "but consciousness by life."

The ideas and actions of people are conditioned by social relations, the development of which does not depend on the subjective will of men and women but takes place according to definite laws which, in the last analysis, reflect the needs of the development of the productive forces. The interrelations between these factors constitute a complex web that is often difficult to see. The study of these relations is the basis of the Marxist theory of history.

Let us cite one example. At the time of the English Revolution, Oliver Cromwell fervently believed that he was fighting for the right of each individual to pray to God according to his conscience. But the further march of history proved that the Cromwellian Revolution was the decisive stage in the irresistible ascent of the English bourgeoisie to power. The concrete stage of the development of the productive forces in 17th Century England permitted no other outcome.

The leaders of the Great French Revolution of 1789-93 fought under the banner of "Liberty, Equality and Fraternity". They believed they were fighting for a regime based on the eternal laws of Justice and Reason. However, regardless of their intentions and ideas, the Jacobins were preparing the way for the rule of the bourgeoisie in France. Again, from a scientific standpoint, no other result was possible at that point of social development.

From the standpoint of the labour movement Marx's great contribution was that he was the first to explain that socialism is not just a good idea, but the necessary result of the development of society. Socialist thinkers before Marx – the utopian socialists – attempted to discover universal laws and formulae that would lay the basis for the triumph of human reason over the injustice of class society. All that was necessary was to discover that idea, and the problems would be solved. This is an idealist approach.

Unlike the Utopians, Marx never attempted to discover the laws of society in general. He analysed the law of movement of a particular society, capitalist society, explaining how it arose, how it evolved and also how it necessarily ceases to exist at a given moment. He performed this huge task in the three volumes of *Capital*.

Historical materialism

Marxism analyses the hidden mainsprings that lie behind the development of human society, from the earliest tribal societies up to the modern day. The way in which Marxism traces this winding road is called the materialist conception of history. This scientific method enables us to understand history, not as a series of unconnected and unforeseen incidents, but rather as part of a clearly understood and interrelated process. It is a series of actions and reactions which cover politics, economics and the whole spectrum of social development. To lay bare the complex dialectical relationship between all these phenomena is the task of historical materialism.

The great English historian Edward Gibbon, the author of *The Decline and Fall of the Roman Empire*, wrote that history is "little more than the register of the crimes, follies and misfortunes of mankind." (Gibbon, *The Decline and Fall of the Roman Empire*, vol 1, p69). In essence, the latest post-modernist interpretation of history has not advanced a single step since then. History is seen as a series of disconnected "narratives" with no organic connection and no inner meaning or logic. No socio-economic system can be said to be better or worse than any other, and there can therefore be no question of progress or retrogression.

History appears here as an essentially meaningless and inexplicable series of random events or accidents. It is governed by no laws that we can comprehend. To try to understand it would therefore be a pointless exercise. A variation on this theme is the idea, now very popular in some academic circles, that there is no such thing as higher and lower forms of social development and culture. They claim that there is no such thing as progress, which they consider to be an old fashioned idea left over from the 19th century, when it was popularised by Victorian liberals, Fabian socialists and – Karl Marx.

This denial of progress in history is characteristic of the psychology of the bourgeoisie in the phase of capitalist decline. It is a faithful reflection of the fact that, under capitalism progress has indeed reached its limits and threatens to go into reverse. The bourgeoisie and its intellectual representatives are, quite naturally, unwilling to accept this fact. Moreover, they are organically incapable of recognising it. Lenin once observed that a man on the edge of a cliff does not reason. However, they are dimly aware of the real situation, and try to find some kind of a justification for the impasse of their system by denying the possibility of progress altogether.

So far has this idea sunk into consciousness that it has even been carried into the realm of non-human evolution. Even such a brilliant thinker as Stephen Jay Gould, whose dialectical theory of punctuated equilibrium transformed the way that evolution is perceived, argued that it is wrong to speak of progress from lower to higher in evolution, so that microbes must be placed on the same level as human beings. In one sense it is correct that all living things are related (the human genome has conclusively proved this). Humankind is not a special creation of the Almighty, but the product of evolution. Nor is it correct to see evolution as a kind of grand design, the aim of which was to create beings like ourselves (teleology – from the Greek telos, meaning an end). However, in rejecting an incorrect idea, it is not necessary to go to the other extreme, leading to new errors.

It is not a question of accepting some kind of preordained plan either related to divine intervention or some kind of teleology, but it is clear that the laws of evolution inherent in nature do in fact determine development from simple forms of life to more complex forms. The earliest forms of life already contain within them the embryo of all future developments. It is possible to explain the development of eyes, legs and other organs without recourse to any preordained plan. At a certain stage we get the development of a central nervous system and a brain. Finally with homo sapiens, we arrive at human consciousness. Matter becomes conscious of itself. There has been no more important revolution since the development of organic matter (life) from inorganic matter.

To please our critics, we should perhaps add the phrase "from our point of view". Doubtless the microbes, if they were able to have a point of view, would probably raise serious objections. But we are human beings and must necessarily see things through human eyes. And we do assert that evolution does in fact represent the development of simple life forms to more complex and versatile ones – in other words progress from lower to higher forms of life. To object to such a formulation seems to be somewhat pointless, not scientific but merely scholastic. In saying this, of course, no offence is intended to the microbes, who after all have been around for a lot longer than us, and if the capitalist system is not overthrown, may yet have the last laugh.

The motor force of history

In *The Critique of Political Economy* Marx explains the relation between the productive forces and the "superstructure" as follows:

> "In the social production which men carry on they enter into definite relations that are indispensable and independent of their will; these relations of production correspond to a definite stage of development of their material powers of production... The mode of production in ma terial life determines the general character of the social, political and spiritual processes of life. It is not the consciousness of men that determines their existence, but, on the contrary, their social existence (which) determines their consciousness."

As Marx and Engels were at pains to point out, the participants in history may not always be aware of what motives drive them, seeking instead to rationalise them in one way or another, but those motives exist and have a basis in the real world.

Just as Charles Darwin explains that species are not immutable, and that they possess a past, a present and a future, changing and evolving, so Marx and Engels explain that a given social system is not something eternally fixed. That is the illusion of every epoch. Every social system believes that it represents the only possible form of existence for human beings, that its institutions, its religion, its morality are the last word that can be spoken.

That is what the cannibals, the Egyptian priests, Marie Antoinette and Tsar Nicolas all fervently believed. And that is what the bourgeoisie and its apologists today wish to demonstrate when they assure us, without the slightest basis, that the so-called system of "free enterprise" is the only possible system – just when it is beginning to sink.

Nowadays, the idea of "evolution" has been generally accepted at least by educated persons. The ideas of Darwin, so revolutionary in his day, are accepted almost as a truism. However, evolution is generally understood as a slow and gradual process without interruptions or violent upheavals. In politics, this kind of argument is frequently used as a justification for reformism. Unfortunately, it is based on a misunderstanding.

The real mechanism of evolution even today remains a book sealed by seven seals. This is hardly surprising since Darwin himself did not understand it. Only in the last decade or so with the new discoveries in palaeontology made by Stephen Jay Gould, who discovered the theory of punctuated equilibria, has it been demonstrated that evolution is not a gradual process. There are long periods in which no big changes are observed, but at a given moment, the line of evolution is broken by an explosion, a veritable biological revolution characterised by the mass extinction of some species and the rapid ascent of others.

The analogy between society and nature is, of course, only approximate. But even the most superficial examination of history shows that the gradualist interpretation is baseless. Society, like nature, knows long periods of slow and gradual change, but also here the line is interrupted by explosive developments – wars and revolutions, in which the process of change is enormously accelerated. In fact, it is these events that act as the main motor force of historical development. And the root cause of revolution is the fact that a particular socio-economic system has reached its limits and is unable to develop the productive forces as before.

A dynamic view of history

Those who deny the existence of any laws governing human social development invariably approach history from a subjective and moralistic standpoint. Like Gibbon (but without his extraordinary talent) they shake their heads at the unending spectacle of senseless violence, the inhumanity of man against man (and woman) and so on and so forth. In place of a scientific view of history we get a parson's view. However, what is required is not a moral sermon but a rational insight. Above and beyond the isolated facts, it is necessary to discern broad tendencies, the transitions from one social system to another, and to work out the fundamental motor forces that determine these transitions.

By applying the method of dialectical materialism to history, it is immediately obvious that human history has its own laws, and that, consequently, the history of humankind is possible to understand it as a process. The rise and fall of different socio-economic formations can be explained scientifically in terms of their ability or inability to develop the means of production, and thereby to push forward the horizons of human culture, and increase the domination of humankind over nature.

Most people believe that society is fixed for all time, and that its moral, religious and ideological values are immutable, along with what we call "human nature". But the slightest acquaintance with history shows that this is false. History manifests itself as the rise and fall of different socio-economic systems. Like individual men and women, societies are born, develop, reach their limits, enter into decline and are then finally replaced by a new social formation.

In the last analysis, the viability of a given socio-economic system is determined by its ability to develop the productive forces, since everything else depends on this. Many other factors enter into the complex equation: religion, politics, philosophy, morality, the psychology of different classes and the individual qualities of leaders. But these things do not drop from the clouds, and a careful analysis will show that they are determined – albeit in a contradictory and dialectical way – by the real historical environment, and by tendencies and processes that are independent of the will of men and women.

The outlook of a society that is in a phase of ascent, which is developing the means of production and pushing forward the horizons of culture and civilisation, is very different to the psychology of a society in a state of stagnation and decline. The general historical context determines everything. It affects the prevailing moral climate, the attitude of men and women towards the existing political and religious institutions. It even affects the quality of individual political leaders.

Capitalism in its youth was capable of colossal feats. It developed the productive forces to an unparalleled degree, and was therefore able to push back the frontiers of human civilisation. People felt that society was advancing, despite all the injustices and exploitation that have always characterised this system. This feeling gave rise to a general spirit of optimism and progress that was the hall mark of the old liberalism, with its firm conviction that today was better than yesterday and tomorrow would be better than today.

That is no longer the case. The old optimism and blind faith in progress have been replaced by a profound sense of discontent with the present and of pessimism with regard to the future. This ubiquitous feeling of fear and insecurity is only a psychological reflection of the fact that capitalism is no longer capable of playing any progressive role anywhere.

In the 19th century, Liberalism, the main ideology of the bourgeoisie, stood (in theory) for progress and democracy. But neo-Liberalism in the modern sense is only a mask that covers the ugly reality of the most rapacious exploitation; the rape of the planet, the destruction of the environment without the slightest concern about the fate of future generations. The sole concern of the boards of the big companies who are the real rulers of the USA and the entire world is to enrich themselves through plunder: asset-stripping, corruption, the theft of public assets through privatisation, parasitism: these are the main features of the bourgeoisie in the phase of its senile decay.

The rise and fall of societies

"The transition from one system to another was always determined by the growth of the productive forces, i.e., of technique and the organisation of labour. Up to a certain point, social changes are quantitative in character and do not alter the foundations of society, i.e., the prevalent forms of property. But a point is reached when the matured productive forces can no longer contain themselves within the old forms of property; then follows a radical change in the social order, accompanied by shocks." (Leon Trotsky, *Marxism in Our Time*, April 1939)

A common argument against socialism is that it is impossible to change human nature; people are naturally selfish and greedy and so on. In reality, there is no such thing as a supra-historical human nature. What we think of as human nature has undergone many changes in the course of human evolution. Men and women constantly change nature through labour, and in so doing, change themselves. As for the argument that people are naturally selfish and greedy, this is disproved by the facts of human evolution.

Our earliest ancestors, who were not yet really human, were small in stature and physically weak compared to other animals. They did not have strong teeth or claws. Their upright stance meant that they could not run fast enough to catch the antelope they wished to eat, or to escape from the lion that wished to eat them. Their brain size was approximately that of a chimpanzee. Wandering on the savannah of East Africa, they were at an extreme disadvantage to every other species – except in one fundamental aspect.

Engels explains in his brilliant essay *The Role Played by Labour in the Transition of Ape to Man* how the upright stance freed the hands, which had originally evolved as an adaptation for climbing trees, for other purposes. The production of stone tools represented a qualitative leap, giving our ancestors an evolutionary advantage. But even more important was the strong sense of community, collective production and social life, which in turn was closely connected to the development of language.

The extreme vulnerability of human children in comparison to the young of other species meant that our ancestors, whose hunter-gatherer existence compelled them to move from one place to another in search of food, had to develop a strong sense of solidarity to protect their offspring and thus ensure the survival of the tribe or clan. We can say with absolute certainty that without this powerful sense of co-operation and solidarity, our species would have become extinct before it was even born.

We see this even today. If a child is seen to be drowning in a river, most people would try to save it even placing their own life at risk. Many people have drowned trying to save others. This cannot be explained in terms of egotistical calculation, or by ties of blood relationships in a small tribal group. The people who act in this way do not know who they trying to save, nor do they expect any reward for doing what they do. This altruistic behaviour is quite spontaneous and comes from a deep-rooted instinct for solidarity. The argument that people are naturally selfish, which is a reflection of the ugly and dehumanised alienation of capitalist society, is a vile label on the human race.

For the immense major part of the history of our species, people lived in societies where private property, in the modern sense, did not exist. There was no money, no bosses and workers, no bankers and landlords, no state, no organised religion, no police and no prisons. Even the family, in our understanding of the word, did not exist. Today, many find it hard to envisage a world without these things; they seem so natural that they could have been ordained by the Almighty. Yet our ancestors managed fairly well without them.

The transition from hunter-gathering to settled agriculture and pastoralism constitutes the first great social revolution, which the great Australian archaeologist (and Marxist) Gordon Childe called the Neolithic Revolution. Agriculture needs water. Once it goes beyond the most basic production on a subsistence level, it requires irrigation, digging, damming and water distribution on a big scale. These are social tasks.

Large-scale irrigation needs organisation on a vast scale. It demands the deployment of large numbers of labourers and a high level of organisation and discipline. The division of labour, which already existed in embryonic form in the elementary division between the sexes arising from the demands of childbirth and the rearing of children, is developed to a higher level. Teamwork needs team leaders, foremen, overseers, etc., and an army of officials to supervise the plan.

Co-operation on such a vast scale demands planning, and the exercise of science and technique. This is beyond the capabilities of the small groups organised in clans that formed the nucleus of the old society. The need to organise and mobilise large numbers of workers led to the rise of a central state, together with a central administration and an army as in Egypt and Mesopotamia.

Time-keeping and measurement were necessary elements of production, and were themselves productive forces. Thus Herodotus traces the beginnings of geometry in Egypt to the need to re-measure the inundated land on an annual basis. The word geometry itself means neither more nor less than earth-measurement. The study of the heavens, astronomy, and mathematics enabled the Egyptian priests to foretell the flooding of the Nile, etc. Thus, science arises from economic necessity.

At the heart of this cleavage into rich and poor, rulers and ruled, educated and ignorant, is the division between mental and manual labour. The foreman is usually exempt from manual labour which now carries a stigma. The Bible speaks of the "hewers of wood and drawers of water," the masses who were excluded from culture, which was wrapped in a cloak of mystery and magic.

Its secrets were closely guarded by the caste of priests and scribes whose monopoly it was.

Here we already see the outlines of class society, the division of society into classes: exploiters and sub-exploiters. In any society where art, science and government are a monopoly of a minority, that minority will use and abuse its position for its own interests. This is the most fundamental secret of class society and has remained so for the last 12,000 years.

During all this time there have been many fundamental changes in the forms of economic and social life. But the fundamental relations between rulers and ruled, rich and poor, exploiters and exploited remained the same. In the same way, although the forms of government experienced many changes, the state remained what it had always been: an instrument of coercion and an expression of class rule.

The rise and fall of slave society was followed in Europe by feudalism, which in turn was dis placed by capitalism. The rise of the bourgeoisie, which began in the towns and cities of Italy and the Netherlands, reached a decisive stage with the bourgeois revolutions in Holland and England in the 16th and 17th centuries, and the Great French Revolution of 1789-93. All these changes were accompanied by profound transformations in culture, art, literature, religion and philosophy.

The state

The state is a special repressive force standing above society and increasingly alienating itself from it. This force has its origin in the remote past. The origins of the state, however, vary according to circumstances. Among the Germans and Native Americans it arose out of the war band that gathered around the person of the war chief. This is also the case with the Greeks, as we see in the epic poems of Homer.

Originally, the tribal chiefs enjoyed authority because of their personal bravery, wisdom and other personal qualities. Today, the power of the ruling class has nothing to do with the personal qualities of leaders as was the case under barbarism. It is rooted in objective social and productive relations and the power of money. The qualities of the individual ruler may be good, bad or indifferent, but that is not the point.

The earliest forms of class society already showed the state as a monster, devouring huge amounts of labour and repressing the masses and depriving them of all rights. At the same time, by developing the division of labour, by organising society and carrying co-operation to a far higher level than ever before, it enabled a huge amount of labour power to be mobilised, and thus raised human productive labour to undreamed-of heights.

At the base, all this depended on the labour of the peasant masses. The state needed a large number of peasants to pay taxes and provide corvée labour – the two pillars upon which society rested. Whoever controls this system of production controls power and the state. The origins of state power are rooted in relations of production, not personal qualities. The state power in such societies was necessarily centralised and bureaucratic. Originally, it had a religious character and was mixed up with the power of the priest caste. At its apex stood the God-king, and under him an army of officials, the Mandarins, the scribes, overseers etc. Writing itself was held in awe as a mysterious art known only to these few.

Thus, from the very beginning, the offices of the state are mystified. Real social relations appear in an alienated guise. This is still the case. In Britain, this mystification is deliberately cultivated through ceremony, pomp and tradition. In the USA it is cultivated by other means: the cult of the President, who represents state power personified. In essence, however, every form of state power represents the domination of one class over the rest of society.

Even in its most democratic form, it stands for the dictatorship of a single class – the ruling class – that class that owns and controls the means of production. The modern state is a bureaucratic monster that devours a colossal amount of the wealth produced by the working class. Marxists agree with the anarchists that the state is a monstrous instrument of oppression that must be eliminated. The question is: How? By whom? And what will replace it? This is a fundamental question for any revolution. In a speech on anarchism during the Civil War that followed the Russian Revolution , Trotsky summarised very well the Marxist position on the state:

> "The bourgeoisie says: don't touch the state power; it is the sacred hereditary privilege of the educated classes. But the Anarchists say: don't touch it; it is an infernal invention, a diabolical device. Don't have anything to do with it. The bourgeoisie says, don't touch it, it's sacred. The Anarchists say: don't touch it, because it's sinful. Both say: don't touch it. But we say: don't just touch it, take it in your hands, and set it to work in your own interests, for the abolition of private ownership and the emancipation of the working class." (Leon Trotsky, *How The Revolution Armed, Volume 1*, 1918)

Marxism explains that that the state consists ultimately of armed bodies of men: the army, police, courts and jails. Against the confused ideas of the anarchists, Marx argued that workers need a state to overcome the resistance of the exploiting classes. But that argument of Marx has been distorted by both the bourgeois and the anarchists. Marx spoke of the "dictatorship of the proletariat", which is merely a more scientifically precise term for "the political rule of the working class."

Nowadays, the word dictatorship has connotations that were unknown to Marx. In an age that has become acquainted with the horrific crimes of Hitler and Stalin, it conjures up nightmarish visions of a totalitarian monster, concentration camps and secret police. But such things did not yet exist even in the imagination in Marx's day. For him the word dictatorship came from the Roman Republic, where it meant a situation where in time of war, the normal rules were set aside for a temporary period.

The Roman dictator ("one who dictates"), was an extraordinary magistrate (magistratus extraordinarius) with the absolute authority to perform tasks beyond the normal authority of a magistrate. The office was originally named *Magister Populi* (Master of the People), that is to say, Master of the Citizen Army. In other words, it was a military role which almost always involved leading an army in the field. Once the appointed period ended, the dictator would step down. The idea of a totalitarian dictatorship like Stalin's Russia, where the state would oppress the working class in the interests of a privileged caste of bureaucrats, would have horrified Marx.

His model could not have been more different. Marx based his idea of the dictatorship of the proletariat on the Paris Commune of 1871. Here, for the first time, the popular masses, with the workers at their head, overthrew the old state and at least began the task of transforming society. With no clearly-defined plan of action, leadership or organisation, the masses displayed an astonishing degree of courage, initiative and creativity. Summing up the experience of the Paris Commune, Marx and Engels explained:

> "One thing especially was proved by the Commune, viz. that 'the working class cannot simply lay hold of the ready-made state machinery, and wield it for its own purposes'..." (Preface to the 1872 German edition of the *Communist Manifesto*).

The transition to socialism – a higher form of society based on genuine democracy and plenty for all – can only be accomplished by the active and conscious participation of the working class in the running of society, of industry, and of the state. It is not something that is kindly handed down to the workers by kind-hearted capitalists or bureaucratic mandarins.

Under Lenin and Trotsky, the Soviet state was constructed in order to facilitate the drawing of workers into the tasks of control and accounting, to ensure the uninterrupted progress of the reduction of the "special functions" of officialdom and of the power of the state. Strict limitations were placed upon the salaries, power, and privileges of officials in order to prevent the formation of a privileged caste.

The workers' state established by the Bolshevik Revolution in 1917 was neither bureaucratic nor totalitarian. On the contrary, before the Stalinist bureaucracy usurped control from the masses, it was the most democratic state that ever existed. The basic principles of the Soviet power were not invented by Marx or Lenin. They were based on the concrete experience of the Paris Commune, and later elaborated upon by Lenin.

Lenin was the sworn enemy of bureaucracy. He always emphasised that the proletariat needs only a state that is "so constituted that it will at once begin to die away and cannot help dying away." A genuine workers' state has nothing in common with the bureaucratic monster that exists today, and even less the one that existed in Stalinist Russia.

The Soviets of Workers' and Soldiers' Deputies were elected assemblies composed not of professional politicians and bureaucrats, but of ordinary workers, peasants and soldiers. It was not an alien a power standing over society, but a power based on the direct initiative of the people from below. Its laws were not like the laws enacted by a capitalist state power. It was an entirely different kind of power from the one that generally exists in the parliamentary bourgeois-democratic republics of the type still prevailing in the advanced countries of Europe and America. This power was of the same type as the Paris Commune of 1871.

It is true that in conditions of appalling backwardness, poverty and illiteracy, the Russian working class was unable to hold onto the power they had conquered. The Revolution suffered a process of bureaucratic degeneration that led to the establishment of Stalinism. Contrary to the lies of bourgeois historians, Stalinism was not the product of Bolshevism but its bitterest enemy. Stalin stands approximately in the same relation to Marx and Lenin as Napoleon to the Jacobins or the Pope to the early Christians.

The early Soviet Union was in fact not a state at all in the sense we normally understand it, but only the organised expression of the revolutionary power of the working people. To use the phrase of Marx, it was a "semi-state", a state so-designed that it would eventually wither away and be dissolved into society, giving way to the collective administration of society for the benefit of all, without force or coercion. That, and only that, is the genuine Marxist conception of a workers' state.

The rise of capitalism

Trotsky pointed out that revolution is the motor force of history. It is no coincidence that the rise of the bourgeoisie in Italy, Holland, England and later in France was accompanied by an extraordinary flourishing of culture, art and science. In those countries where the bourgeois revolution triumphed in the 17th and 18th centuries, the development of the productive forces and technology was complemented by a parallel development of science and philosophy, which undermined the ideological domination of the Church forever.

In contrast, those countries where the forces of feudal-Catholic reaction strangled the embryo of the new society in the womb were condemned to suffer the nightmare of a long and inglorious period of degeneration, decline and decay. The example of Spain is perhaps the most graphic in this regard.

The rise of capitalism began in the Netherlands and the cities of northern Italy. It was accompanied by new attitudes, which gradually solidified into a new morality and new religious beliefs. Under feudalism economic power was expressed as the ownership of land. Money played a secondary role. But the rise of trade and manufacture and the incipient market relations that accompanied them made Money an even greater power. Great banking families like the Fuggers arose and challenged the might of kings.

The bloody wars of religion in the 16th and 17th century were merely the outward expression of deeper class conflicts. The only possible result of these struggles was the rise to power of the bourgeoisie and new (capitalist) relations of production. But the leaders of these struggles had no prior knowledge of this.

The English Revolution of 1640-60 was a great social transformation. The old feudal regime was destroyed and replaced with a new capitalist social order. The Civil War was a class war which overthrew the despotism of Charles I and the reactionary feudal order that stood behind him. Parliament represented the new rising middle classes of town and country which challenged and defeated the old regime, cutting off the head of the king and abolishing the House of Lords in the process.

Objectively, Oliver Cromwell was laying the basis for the rule of the bourgeoisie in England. But in order to do this, in order to clear all the feudal-monarchical rubbish out of the way, he was first obliged to sweep aside the cowardly bourgeoisie, dissolve its parliament and base himself on the petty bourgeoisie, the small farmers of East Anglia, the class to which he belonged, and the plebeian and semi-proletarian masses of town and country.

Placing himself at the head of a revolutionary army, Cromwell aroused the fighting spirit of the masses by appealing to the Bible, the Saints and the Kingdom of God on Earth. His soldiers did not go into battle under the banner of Rent, Interest and Profit, but singing religious hymns. This evangelistic spirit, which was soon filled with a revolutionary (and even sometimes a communistic) content, was what inspired the masses to fight with tremendous courage and enthusiasm against the Hosts of Baal.

However, once in power, Cromwell could not go beyond the bounds established by history and the objective limits of the productive forces of the epoch. He was compelled to turn against the Left Wing, suppressing the Levellers by force, and to pursue a policy that favoured the bourgeoisie and the reinforcement of capitalist property relations in England. In the end, Cromwell dismissed parliament and ruled as dictator until his death, when the English bourgeoisie, fearful that the Revolution had gone too far and might pose a threat to property, restored the Stuarts to the throne.

The French Revolution of 1789-93 was on a qualitatively higher level. Instead of religion, the Jacobins appealed to Reason. They fought under the banner of Liberty, Equality and Fraternity in order to rouse the plebeian and semi-proletarian masses against the feudal aristocracy and the monarchy.

Long before it brought down the formidable walls of the Bastille, it had overthrown the invisible, but no less formidable, walls of the Church and religion. But when the French bourgeoisie became the ruling class, faced with the new revolutionary class, the proletariat, the bourgeoisie quickly forgot the rationalist and atheist intoxication of its youth.

After the fall of Robespierre, the victorious men of property longed for stability. Searching for stabilising formulae and a conservative ideology that would justify their privileges, they quickly rediscovered the charms of Holy Mother Church. The latter, with her extraordinary ability to adapt, has managed to survive for two millennia, despite all the social changes that have taken place. The Catholic Church soon welcomed its new master and protector, sanctifying the domain of Big Capital, in the same way as before the same church had sanctified the power of feudal monarchs and the slave owners of the Roman Empire.

Marxist philosophy

In the writings of Marx and Engels we do not have a philosophical system, like that of Hegel, but a series of brilliant insights and pointers, which, if they were developed, would provide a valuable addition to the methodological armoury of science. Unfortunately, such a work has never been seriously undertaken.

There is a difficulty for anyone who wishes to study dialectical materialism thoroughly. Despite the immense importance of the subject, there is no single book of Marx and Engels that deals with the question in a comprehensive manner. However, the dialectical method is in evidence in all the writings of

Marx. Probably the best example of the application of dialectics to a particular field (in this case political economy) consists of the three volumes of *Capital*.

For a long time, Marx had intended to write a book on dialectical materialism, but it proved impossible because of his work on *Capital*. In addition to this monumental task, Marx produced numerous political writings and was constantly engaged in active participation in the labour movement, particularly in the construction of the International Workingmen's Association (the First International). This occupied every moment of his time, and even this work was frequently interrupted by bouts of illness brought on by his miserable living conditions, poor diet and exhaustion.

After Marx's death Engels planned to write the book on philosophy that his friend was unable to produce. He left us a precious legacy of writings on Marxist philosophy, such as *Ludwig Feuerbach and the End of Classical German Philosophy*, *Anti-Dühring* and *Dialectics of Nature*. But unfortunately, Engels also failed to write the definitive book on Marxist philosophy for various reasons.

First, the emergence of an opportunist trend within the Social Democratic Party in Germany forced him to leave his scientific research to one side in order to write a polemic against opportunism that has become one of the most important classics of Marxism. This was the celebrated *Anti-Dühring* which, among other things, contains a contribution to Marxist philosophy of the first order of importance.

Later on, Engels returned to his preparatory studies for a comprehensive book on philosophy. But with the death of Marx, on March 14, 1883, he was again obliged to suspend this work in order to prioritise the difficult task of putting in order and completing the manuscripts of *Volumes Two* and *Three* of *Capital* that had been left unfinished.

Marx and Hegel

Dialectical philosophy reached its highest point in the philosophy of the German idealist Georg Hegel. His great contribution was to rediscover dialectics, originally invented by the Greeks. He developed this to new heights. But he did this on the basis of idealism. This was, in Engels' words, the greatest miscarriage in history. Reading Hegel, one has the sensation of a truly great idea that is struggling to escape from the straitjacket of idealist mystification. Here we find extraordinarily profound ideas and flashes of great insight, but buried amidst a heap of idealist nonsense. It is a very frustrating experience to read Hegel!

Time and again this great thinker drew tantalisingly close to a materialist position. But at the last minute he always drew back, fearful of the consequences. For that reason, Hegelian philosophy was unsatisfactory, contradictory, botched and incomplete. It was left to Marx and Engels to dot the Is and cross the Ts, to carry the Hegelian philosophy to its logical conclusions, and, in so doing, to negate it utterly and replace it with something qualitatively superior.

Hegel carried traditional philosophy as far as it could go. In order to carry it further, it had to go beyond its bounds, negating itself in the process. Philosophy had to return from the nebulous realms of speculation back to the real world of material things, of living men and women, of real history and struggle from which it had been separated for so long.

The problem with Feuerbach and some other Left Hegelians, like Moses Hess, is that they merely said no to Hegel, negating his philosophy by simply denying it. Hess' move to materialism was a bold one. It required courage, especially in the given context of general European reaction and the repressive Prussian state. It provided inspiration to the young Marx and Engels. But ultimately, it failed.

One can negate a grain of wheat by crushing it underfoot. But the dialectical concept of negation is not merely to destroy: it is to destroy while simultaneously preserving all that deserves to be preserved. A grain of wheat can also be negated by allowing it to germinate.

Hegel pointed out that the same words in the mouth of an adolescent do not carry the same weight as on the lips of an old man, who has lived life and accumulated great experience. It is the same with philosophy. In returning to its starting point, philosophy does not merely repeat a long-surpassed stage. It does not become childish by returning in old age to its infancy, but it returns to the old ideas of the Ionic Greeks enriched by 2,000 years of history and the development of science and culture.

This is not the mechanical movement of a gigantic wheel, the senseless repetition of previous stages, like the endless process of rebirth that features in certain Oriental religions, but the negation of the negation, which posits the return to an earlier phase of development, but on a qualifiedly higher level. It is the same, and not the same.

However, although he reached some deep and important conclusions, at times drawing close to materialism (for example in *The Philosophy of History*), Hegel remained a prisoner of his idealist outlook. He never managed to apply his dialectical method correctly to the real world of society and nature, because for him, the only real development was the development of the world of ideas.

Marx's philosophical revolution

Of all the theories of Marx, no other has been so attacked, distorted and slandered as dialectical materialism. And this is no accident, since this theory is the basis and foundation of Marxism. It is, more or less, the method of scientific socialism. Marxism is much more than a political programme and an economic theory. It is a philosophy, the vast scope of which covers not only politics and the class struggle, but the whole of human history, economics, society, thought and nature.

Today, the ideology of the bourgeoisie is in the process of disintegration, not only in the field of economics and politics but also in that of philosophy. In the period of its ascent the bourgeoisie was capable of producing great thinkers like Hegel and Kant. In the period of its senile decay it produces nothing of value. It is impossible to read the barren products of the university philosophy departments without a feeling of tedium and irritation in equal measure.

The fight against the power of the ruling class cannot stop in the factories, the streets, parliament and local councils. We must also carry out the battle in the ideological field, where the influence of the bourgeoisie is no less pernicious and harmful by being hidden under the guise of a false impartiality and a superficial objectivity. Marxism has a duty to provide a comprehensive alternative to the old and discredited schemes.

The young Marx was heavily influenced by Hegelian philosophy that dominated the German universities at that time. The whole of Hegel's doctrine was based on the idea of constant change and development through contradictions. In that sense it represented a real revolution in philosophy. It is this dynamic, revolutionary side that inspired the young Marx and is the starting point for all his ideas.

Marx and Engels negated Hegel and turned his system of ideas into its opposite. But they did so while simultaneously preserving all that was valuable in his philosophy. They based themselves on the "rational kernel" of Hegel's ideas and carried them to a higher level by developing and making actual what was always implicit in them.

In Hegel, the real struggle of historical forces is expressed in the shadowy form of the struggle of ideas. But, as Marx explains, ideas in themselves have no history and no real existence. Therefore, reality appears in Hegel in a mystified, alienated form. In Feuerbach things are really not much better, since Man here appears also in a one-sided, idealistic and unreal manner. The real, historical men and women only appear with the advent of Marxist philosophy.

With the philosophy of Marx, philosophy at last returns to its roots. It is both dialectical and materialist. Here theory and practice once again join hands and rejoice together. Philosophy comes out of its dark and airless study and enjoys the sun and air. It becomes an inseparable part of life. In place of the obscure conflict of ideas without substance, we have the real contradictions of the material world and society. Instead of a remote and incomprehensible Absolute, we have real men and women, living in real society, making real history and fighting real battles.

The dialectic appears in the work of Hegel in a fantastic and semi-mystical guise. It is "upside down", so to speak. Here we do not find the real processes taking place in nature and society, but only the pale reflection of those processes in the minds of men, especially of philosophers. In the words of Engels, the dialectic in Hegel's hands, despite his great genius, was a colossal miscarriage.

He points out that Marx was the only one who could strip away the mysticism contained in Hegelian logic and extract the dialectical kernel. This represented the real discoveries in this field. Through the reconstruction of the dialectical method, Marx managed to provide the only true development of thought.

While the philosophy of Hegel interpreted things only from the point of view of the mind and spirit (i.e. from the idealist standpoint), Marx showed that the development of ideas in the minds of men is only a reflection of developments that occur in nature and society. As Marx says:

"Hegel's dialectic is the basic form of all dialectic, but only after being stripped of its mystical form, and it is precisely this which distinguishes my method." (*Letter to Kugelmann, 6 March 1868, MECW*, Volume 42, p543)

What is dialectics?

Trotsky, in his brilliant little article *The ABC of Dialectical Materialism*, defined dialectics thus:

> "The dialectic is neither fiction nor mysticism, but a science of the forms of our thinking insofar as it is not limited to the daily problems of life but attempts to arrive at an understanding of more complicated and drawn-out processes. The dialectic and formal logic bear a relationship similar to that between higher and lower mathematics."

The combination of the dialectical method with materialism created an extremely powerful analytical tool. But what is the dialectic? For reasons of space, it is impossible to explain here all the laws of dialectics developed by Hegel and perfected by Marx. I have attempted to do this elsewhere, in *Reason in Revolt: Marxist Philosophy and Modern Science*, published by Wellred Books. In a few lines I can only give the sketchiest of outlines.

In his book *Anti-Dühring* Engels characterised it as follows: "The dialectic is simply the science of the general laws of motion and development of nature, human society and thought." In *Dialectics of Nature* Engels also sketches in outline the main laws of dialectics:

1. The law of transformation of quantity into quality.

2. The law of the unity and struggle of opposites and transformation into each other when they are taken to extremes.

3. The law of development through contradictions, or put another way, the negation of the negation.

Despite its unfinished and fragmentary nature, Engels's book *Dialectics of Nature* is very important, along with *Anti-Dühring*, for the student of Marxism. Obviously, Engels had to rely on the knowledge and scientific discoveries of the time. Consequently, certain aspects of the content have a mainly historical interest. But what is surprising in *Dialectics of Nature* is not this or that detail or fact that has been inevitably overtaken by the march of science. On the contrary, what is astonishing is the number of ideas advanced by Engels – often ideas that ran counter to the scientific theories of his day – which have been corroborated brilliantly by modern science.

Throughout the book, Engels emphasises the idea that matter and motion (now we would call it energy) are inseparable. Motion is the mode of existence of matter. This dynamic view of matter, of the universe, contains a profound truth that was already understood, or rather guessed as, by the early Greek philosophers like Heraclitus. For him "everything is and is not, because everything is in flux". Everything is constantly changing, coming into being and passing away.

For common sense, the mass of an object never changes. For example, a spinning top when rotating, has the same weight as one that is motionless. Mass was therefore considered to be constant, regardless of speed. Later it was discovered that this is wrong. In fact, mass increases with speed, but such an increase is only appreciable in cases where the velocity is approaching that of light. For the practical purposes of everyday life, we can accept that the mass of an object is constant regardless of the speed with which it moves. However, for very high speeds, this claim is false, and the higher the speed, the falser is the claim.

Commenting on this law, Professor Feynman's says: "[…] philosophically we are completely wrong with the approximate law. Our entire picture of the world has to be altered even though the mass changes only a little. This is a very peculiar thing about the philosophy, or the ideas, behind the laws. Even a very small effect sometimes requires profound changes in our ideas…" (R. Feynman, *Lectures on Physics*)

This example clearly demonstrates the fundamental difference between elementary mechanics and advanced modern physics. Similarly, there is a big difference between elementary mathematics, used for simple everyday calculations, and higher mathematics (the differential and integral calculus), discussed by Engels in *Anti-Dühring* and *Dialectics of Nature*.

The same difference exists between formal logic and dialectics. For everyday life, the laws of formal logic are more than enough. However, for more complex processes, these laws are often turned upside down. Their limited truth becomes false.

Quantity and quality

From the point of view of dialectical materialism, the material universe has no beginning or end, but consists of a mass of material (or energy) in a constant state of movement. This is the fundamental idea of Marxist philosophy and it is completely supported by the discoveries of modern science over the last one hundred years.

Take any example from everyday life: any phenomenon apparently stable, and we will see below the surface it is in a state of flux, although this change is invisible at first glance. For example, a glass of water: "To our eyes, our crude eyes, nothing is changing, but if we could see it a billion times magnified, we would see that from its own point of view it is always changing: molecules are leaving the surface, molecules are coming back." (Richard P Feynman, *The Feynman Lectures on Physics*, Chapter 1, p8)

These words are not of Engels, but a renowned scientist, the late Professor Richard P Feynman, who used to teach theoretical physics at the California Institute of Technology. The same author repeats Engels' famous example of the law of transformation of quantity into quality.

Water is composed of hydrogen and oxygen atoms in a state of constant motion. Water does not break up into its component parts due to the mutual attraction of the molecules. However, if it is heated to 100 ° C at normal atmospheric pressure, it reaches a critical point where the attractive force between the molecules is insufficient and they fly apart suddenly.

This example may seem trivial, but it has tremendously important consequences for science and industry. It is part of a very important branch of modern physics: the study of phase transitions. Matter can exist in four phases (or states), solid, liquid, gas, and plasma, plus a few other extreme phases, like critical fluids and degenerate gases.

Generally, as a solid is heated (or as pressure decreases), it will change to a liquid form, and will eventually become a gas. For example, ice (frozen water) melts into liquid water when it is heated. As the water boils, the water evaporates and becomes water vapour. But if this vapour is heated to a very high temperature, a further phase transition occurs. At 12,000 K = 11,726.85 Celsius, steam becomes plasma.

This is what Marxists call the transformation of quantity into quality. That is to say, a large number of very small changes finally produces a qualitative leap – a phase transition. Examples may be cited at will: If one cools a substance such as lead or niobium, there is a gradual reduction of its electrical resistance, up to a critical temperature (usually a few degrees above -273 ° C). Precisely at this point, all resistance will suddenly disappear. There is a kind of "quantum leap", the transition from having a small resistance to having none.

One can find a limitless number of similar examples in all the natural sciences. The American scientist Marc Buchanan wrote a very interesting book called Ubiquity. In this book, he gives a long series of examples: heart attacks, forest fires, avalanches, the rise and fall of animal populations, stock exchange crises, wars, and even changes in fashion and different schools of art (I would add revolutions to this list).

All these things seem to have no connection, yet are subject to the same law, which can be expressed by a mathematical equation known as a power law. What this is, in Marxist terminology, is the law of the transformation of quantity into quality. And what this study shows is that this law is ubiquitous, that is to say, it is present at all levels in the universe. It is a truly universal law of nature, just as Engels said.

Dialectics versus empiricism

"Give us the facts"! This imperious demand appears to be the acme of practical realism. What can be more solid than the facts? Only what appears to be realism turns out to be just the opposite. What are established facts at one time, can turn out to be something very different. Everything is in a constant state of change, and sooner or later everything changes into its opposite. What appears to be solid dissolves into thin air.

The dialectical method allows us to penetrate beyond appearances and see the processes that are taking place beneath the surface. The dialectic is first of all the science of universal interconnection. It provides a comprehensive and dynamic view of phenomena and processes. It analyses things in their relationship, not separately; in their motion, not statically; in their life, not death.

Knowledge of dialectics means freedom from the slavish worship of the established fact, of things as they are, which is the chief characteristic of superficial empirical thinking. In politics this is typical of reformism that seeks to cloak its conservatism, myopia and cowardice in the philosophical language of pragmatism, the art of the possible, "realism" and so on.

Dialectics permits us to penetrate beyond the "given", the immediate, that is, the world of appearance, and to uncover the hidden processes that are taking place beneath the surface. We point out that behind the appearance of calm and absence of movement, there is a process of molecular change, not only in physics but also in society and in the psychology of the masses.

It was not so long ago that most people thought the boom was going to last forever. That was, or appeared to be, an unquestionable fact. Those who did question it were regarded as deluded cranks. But now that unquestionable truth lies in ruins. The facts have changed into their opposite. What seemed to be an indisputable truth turns out to be a lie. To quote the words of Hegel: Reason becomes unreason.

Using this method more than a century ago, Frederick Engels was able, in a number of instances, to see further than most contemporary scientists, anticipating many of the discoveries of modern science. Engels was not a professional scientist, but had a fairly extensive knowledge of the natural sciences of his time.

However, based on a deep understanding of the dialectical method of analysis, Engels made a number of very important contributions to the philosophical interpretation of science today, although they have remained unknown to the overwhelming majority of scientists until now.

Of course, philosophy cannot dictate the laws of the natural sciences. These laws can only be developed on the basis of a serious and rigorous analysis of nature. The progress of science is characterised by a series of approximations. Through experiment and observation we get closer and closer to the truth, without ever being able to get to know the whole truth. It is a never-ending process of a deepening penetration of the secrets of matter and the universe. The truth of scientific theories can only be established through practice, observation and experiment, not by any commandments of philosophers.

Most of the questions with which philosophers have wrestled in the past have been solved by science. Nevertheless, it would be a serious mistake to suppose that philosophy has no role to play in science. There remain only two aspects of philosophy which remain valid today which have not been absorbed by the different branches of science: formal logic and dialectics.

Engels insisted that "the dialectic, stripped of mysticism, becomes an absolute necessity" for science. The dialectic, of course, has no magical quality to solve the problems of modern physics. Nevertheless, a comprehensive and coherent philosophy would be of inestimable help in guiding scientific investigation onto the most fruitful lines and prevent it from falling into all manner of arbitrary and mystical hypotheses that lead nowhere. Many of the problems facing science today arise precisely because of its lack of a firm philosophical foundation.

Dialectics and science

Many scientists treat philosophy with contempt. As far as modern philosophy is concerned, this contempt is well deserved. For the past one and a half centuries the realm of philosophy resembles an arid desert with only traces of life. The treasure trove of the past, with its ancient glories and flashes of illumination, seems utterly extinguished. Not only scientists but men and women in general will search in vain in this wasteland for any source of illumination.

Yet on closer inspection the contempt displayed by scientists to philosophy is not well grounded. For if we look seriously at the state of modern science – or more accurately at its theoretical underpinnings and assumptions, we see that science has in fact never freed itself from philosophy. Unceremoniously expelled by the front door, philosophy slyly gains an entry through the back window.

Scientists who proudly assert their complete indifference to philosophy in reality make all kinds of assumptions that are philosophical in character. And in fact, this kind of unconscious and uncritical philosophy is not superior to the old fashioned kind but immeasurably inferior to it. Moreover, it is the source of many errors in practice.

The remarkable advances of science over the past century seem to have made philosophy redundant. In a world where we can penetrate the deepest mysteries of the cosmos and follow the complex motions of sub-atomic particles, the old questions which absorbed the attention of philosophers have been resolved. The role of philosophy has been correspondingly reduced. However, to repeat the point, there are two areas where philosophy retains its importance: formal logic and dialectics.

A major advance in the application of the dialectical method to the history of science was the publication in 1962 of TS Kuhn's remarkable book *The Structure of Scientific Revolutions*. This demonstrated the inevitability of scientific revolutions and showed the approximate mechanism whereby these occur. "All that exists deserves to perish" holds good not only for living organisms but also to scientific theories, including those which we currently hold to be of absolute validity.

As a matter of fact, Engels was far ahead of his contemporaries (most scientists included) in his attitude towards the natural sciences. He not only explained motion (energy) as inseparable from matter, but also explained that the difference between the sciences consisted only in the study of the various forms of energy and the dialectical transition from one form of energy into another. This is what is now known as phase transitions.

The whole evolution of science in the twentieth century has rejected the old compartmentalisation, recognising the dialectical transition from one science to another. Marx and Engels in their day caused great indignation amongst their opponents, when they said that the difference between organic and inorganic matter was only relative. They explained that organic matter – the first living organisms – arose from inorganic matter at a given time, representing a qualitative leap in evolution. They said that animals, including man with his mind, his ideas and beliefs were simply matter organised in a certain way.

The difference between organic and inorganic matter, which Kant considered an insurmountable barrier, has been eliminated, as Feynman points out:

> "Everything is constituted by atoms. This is the key assumption. For example, the most important assumptions in biology are that everything that animals do, atoms do. In other words, there is nothing living things do that cannot be understood from the point of view that they are made of atoms, acting in accordance with the laws of physics." (R. Feynman, *Lectures on Physics*)

From the scientific perspective, men and women are aggregations of atoms arranged in a particular way. But we are not merely agglomeration of atoms. The human body is an extraordinarily complex organism, in particular the brain, the structure and functioning of which we are only now beginning to understand. This is something far more beautiful and wonderful than all the old fairy stories of religion.

At the same time that Marx was carrying out a revolution in the field of political economy, Darwin was doing the same in the field of biology. It is no accident that while Darwin's work aroused a storm of indignation and incomprehension, it was immediately recognised by Marx and Engels as a masterpiece of the dialectic, although Darwin himself was unaware of it. The explanation for this apparent paradox is that the laws of dialectics are not an arbitrary invention, but reflect processes that actually exist in nature and society.

The discovery of genetics has revealed the exact mechanism that determines the transformation of one species into another. The human genome has provided a new dimension to Darwin's work, showing that humans share our genes not just with the humble fruit fly but with the most basic forms of life, the bacteria. In the next few years, scientists will carry out an act of creation in a laboratory, producing a living organism from inorganic matter. The last patch of ground will be cut from under the feet of the Divine Creator, who will finally be rendered utterly redundant.

For a long time scientists argued as to whether the creation of new species was the result of a long period of accumulation of slow changes or arose from a sudden violent change. From a dialectical point of view, there is no contradiction between the two. A long period of molecular changes (quantitative changes) reaches a critical point where it suddenly produces what is now termed a quantum leap.

Marx and Engels believed the theory of evolution of species was clear proof of the fact that nature ultimately works in a dialectical way, i.e. through development, through contradictions. Three decades ago, this statement received a powerful boost from such a prestigious institution as the British Museum, where a furious debate broke the decorous silence of centuries. One of the arguments against the defenders of the idea of qualitative leaps in the chain of evolution was that it represented Marxist infiltration in the British Museum!

However, despite itself, modern biology has had no choice but to correct the old idea of evolution as a gradual, linear, uninterrupted process, without abrupt changes, and admit the existence of qualitative leaps, characterised by the mass extinction of some species and the emergence of new ones. On 17 April 1982 *The Economist* published an article on the centenary of Darwin that said:

> "It will be increasingly clear that fairly small mutations that affect what happens at a key stage of development can cause major evolutionary changes (for example, a small change in the mode of operation of certain genes could lead to a significant increase in brain size). Evidence is also accumulating that many genes undergo a slow but steady mutation. Thus, little by little, scientists solve the ongoing controversy of whether species change slowly and continuously for long periods, or remain unchanged for a long time and then experience a rapid evolution. Probably both types of changes occur."

The old version of evolutionary theory (phyletic gradualism) maintained that species change only gradually as individual genetic mutations arise and are selected. However, a new theory was put forward by Stephen Jay Gould and Niles Eldridge called "punctuated equilibrium" according to which genetic change can take place through sudden leaps. Incidentally, the late Stephen Jay Gould pointed out that if the scientists had paid attention to what Engels had written about human origins, they would have saved themselves a hundred years of error.

Whole nations bankrupt

The first phase of the crisis that began in 2008 was characterised by the default of big banks. The entire banking system of the USA and the rest of the world was only saved by the massive injection of billions of dollars and euros by the state. But the question must be asked: what is left of the old idea that the free market, if left to itself, will solve all problems? What is left of the old idea that the state must not interfere in the workings of the economy?

The massive injection of public money solved nothing. The crisis has not been resolved. It has merely been shifted onto states. All that happened is that in place of a massive deficit of the banks we have a gaping black hole in public finances. And who will pay for this? Not those well-heeled bankers who, having presided over the wrecking of the world financial order, have calmly pocketed the public's hard-earned money and are now awarding themselves lavish bonuses with the proceeds.

No! The deficits about which the economists and politicians are complaining so bitterly must be paid for by the poorest and most defenceless sections of society. Suddenly there is no money for the old, the sick, the unemployed, but there is always plenty of money for the bankers. This means a regime of permanent austerity. But this merely creates new contradictions. By cutting demand, it reduces the market still further, and thus aggravates the crisis of overproduction.

Now the economists are predicting a new collapse, when currencies and governments will go under, threatening the very fabric of the world financial system. And despite what the politicians say about the need to curb the deficit, debts on the scale that have been run up cannot be repaid. Greece provides a graphic example of this fact. The future is one of even deeper crises, falling living standards, painful adjustments and increasing impoverishment for the majority. This is a finished recipe for further upheavals and class struggle on an even higher level. It is a systemic crisis of capitalism on a world scale.

Some sophists ask: if socialism is inevitable, why should one have to struggle to achieve it? As a matter of fact, it is possible to be a convinced determinist and yet be committed to an active revolutionary role. In the seventeenth century the Calvinists were determinists of the most categorical and absolute kind. They believed fervently in predestination, that the fate and salvation of every man and woman was determined before they were born.

Nevertheless, this iron determinism did not prevent the Calvinists from playing a most revolutionary role in the struggle against decaying feudalism and its main ideological expression, the Roman Catholic Church. Precisely because they were convinced of the justice and inevitable triumph of their cause, they fought all the more bravely to speed up its victory.

The old society is dying on its feet, and a new society is struggling to be born. But those who have derived vast riches from it will never accept the inevitability of its demise. Sooner than see it sink into oblivion, the ruling class would prefer to drag the whole of society down with it. The prolongation of the death agony of capitalism constitutes a mortal threat to human culture and civilisation. Our task is to assist in the birth of the new society, to ensure that it takes place as swiftly and painlessly as possible, with the smallest cost to humanity.

Contrary to the calumnies of our enemies, Marxists do not advocate violence, but we are realists, and we know that the whole history of the last ten thousand years proves that no ruling class or caste ever surrenders its wealth, power and privileges without a fight, and that usually means a fight with no holds barred. And that remains the case today.

It is the decay of capitalism that threatens to unleash the most terrible violence on the world. In order to reduce the possibility of violence, to put an end to chaos and wars, to ensure the most peaceful and orderly transition to socialism, the prior condition is that the working class must be mobilised for struggle and be prepared to fight to the end.

"All roads lead to ruin"

Contrary to the comforting picture that used to be presented of the capitalist system offering a secure and prosperous future for all, we see the reality of a world in which millions suffer poverty and hunger, while the super rich become richer every day. People live in constant fear of an insecure future that will be decided, not by the rational decisions of people but solely by the wild gyrations of the market.

Financial crises, mass unemployment and constant social and political upheavals turn many things upside down. What appeared to be fixed and permanent dissolves overnight and people begin to question things they always took for granted. This state of perpetual unrest is what prepares the ground psychologically for revolution, which in the end becomes the only option that is realistically imaginable. In order to see this in practice one only has to look at present-day Greece.

Everybody knows that the capitalist system is in crisis. But what is the antidote to the crisis? If capitalism is an anarchic and chaotic system that inevitably ends in crises, then one must conclude that in order to eliminate crises it is necessary to abolish the capitalist system itself. If you say "A", you must also say "B", "C" and "D". But this is what the bourgeois economists refuse to do.

Are there no mechanisms that could allow the bourgeois to get out of a crisis of overproduction? Of course there are! One method would be to lower the rate of interest in order to boost profit margins and stimulate investment. But the rate of interest is already close to zero. Reduce it any further and we would be talking about a negative rate of interest: the banks would pay people to borrow money. This is completely crazy, but they are even discussing it. That shows that they are becoming desperate.

The other method is to increase state spending. This is what all the Keynesians and reformists are advocating. In the first place, this exposes the bankruptcy of free market economics. The private sector is so feeble, decrepit, so bankrupt in the literal sense of the word that it must rely on the state just as a man with no legs relies on crutches. But even that option does not offer a way out.

It is an obvious fact that the banks and big monopolies are now dependent on the state for their survival. As soon as they were in difficulties, the same people who used to insist that the state must play no role in the economy, ran to the government with their hands out, demanding huge sums of money. And the government immediately gave them a blank cheque. Trillions of pounds of public money has been handed over to the banks, totalling some $14trillion. But the crisis continues to deepen.

All that has been achieved in the last four years is to transform what was a black hole in the finances of the banks into a black hole in public finances. In order to save the bankers, everybody is expected to sacrifice, but for the bankers and capitalists no sacrifices are demanded. They pay themselves lavish bonuses with the money of the taxpayer. This is Robin Hood in reverse.

The existence of huge deficits means that the Keynesian argument about increasing state spending falls under its own weight. How can the state spend money it does not possess? The one avenue still open to them is printing money, or, as it is euphemistically known, Quantitative Easing (QE). The injection of large amounts of fictitious capital into the economy is subject to the law of diminishing returns. It has a similar effect to that of a junkie who has to inject himself with ever bigger quantities of a drug in order to get the same effect. In the process they are poisoning the system and undermining its health.

This is a really desperate measure that must result sooner or later in an increase in inflation. In this way, they are preparing for an even deeper slump in the coming period. This is the inevitable result of the fact that in the previous period the capitalist system went beyond its limits. In order to postpone a slump, they used up the very mechanisms that they need to get out of the present crisis. This is the reason why the crisis is so deep and so intractable. As Marx explains, the capitalists can only solve their crises "by paving the way for more extensive and more destructive crises, and by diminishing the means whereby crises are prevented." (*The Communist Manifesto*)

In the olden days the Church used to say: "All roads lead to Rome." Now the bourgeoisie has a new motto: All roads lead to ruin. It is unthinkable that a crisis that is throwing the whole world into chaos, that condemns millions of people to unemployment, poverty and despair, that robs the youth of a future and destroys health, housing, education and culture – that all this can occur without producing a social and political crisis. The crisis of capitalism is preparing the conditions for revolution everywhere.

This is no longer a theoretical proposition. It is a fact. If we take just the last twelve months, what do we see? Revolutionary movements have occurred in one country after another: Tunisia, Egypt, Greece, Spain. Even in the United States we have the #Occupy movement and the earlier mass protests in Wisconsin.

These dramatic events are a clear expression of the fact that the crisis of capitalism is producing a massive backlash on a world scale, and that a growing number of people are beginning to draw revolutionary conclusions. As long as a tiny minority holds in its hands the land, the banks and the big corporations, it will continue to take all the fundamental decisions that affect the lives and destinies of millions of people on the planet.

The intolerable gap that has developed between rich and poor is placing an increasing strain on social cohesion. The basis of the old Social Democratic dream of class peace and social partnership has broken down irremediably. This fact was summed up by the Occupy Wall Street slogan: "The one thing we all have in common is that we are the 99% that will no longer tolerate the greed and corruption of the 1%."

The problem is that the present protest movement is confused in its aims. It lacks a coherent programme and a bold leadership. But it reflects a general mood of anger that is building up under the surface and which sooner or later must find a way out. But they are definitely anti-capitalist movements, and sooner or later, in one country or another, the question of the revolutionary overthrow of capitalism will be posed.

Under capitalism, as Marx explained, the productive forces have experienced the most spectacular development in history. Yet the ideas of the ruling class, even in its most revolutionary epoch, lagged far behind the advances in production, technology and science.

The threat to culture?

The contrast between the rapid development of technology and science, and the extraordinary delay in the development of human ideology, is presented in a clear manner in the most advanced capitalist country of the world: the USA. This is the land where science has achieved its most spectacular results. The steady progress of technology is the precondition for the final emancipation of man, the abolition of poverty and illiteracy, ignorance, disease and the domination of nature by man through the conscious planning of the economy. The road is open to conquest, not only on Earth, but in space. And yet, in this technologically advanced country, the most primitive superstitions reign supreme. Nine out of ten Americans believe in the existence of a divine being and seven out of ten believe in life after death.

On Christmas Day 1968, when the first man to fly around the Moon had to choose a message to convey to the American people from his spaceship, out of the entire corpus of world literature, he chose the first book of Genesis. As he hurtled through space in a spaceship crammed full of the most modern gadgets, he pronounced the words: "In the beginning God created the heaven and the earth." It is more than 130 years since Darwin's death. Nevertheless, there are still many people in the USA who believe that every word of the Bible is literally correct, and who wish the schools to teach the version of human origins contained in Genesis, rather than the theory of evolution based on natural selection. In an attempt to make Creationism more respectable, its proponents have renamed it "intelligent design." The question immediately arises: who designed the intelligent designer? To this entirely reasonable question they have no answer. Nor can they explain why their "intelligent designer" made such a hopeless botch of the job when he created the world in the first place.

Why design a world with things like cancer, bubonic plague, aids, menstruation and migraine? Why design vampire bats, leeches and investment bankers? Come to think of it, why is it that apparently most of our genes are made of useless junk? Our intelligent designer turns out to be not so intelligent after all. In the words of Alfonso the Wise, King of Castile (1221-1284): "Had I been present at the Creation, I would have given some useful hints for the better ordering of the universe." Indeed, an eleven year old of average intelligence could probably have done a better job.

It is true that the authority of the Church is in decline in all Western countries. The number of practicing believers is decreasing. In countries like Spain and Ireland the Church is finding it difficult to recruit new priests. Attendance at mass has suffered a sharp decline in recent times, especially among the youth. ?However, the decline of the Church has opened the door to a real Egyptian plague of religious sects of the weirdest varieties, and a flowering of mysticism and superstitions of all kinds. Astrology, that remnant of medieval barbarism – is back in fashion. Cinemas, television and bookstores are full of works based on the most brazen mysticism and superstition. ?

These are only the outward signs of the putrefaction of a social system that has outlived itself, that has ceased to be a historically progressive force and that has definitely entered into conflict with the needs of the development of the productive forces. In this sense, the struggle of the working class to surgically cut short the agony of bourgeois society is also the struggle to defend the achievements of science and culture against the encroaching forces of barbarism.

The only alternatives open to humanity are clear: either the socialist transformation of society, the elimination of the political and economic power of the bourgeoisie and the initiation of a new stage in the development of human civilisation, or the destruction of civilisation, and even of life itself. The ecologists and Greens moan continually about the degradation of the environment and warn of the threat this poses for humanity. They are right. But they resemble an inexperienced doctor who points to the symptoms but is unable to diagnose the nature of the disease, or to suggest a cure.

The degeneration of the system is felt at all levels, not only in the economic field, but in the realm of morality, culture, art, music and philosophy. The existence of capitalism is being extended at the expense of the destruction of the productive forces, but it is also undermining culture, boosting demoralisation and the lumpenisation of entire layers of society, with disastrous consequences for the future. Ultimately, the existence of capitalism will enter into conflict with the existence of the democratic and trade union rights of the working class.

The increase in crime and violence, pornography, bourgeois selfishness and the brutal indifference to the sufferings of others, sadism, disintegration of the family and the collapse of traditional morality, drug addiction and alcoholism – all those things provoking the hypocritical wrath and indignation of reactionaries – are only symptoms of the senile degeneration of capitalism. In the same way that similar phenomena accompanied the period of decline of slave society under the Roman Empire.

The capitalist system, which puts profit before any other consideration, is poisoning the air we breathe, the water we drink and the food we eat. The latest scandal of the massive adulteration of meat products in Europe is only the tip of the iceberg. If we allow the rule of the big banks and monopolies to continue for another five decades or more, it is entirely possible that the destruction of the planet may reach a point where irreversible damage is done that will threaten the future existence of humankind. The struggle to change society is therefore a life and death question.

The need for a planned economy

For the past two decades we have been fed a steady diet of economic propaganda which assured us that the idea of a planned socialist economy was dead, and that the "market", left to its own devices, would solve the problem of unemployment, bringing about a world of peace and prosperity.

Now, following the crash of 2008, the truth is beginning to dawn on people that the existing order is incapable of assuring even the most basic of human needs – a job, a living wage, a home, decent education and health provisions, a proper pension, a safe environment, clean air and water – for the great majority, and not only for those in the Third World.

Such a system must surely stand condemned by all thinking people who are not blinded by the constant avalanche of spurious arguments, the sole purpose of which is to defend the vested interests of those who are doing extremely well out of the present set-up and cannot or will not believe that it will not last forever and a day.

The central point of the *Communist Manifesto* – and herein lies its revolutionary message – is precisely that the capitalist system is not forever. This is the element which the apologists of our present system find most difficult to swallow. Naturally! It is the common delusion of every socio-economic system throughout history that it represents the very last word in social progress. Yet even from the standpoint of commonsense, such a view is clearly flawed. If we accept that everything in nature is mutable, why should society be any different?

These facts indicate that the capitalist system had already exhausted its progressive mission. Every intelligent person realises that the free development of the productive forces demands the unification of the economies of all countries through a common plan which would permit the harmonious exploitation of the resources of our planet for the benefit of all.

This is so evident that it is recognised by scientists and experts who have nothing to do with socialism, but are filled with indignation at the nightmare conditions in which two thirds of the human race live, and are worried by the effects of the destruction of the environment. Unfortunately, their well-intentioned recommendations fall on deaf ears, since they conflict with the vested interests of the big multinationals that dominate the world economy and whose calculations are not based on the welfare of humanity or the future of the planet, but exclusively on greed and the search for profit above all other considerations.

The superiority of economic planning over capitalist anarchy is understood even by the bourgeois themselves, although they cannot admit it. In 1940, when Hitler's armies had smashed France, and Britain had its back against the wall, what did they do? Did they say: "Let market forces decide"? No! They centralised the economy, nationalised essential industries and introduced sweeping government controls, including economic conscription and rationing. Why did they opt for centralisation and planning? For the very simple reason that it gives better results.

Of course, it is impossible to have a real plan of production under capitalism. Nevertheless, even the measures of state capitalist planning introduced by Churchill's wartime coalition were essential for defeating Hitler. An even more striking example was the Soviet Union. The Second World War in Europe was in reality a gigantic conflict between Hitler's Germany, with all the resources of Europe behind it, and the Soviet Union.

It was the Soviet Union that defeated Hitler's armies. The reason for this extraordinary victory can never be admitted by the defenders of capitalism, but it is a self-evident fact. The existence of a nationalised planned economy gave the USSR an enormous advantage in the war. Despite the criminal policies of Stalin, which nearly brought about the collapse of the USSR at the beginning of the war, the Soviet Union was able to swiftly recover and rebuild its industrial and military capacity.

The Russians were able to dismantle all their industries in the West – 1,500 factories and a million workers – put them on trains and ship them east of the Urals where they were beyond the reach of the Germans. In a matter of months the Soviet Union was out-producing the Germans in tanks, guns and airplanes. This demonstrates beyond doubt the colossal superiority of a nationalised planned economy, even under Stalin's bureaucratic regime.

The USSR lost 27 million people in the Second World War – half the total deaths on a world scale. Its industries and agricultures suffered terrible devastation. Yet within ten years everything had been rebuilt, and without the kind of vast amounts of foreign money that were channelled into Western Europe by the Americans under Marshall Aid. That, and not Germany and Japan, is the real post-war economic miracle.

Of course, real socialism must be based on democracy – not the fake formal democracy that exists in Britain and the USA, where anybody can say what they want as long as the big banks and monopolies decide what happens – but a genuine democracy based on the control and administration of society by working people themselves.

There is nothing utopian about such an idea. It is based on what already exists. Let us take just one example. It is a never-ending source of amazement to the author of these lines how a big supermarket like Tesco can calculate precisely the amount of sugar, bread and milk that is required by an area of London with tens of thousands of inhabitants. They do this by scientific planning, and it never fails. If planning on such a level can work for a large supermarket, why cannot the same methods of planning be applied to society as a whole?

Socialism and internationalism

Anyone who reads the *Communist Manifesto* can see that Marx and Engels anticipated this situation more than 150 years ago. They explained that capitalism must develop as a world system. Today, this analysis has been brilliantly confirmed by events. At the present time nobody can deny the crashing domination of the world market. It is in fact the most decisive phenomenon of the age in which we live.

Yet when the *Manifesto* was written, there was practically no empirical data to support such a hypothesis. The only really developed capitalist economy was England. The infant industries of France and Germany (the latter did not even exist as a united entity) still sheltered behind high tariff walls – a fact which is conveniently forgotten today, as Western governments and economists deliver stern lectures to the rest of the world on the need to open up their economies.

In the last few years economists have talked a lot about "globalisation", imagining that this was the panacea which would permit them to abolish the cycle of booms and slumps altogether. These dreams were shattered by the collapse of 2008.

This has profound implications for the rest of the world. It shows the reverse side of "globalisation". To the degree that the capitalist system develops the world economy, it also prepared the conditions for a devastating world slump. A crisis in any part of the world economy rapidly extends to all the others. Far from abolishing the boom-slump cycle, globalisation has invested it with an even more convulsive and universal character than at any previous period.

The fundamental problem is the system itself. In the words of Marx, "The real barrier of capitalist production is capital itself." (*Capital Volume III, Part III*) The economic pundits who argued that Marx was wrong and capitalist crises were things of the past (the "new economic paradigm") have themselves been proved wrong. The present boom has all the features of the economic cycle Marx described long ago. The process of the concentration of capital has reached staggering proportions. There is an orgy of takeovers and ever-increasing monopolisation. This does not lead to the development of the productive forces as in the past. On the contrary, factories are closed as if they were matchboxes and thousands of people are thrown out of work.

The economic theories of monetarism – the Bible of neo-Liberalism – were summed up by John Kenneth Galbraith in the following way: "the poor have too much money, and the rich do not have enough." Record profit levels are accompanied by record inequality. The Economist has pointed out that "the one truly continuous trend over the past 25 years has been towards greater concentration of income at the very top."

A tiny minority are obscenely rich, while the share of the workers in the national income is constantly reduced and the poorest sections sink into ever deeper poverty. Hurricane Katrina revealed to the whole world the existence of a subclass of deprived US citizens living in third world conditions.

In the USA workers now produce 30% more than ten years ago, yet wages have hardly increased. The social fabric is increasingly strained. There is an enormous increase in tensions in society, even in the richest country in the world. This is preparing the ground for an even greater explosion of the class struggle.

This is not only the case in the USA. Around the world, the boom is accompanied by high unemployment. Reforms and concessions are being taken back. In order to become competitive in world markets, Italy would need to sack 500,000 workers and the remainder would have to accept a wage reduction of 30%.

For a time, capitalism succeeded in overcoming its contradictions by increasing world trade (globalisation). For the first time in history, the entire world has been drawn into the world market. The capitalists found new markets and avenues of investment in China and other countries. But this has now reached its limits.

The American and European capitalists are no longer so enthusiastic about globalisation and free trade, when mountains of cheap Chinese goods are piling up on their doorstep. In the US Senate protectionist voices are raised and are becoming increasingly insistent. The Doha round of talks about world trade has been suspended and so great are the contradictions that there is no agreement possible.

The current unstable economic boom is already running out of steam. The consumer boom in the USA is based on relatively low interest rates and a vast extension of credit and debt. These factors will turn into their opposite. A new crisis is being prepared on a world scale. Thus, globalisation reveals itself as a global crisis of capitalism.

Is there no alternative?

Bourgeois economists are so blinkered and narrow minded that they cling to the outmoded capitalist system even when they are forced to admit that it is terminally diseased and condemned to collapse. To imagine that the human race is incapable of discovering a viable alternative to this rotten, corrupt and degenerate system is frankly an affront to humanity.

Is it really true that there is no alternative to capitalism? No, it is not true. The alternative is a system based on production for the needs of the many and not the profit of the few; a system that replaces chaos and anarchy with harmonious planning; that replaces the rule of a minority of wealthy parasites with the rule of the majority who produce all the wealth of society. The name of this alternative is socialism.

One may quibble over words, but the name of this system is socialism – not the bureaucratic and totalitarian caricature that existed in Stalinist Russia, but a genuine democracy based on the ownership, control and management of the productive forces by the working class. Is this idea really so very difficult to understand? Is it really utopian to suggest that the human race can take hold of its own fate and run society on the basis of a democratic plan of production?

The need for a socialist planned economy is not an invention of Marx or any other thinker. It flows from objective necessity. The possibility of world socialism flows from the present conditions of capitalism itself. All that is necessary is for the working class, which constitutes the overwhelming majority of society, to take over the running of society, expropriate the banks and giant monopolies and mobilise the vast unused productive potential to solve the problems of society.

Marx wrote: "No social order is ever destroyed before all the productive forces for which it is sufficient have been developed." (Karl Marx, Preface to *A Contribution to the Critique of Political Economy*) The objective conditions for the creation of a new and higher form of human society have already been established by the development of capitalism. For the last 200 years the development of industry, agriculture, science and technology has acquired a speed and intensity without historical precedent:

> "The bourgeoisie cannot exist without constantly revolutionising the instruments of production, and thereby the relations of production, and with them the whole relations of society. Conservation of the old modes of production in unaltered form, was, on the contrary, the first condition of existence for all earlier industrial classes. Constant revolutionising of production, uninterrupted disturbance of all social conditions, everlasting uncertainty and agitation distinguish the bourgeois epoch from all earlier ones." (Marx and Engels, *The Communist Manifesto, Chapter I: Bourgeois and Proletarians*)

How true are these words of Marx and how applicable to our time! The solutions to the problems we face are already in existence. Over the last 200 years capitalism has built up a colossal productive power. But it is unable to utilise this potential to the full. The present crisis is only a manifestation of the fact that industry, science and technology have grown to the point where they cannot be contained within the narrow confines of private ownership and the nation state.

The development of the productive forces, especially since the Second World War, has been unprecedented in history: nuclear energy, microelectronics, telecommunications, computers, industrial robots ... have meant a dramatic increase in productivity at work to a level much higher than could have been imagined in Marx's time, giving us a very clear idea of what would be possible in the future under socialism, based on a socialist planned economy, above all on a global scale. The present crisis is merely a manifestation of the revolt of the productive forces against these suffocating limitations. Once industry, agriculture, science and technology are freed from the suffocating restraints of capitalism, the productive forces would be capable of immediately satisfying all human wants without any difficulty. For the first time in history, humanity would be free to realise its full potential. A general reduction in working hours would provide the material basis for a genuine cultural revolution. Culture, art, music, literature and science would soar to unimaginable heights.

The only road

Twenty years ago Francis Fukuyama spoke of the end of history. But history has not ended. In fact, the real history of our species will only begin when we have put an end to the slavery of class society and begun to establish control over our lives and destinies. This is what socialism really is: humanity's leap from the realm of necessity to the realm of freedom.

In the second decade of the 21st century, the human race stands at the crossroads. On the one hand, the achievements of modern science and technology have provided us with the means of solving all the problems that have plagued us for all of history. We can eradicate diseases, abolish illiteracy and homelessness and make deserts bloom.

On the other hand, reality seems to mock these dreams. The discoveries of science are used to produce ever more monstrous weapons of mass destruction. Everywhere there is poverty, hunger, illiteracy and disease. There is human suffering on a massive scale. Obscene riches flourish side by side with misery. We can put a man on the moon, but every year eight million people die simply because they do not have enough money to live. 100 million children are born, live and die on the streets, and they do not know what it is like to have a roof over their head.

The most striking aspect of the present situation is the chaos and turbulence that has gripped the entire planet. There is instability at all levels: economic, social, political, diplomatic and military.

Most people turn away from these barbarities in disgust. It seems that the world has suddenly gone mad. However, such a response is useless and counterproductive. Marxism teaches us that history is not meaningless. The present situation is not an expression of the madness or the inherent wickedness of men and women. The great philosopher Spinoza once said: "neither weep nor laugh, but understand!" That is very sound advice, for if we are not able to understand the world we live in, we will never be able to change it.

When Marx and Engels wrote the *Manifesto*, they were two young men, 29 and 27 years old respectively. They were writing in a period of black reaction. The working class was apparently immobile. The *Manifesto* itself was written in Brussels, where its authors had been forced to flee as political refugees. And yet at the very moment when the Communist *Manifesto* first saw the light of day in February 1848, revolution had already erupted onto the streets of Paris, and over the following months had spread like wildfire through virtually the whole of Europe.

After the fall of the Soviet Union, the defenders of the old order were jubilant. They spoke of the end of socialism, and even the end of history. They promised us a new era of peace, prosperity and democracy, thanks to the miracles of the free market economy. Now, only fifteen years later, those dreams are reduced to a heap of smoking rubble. Not one stone upon another remains of these illusions

What is the meaning of all of this? We are witnessing the painful death agonies of a social system that does not deserve to live, but which refuses to die. That is the real explanation of the wars, terrorism, violence and death that are the main features of the epoch in which we live.

But we are also witnessing the birth-pangs of a new society – a new and just society, a world fit for men and women to live in. Out of these bloody events, in one country after another, a new force is being born – the revolutionary force of the workers, peasants, and youth. At the UN President Chavez of Venezuels warned that "the world is waking up. And people are standing up".

These words express a profound truth. Millions of people are beginning to react. The massive demonstrations against the Iraq war brought millions onto the streets. That was an indication of the beginnings of an awakening. But the movement lacked a coherent programme to change society. That was its great weakness.

The cynics and sceptics have had their day. It is time to push them out of our way and carry the fight forward. The new generation is willing to fight for its emancipation. They are looking for a banner, an idea and a programme that can inspire them and lead them to victory. That can only be the struggle for socialism on a world scale. Karl Marx was right: The choice before the human race is socialism or barbarism.

1. Dialectical Materialism

What Is Dialectical Materialism?

Rob Sewell

Do we need a philosophy?

Scientific socialism or Marxism is composed of three component parts: dialectical materialism, historical materialism and Marxist economics. We begin with an explanation of the method of Marxism, namely dialectical materialism.

For those unacquainted with Marxist philosophy, dialectical materialism may seem an obscure and difficult concept. However, for those prepared to take the time to study this new way of looking at things, they will discover a revolutionary outlook that will allow them an insight into and understanding of the mysteries of the world in which we live. A grasp of dialectical materialism is an essential prerequisite in understanding the doctrine of Marxism. Dialectical materialism is the philosophy of Marxism, which provides us with a scientific and comprehensive world outlook. It is the philosophical bedrock – the method – on which the whole of Marxist doctrine is founded.

According to Engels, dialectics was "our best working tool and our sharpest weapon." And for us also, it is a guide to action and our activities within the working class movement. It is similar to a compass or map, which allows us to get our bearings in the turmoil of events, and permits us to understand the underlying processes that shape our world.

Whether we like it or not, consciously or unconsciously, everyone has a philosophy. A philosophy is simply a way of looking at the world. Under capitalism, without our own scientific philosophy, we will inevitably adopt the dominant philosophy of the ruling class and the prejudices of the society in which we live. "Things will never change" is a common refrain, reflecting the futility of changing things and of the need to accept our lot in life. There

3

are other such proverbs as "There is nothing new under the sun", and "History always repeats itself", which reflect the same conservative outlook. Such ideas, explained Marx, form a crushing weight on the consciousness of men and women.

Just as the emerging bourgeoisie in its revolution against feudal society challenged the conservative ideas of the old feudal aristocracy, so the working class, in its fight for a new society, needs to challenge the dominant outlook of its own oppressor, the capitalist class. Of course, the ruling class, through its monopoly control of the mass media, the press, school, university and pulpit, consciously justifies its system of exploitation as the most "natural form of society". The repressive state machine, with its "armed bodies of men", is not sufficient to maintain the capitalist system. The dominant ideas and morality of bourgeois society serve as a vital defence of the material interests of the ruling class. Without this powerful ideology, the capitalist system could not last for any length of time. Lenin states:

> "In one way or another, all official and liberal science defends wage-slavery... To expect science to be impartial in a wage-slave society is as foolishly naïve as to expect impartiality from manufacturers on the question of whether workers' wages ought not to be increased by decreasing the profits of capital."

Official bourgeois ideology conducts a relentless war against Marxism, which it correctly sees as a mortal danger to capitalism. The bourgeois scribes and professors pour out a continual stream of propaganda in an attempt to discredit Marxism – particularly the dialectic. This has especially been the case since the collapse of the Berlin Wall, and the ferocious ideological offensive against Marxism, communism, revolution, and such like. "Marxism is dead," they repeatedly proclaim like some religious incantation. But Marxism refuses to lie down in front of these witch doctors! Marxism reflects the unconscious will of the working class to change society. Its fate is linked to that of the proletariat.

The apologists of capitalism, together with their shadows in the labour movement, constantly assert that their system is a natural and permanent form of society. On the other hand, the dialect asserts that nothing is permanent and all things perish in time. Such a revolutionary philosophy constitutes a profound threat to the capitalist system and therefore must be discredited at all cost. This explains the daily churning out of anti-Marxist propaganda.

But each real step forward in science and knowledge serves to confirm the correctness of the dialectic. For millions of people the growing crisis of capitalism increasingly demonstrates the validity of Marxism. The objective situation is forcing working people to seek a way out of the impasse. "Life teaches," remarked Lenin. Today, to use the famous words of the *Communist Manifesto*, "A spectre is haunting Europe, the spectre of communism."

In the fight for the emancipation of the working class, Marxism also wages a relentless war against capitalism and its ideology, which defends and justifies its system of exploitation, the "market economy". But Marxism does more than this. Marxism provides the working class with "an integral world outlook irreconcilable with any form of superstition, reaction, or defence of bourgeois oppression" (Lenin). It seeks to reveal the real relationships that exist under capitalism and arms the working class with an understanding of how it can achieve its own emancipation. Dialectical materialism, to use the words of the Russian Marxist Plekhanov, is more than an outlook, it is a "philosophy of action".

The limits of formal logic

Men and women attempt to think in a rational manner. Logic (from the Greek *logos*, meaning "word" or "reason") is the science of the laws of thinking. Whatever thoughts we think, and whatever language they are expressed in, they must satisfy the requirements of reasoning. These requirements give rise to laws of thought, to the principles of logic. It was the Greek philosopher Aristotle (384 – 322BC) more than 2,000 years ago who formulated the present system of formal logic – a system that is the basis of our educational establishments to this very day. He categorised the method of how we should reason correctly and how statements are combined to arrive at judgements, and from them, how conclusions are drawn. He laid down three basic laws of logic: the principle of Identity ($A = A$), of non-contradiction (A cannot be A and not-A), and the excluded middle (A is either A or non-A; there is no middle alternative).

Formal logic has held sway for more than two millennia and was the basis of experiment and the great advances of modern science. The development of mathematics was based on this logic. You cannot teach a child to add up without it. One plus one equals two, not three. Formal logic may seem like common sense and is responsible for the execution of a million and one everyday things, but – and this is the big but – it has its limits. When dealing with drawn out processes or complicated events, formal logic becomes a totally inadequate way of thinking. This is particularly the case in dealing with movement, change and contradiction. Formal logic regards things as fixed and motionless. Of course, this is not to deny the everyday usefulness of formal logic – on the contrary – but we need to recognise it limits.

> "The dialectic is neither fiction nor mysticism," wrote Leon Trotsky, "but a science of the forms of our thinking insofar as it is not limited to the daily problems of life but attempts to arrive at an understanding of more complicated and drawn-out processes. The dialectic and formal logic bear a relationship similar to that between higher and lower mathematics." (*The ABC of Materialist Dialectics*).

With the development of modern science, the system of classification (of Linnaeus) was based on formal logic, where all living things were divided into species and orders. This constituted a great leap forward for biology compared to the past. However, it was a fixed and rigid system, with its rigid categories, which over time revealed its limits. Darwin in particular showed that through evolution it was possible for one species to be transformed into another species. Consequently, the rigid system of classification had to be changed to allow for this new understanding of reality.

In effect, the system of formal logic broke down. It could not cope with these contradictions. On the other hand, dialectics – the logic of change – explains that there are no absolute or fixed categories in nature or society. Engels had great fun in pointing to the duck-billed platypus, this transitional form, and asking where it fitted into the rigid scheme of things!

Only dialectical materialism can explain the laws of evolution and change, which sees the world not as a complex of ready-made things, but as a complex of processes, which go through an uninterrupted transformation of coming into being and passing away. For Hegel, the old logic was exactly like a child's game, which sought to make pictures out of jigsaw pieces. "The fundamental flaw in vulgar thought," wrote Trotsky, "lies in the fact that it wishes to content itself with motionless imprints of reality which consists of eternal motion."

Before we look at the main laws of dialectical materialism, let us take a look at the origins of the materialist outlook.

Materialism versus idealism

"The philosophy of Marxism is materialism," wrote Lenin. Philosophy itself fits into two great ideological camps: materialism and idealism. Before we proceed, even these terms need an explanation. To begin with, materialism and idealism have nothing whatsoever in common with their everyday usage, where materialism is associated with material greed and swindling (in short, the morality of present-day capitalism) and idealism with high ideals and virtue. Far from it!

Philosophical materialism is the outlook which explains that there is only one material world. There is no Heaven or Hell. The universe, which has always existed and is not the creation of any supernatural being, is in the process of constant flux. Human beings are a part of nature, and evolved from lower forms of life, whose origins sprung from a lifeless planet some 3.6 billion or so years ago. With the evolution of life, at a certain stage, came the development of animals with a nervous system, and eventually human beings with a large brain. With humans emerged human thought and consciousness. The human brain alone is capable of producing general ideas, i.e. thinking. Therefore matter, which existed eternally, has always existed independently of the mind and human beings. Things existed long before any awareness of them arose or could have arisen on the part of living organisms.

For materialists there is no consciousness apart from the living brain, which is part of a material body. A mind without a body is an absurdity. Matter is not a product of mind, but mind itself is the highest product of matter. Ideas are simply a reflection of the independent material world that surrounds us. Things reflected in a mirror do not depend on this reflection for their existence. "All ideas are taken from experience, are reflections – true or distorted – of reality," states Engels. Or to use the words of Marx, "Life is not determined by consciousness, but consciousness by life."

Marxists do not deny that mind, consciousness, thought, will, feeling or sensation are real. What materialists deny is that the thing called "the mind" exists separately from the body. Mind is not distinct from the body. Thinking is the product of the brain, which is the organ of thought.

Yet this does not mean that our consciousness is a lifeless mirror of nature. Human beings relate to their surroundings; they are aware of their surroundings and react accordingly; in turn, the environment reacts back upon them. While rooted in material conditions, human beings generalise and think creatively. They in turn change their material surroundings.

On the other hand, philosophical idealism states that the material world is not real but is simply the reflection of the world of ideas. There are different forms of idealism, but all essentially explain that ideas are primary and matter, if it exists at all, secondary. For the idealists, ideas are dissevered from matter, from nature. This is Hegel's conception of the Absolute Idea or what amounts to God. Philosophical idealism opens the road, in one way or another, to the defence of or support for religion and superstition. Not only is this outlook false, it is also profoundly conservative, leading us to the pessimistic conclusion that we can never understand the "mysterious ways" of the world. Whereas materialism understands that human beings not only observe the real world, but can change it, and in doing so, change themselves.

The idealist view of the world grew out of the division of labour between physical and mental labour. This division constituted an enormous advance as it freed a section of society from physical work and allowed them the time to develop science and technology. However, the further they were removed from physical labour, the more abstract became their ideas. And when thinkers separate their ideas from the real world, they become increasingly consumed by abstract "pure thought" and end up with all types of fantasies. Today, cosmology is dominated by complex abstract mathematical conceptions, which have led to all sorts of weird and wonderful erroneous theories: the Big Bang, beginning of time, parallel universes, etc. Every break with practice leads to a one-sided idealism.

The materialist outlook has a long history stretching back to the ancient Greeks of Anaxagoras (c.500-428 BC) and Democritus (c.460-c.370 BC). With the collapse of Ancient Greece, this rational outlook was cut across for a whole historical epoch, and only after the reawakening of thought following the demise of the Christian Middle Ages was there a revival of philosophy and natural science. From the seventeenth century, the home of modern materialism was England. "The real progenitor of English materialism is Bacon," wrote Marx. The materialism of Francis Bacon (1561-1626) was then systemised and developed by Thomas Hobbes (1588-1679), whose ideas were in turn developed by John Locke (1632-1704). The latter already thought it possible that matter could posses the faculty of thinking. It is no accident that these advances in human thought coincided with the rise of the bourgeoisie and great advances in science, particularly mechanics, astronomy and medicine. These great thinkers in turn provided the breakthrough for the brilliant school of French materialists of the eighteenth century, most notably René Descartes (1596-1650).

It was their materialism and rationalism that became the creed of the Great French Revolution of 1789. These revolutionary thinkers recognised no external authority. Everything from religion to natural science, from society to political institutions, was subjected to the most searching criticism. Reason became the measure of everything.

This materialist philosophy, consistently championed by Holbach (1723-1789) and Helvetius, was a revolutionary philosophy. "The universe is the vast unity of everything that is, everywhere it shows us only matter in movement," states Holbach. "This is all that there is and it displays only an infinite and continuous chain of causes and actions; some of these causes we know, since they immediately strike our senses; others we do not know since they act on us only by means of consequences, quite remote from first causes."

This rational philosophy was an ideological reflection of the revolutionary bourgeoisie's struggle against the church, the aristocracy and the absolute monarchy. It represented a fierce attack on the ideology of the Old Order. In the end, the kingdom of Reason became nothing more than the idealised kingdom of the bourgeoisie. Bourgeois property became one of the essential rights of man. The revolutionary materialists paved the way for the new bourgeois society and the domination of new forms of private property. "Different times, different circumstances, a different philosophy," stated Denis Diderot (1713-1784).

The new materialism, although a revolutionary advance, tended to be very rigid and mechanical. These new philosophers attacked the church and denied the self-sufficiency of the soul and held that man was simply a material body as all other animals and inorganic bodies. Man was regarded as a more complex and more delicate mechanism than other bodies. According to La Mettrie (1709-1751) in his principal work Man the Machine, "We are instruments endowed with feeling and memory."

For the French materialists the origin of knowledge – the discovery of objective truth – lay through the action of nature on our senses. The planets and man's place within the solar system and nature itself was fixed. For them, it was a clockwork world, where everything had its logical static place, and where the impulse for movement came from outside. The whole approach, while materialist, was mechanical, and failed to grasp the living reality of the world. It could not grasp the universe as a process, as matter undergoing continuous change. This weakness led to the false dichotomy between the material world and the world of ideas. And this dualism opened the door to idealism.

Others held to a monist view that the universe was one system which was not pure spirit or pure matter. Spinoza was the first to work out such a system. While he saw the need for a God, the universe was one system, which was wholly material from end to end.

Dialectics and metaphysics

The Marxist view of the world is not only materialist, but also dialectical. For its critics, the dialectic is portrayed as something totally mystical, and therefore irrelevant. But this is certainly not the case. The dialectical method is simply an attempt to understand more clearly our real interdependent world. Dialectics, states Engels in *Anti-Dühring*, "is nothing more than the science of the general laws of motion and development of nature, human society and thought." Put simply, it is the logic of motion.

It is obvious to most people that we do not live in a static world. In fact, everything in nature is in a state of constant change. "Motion is the mode of existence of matter," states Engels. "Never anywhere has there been matter without motion, nor can there be." The earth revolves continually around its axis, and in turn itself revolves around the sun. This results in day and night, and the different seasons that we experience throughout the year. We are born, grow up, grow old and eventually die. Everything is moving, changing, either rising and developing or declining and dying away. Any equilibrium is only relative, and only has meaning in relation to other forms of motion.

> "When we consider and reflect upon nature at large or the history of mankind or our own intellectual activity, at first we see the picture of an endless entanglement of relations and reactions, permutations and combinations, in which nothing remains what, where, and as it was, but everything moves, changes, comes into being, and passes away," remarks Engels.

> "We see, therefore, at first the picture as a whole, with its individual parts still more or less kept in the background; we observe the movements, transitions, connections rather than the things that move, combine, and are connected. This

primitive, naïve but intrinsically correct conception of the world is that of ancient Greek philosophy, and was first clearly formulated by Heraclitus: everything is and is not, for everything is fluid, is constantly changing, constantly coming into being and passing away."

The Greeks made a whole series of revolutionary discoveries and advances in natural science. Anaximander made a map of the world, and wrote a book on cosmology, from which only a few fragments survive. The Antikythera mechanism, as it is called, appears to be the remains of a clockwork planetarium dating back to the first century BC. Given the limited knowledge of the time, many were anticipations and inspired guesses. Under slave society, these brilliant inventions could not be put to productive use and were simply regarded as playthings for amusement. The real advances in natural science took place in the mid-fifteenth century. The new methods of investigation meant the division of nature into its individual parts, allowing objects and processes to be classified. While this provided massive amounts of data, objects were analysed in isolation and not in their living environment. This produced a narrow, rigid, metaphysical mode of thought that has become the hallmark of empiricism. "The Facts" became the all important feature. "Now, what I want is, Facts. Teach these boys and girls nothing but Facts. Facts alone are wanted in life," states the Dickensian character Thomas Gradgrind in *Hard Times.*

"To the metaphysician things and their mental reflexes, ideas, are isolated, are to be considered one after the other and apart from each other, are objects of investigation fixed, rigid, given once and for all," states Engels. "He thinks in absolutely irreconcilable antitheses. 'His communication is "yea, yea; nay, nay"; for whatsoever is more than these cometh of evil.' For him a thing either exists or does not exist; a thing cannot at the same time be itself and something else. Positive and negative absolutely exclude one another; cause and effect stand in rigid antithesis one to another.

"At first sight this mode of thinking seems to us very luminous, because it is that of so-called sound common sense. Only sound common sense, respectable fellow that he is, in the homely realm of his own four walls, has very wonderful adventures directly he ventures out into the wide world of research. And the metaphysical mode of thought, justifiable and necessary as it is in a number of domains whose extent varies according to the nature of the particular object of investigation, sooner or later reaches a limit beyond which it becomes one-sided, restricted, abstract, lost in insoluble contradictions. In the contemplation of individual things it forgets the connection between them; in the contemplation of their existence it forgets the beginning and the end of that existence; of their repose, it forgets their motion. It cannot see the wood for the trees."

Engels goes on to explain that for everyday purposes we know whether an animal is alive or not. But upon closer examination, we are forced to recognise that is not a simple straightforward question. On the contrary, it is a complex question. There are raging debates even today as to when life begins in the mothers' womb. Likewise, it is just as difficult to say when the exact moment of death occurs, as physiology proves that death is not a single instantaneous act, but a protracted process. In the brilliant words of the Greek philosopher Heraclitus:

> "It is the same thing in us that is living and dead, asleep and awake, young and old; each changes place and becomes the other. We step and we do not step into the same stream; we are and we are not."

Not everything is as appears on the surface of things. Every species, every aspect of organic life, is every moment the same and not the same. It develops by assimilating matter from without and simultaneously discards other unwanted matter; continually some cells die, while others are renewed. Over time, the body is completely transformed, renewed from top to bottom. Therefore, every organic entity is both itself and yet something other than itself.

This phenomenon cannot be explained by metaphysical thought or formal logic. This approach is incapable of explaining contradiction. This contradictory reality does not enter the realm of common sense reasoning. Dialectics, on the other hand, comprehends things in their connection, development, and motion. As far as Engels was concerned, "Nature is the proof of dialectics."

Here is how Engels described the rich processes of change in his book the *Dialectics of Nature*:

> "Matter moves in an eternal cycle, completing its trajectory in a period so vast that in comparison with it our earthly year is as nothing; in a cycle in which the period of highest development, namely the period of organic life with its crowning achievement – self-consciousness, is a space just as comparatively minute in the history of life and self-consciousness; in a cycle in which every particular form of

the existence of matter – be it the sun or a nebular, a particular animal or animal-species, a chemical combination or decomposition – is equally in transition; in a cycle in which nothing is eternal, except eternally changing, eternally moving matter and the laws of its movement and change. But however often and pitilessly this cycle may be accomplished in time and space, however many countless suns and earths may arise and fall, however long it may be necessary to wait until in some solar system, on some planet appear conditions suitable for organic life, however many countless beings may fall and rise before, out of their midst, develop animals with a thinking brain that find an environment that permits them to live, be it even only for a short period, we are, nevertheless, assured that matter in all its changes remains eternally one and the same, that not one of its attributes may perish, and that that same iron necessity which compels the destruction of the highest early bloom of matter – the thinking spirit – also necessitates its rebirth at some other place, at some other time."

Along with, and following the French philosophy of the eighteenth century, arose a new radical German philosophy. Through Emmanuel Kant, the culmination of this philosophy was epitomised by the system of George F. Hegel, who had greatly admired the French Revolution. Hegel, although an idealist, was the most encyclopaedic mind of his age. The great contribution of this genius was the rescuing of the dialectical mode of thought originally developed by the ancient Greek philosophers some 2,000 years before.

"Changes in being consist not only in the fact that one quantity passes into another quantity, but also that quality passes into quantity, and vice versa," wrote Hegel. "Each transition of the latter kind represents an interruption, and gives the phenomenon a new aspect, qualitatively distinct from the previous one. Thus water when cooled grows hard, not gradually… but all at once; having already cooled to freezing-point, it can still remain a liquid only if preserves a tranquil condition, and then the slightest shock is sufficient for it suddenly to become hard… In the world of moral phenomena… there take place the same changes of quantitative into qualitative, and differences in qualities there also are founded upon quantitative differences. Thus, a little less, a little more constitutes that limit beyond which frivolity ceases and there appears something quite different, crime…" (*The Science of Logic*).

Hegel's works are full of references and examples of dialectics. Unfortunately, Hegel was not only an idealist, but wrote in the most obscure and abstruse fashion imaginable, making his works very difficult to read. Lenin, while re-reading Hegel in exile during the First World War, wrote:

> "I am in general trying to read Hegel materialistically: Hegel is materialism which has been stood on its head (according to Engels) – that is to say, I cast aside for the most part God, the Absolute, the Pure Idea, etc."

Lenin was greatly impressed by Hegel, and, despite his idealism, later recommended that young communists study his writings for themselves.

The young Marx and Engels were followers of the great Hegel. They learned a colossal amount from this teacher. He opened their eyes to a new outlook on the world epitomised by the dialectic. By embracing the dialectic, Hegel freed history from metaphysics. For the dialectic, there is nothing final, absolute, or sacred. It reveals the transitory character of everything. However, Hegel was limited by his knowledge, the knowledge of his age, and the fact he was an idealist. He regarded thoughts within the brain not as more or less abstract pictures of real things and processes, but as realisations of the "Absolute Idea", existing from eternity. Hegel's idealism turned reality on its head.

Nevertheless, Hegel systematically outlined the important laws of change, touched upon earlier.

The law of quantity into quality (and vice versa)

> "It has been said that there are no sudden leaps in nature, and it is a common notion that things have their origin through gradual increase or decrease," states Hegel. "But there is also such a thing as sudden transformation from quantity to quality. For example, water does not become gradually hard on cooling, becoming first pulpy and ultimately attaining a rigidity of ice, but turns hard at once. If temperature be lowered to a certain degree, the water is suddenly changed into ice, i.e., the quantity – the number of degrees of temperature – is transformed into quality – a change in the nature of the thing." (*The Science of Logic*).

This is the cornerstone of understanding change. Change or evolution does not take place gradually in a straight smooth line. Marx compared the social revolution to an old mole burrowing busily beneath the ground, invisible for long periods, but steadily undermining the old order and later emerging into the light in a sudden overturn. Even Charles Darwin believed that his theory of evolution was essentially gradual and that the gaps in the fossil record did not represent any breaks or leaps in evolution, and would be "filled in" by further discoveries. In this Darwin was wrong. Today, new theories, essentially dialectical, have been put forward to explain the leaps in evolution. Stephen Jay Gould and Niles Eldredge termed their dialectical theory of evolution "punctuated equilibria". They explained that there were long periods of evolution where there were no apparent changes taking place, then suddenly, a new life form or forms emerged. In other words, quantitative differences gave rise to a qualitative change, leading to new species. The whole of development is characterised by breaks in continuity, leaps, catastrophes and revolutions.

The emergence of single-cellular life in the earth's oceans some 3.6 billion years ago was a qualitative leap in the evolution of matter. The "Cambrian explosion", some 600 million years ago, where complex multicellular life with hard parts exploded onto the scene was a further qualitative leap forward in evolution. In the lower Palaeozoic, some 400 to 500 million years ago, the first vertebrate fish emerged. This revolutionary design became dominant and advanced through the amphibians (which lived both in water and on land), through reptiles, and finally branched off into warm-blooded creatures: birds and mammals. Such revolutionary leaps culminated in human beings that have the capacity to think. Evolution is a long process whereby an accumulation of changes inside and outside the organism leads to a leap, a qualitatively higher state of development.

Just as colossal subterranean pressures that accumulate and periodically break through the earth's crust in the form of earthquakes, so gradual changes in the consciousness of workers lead to an explosion in the class struggle. A strike in a factory is not caused by outside "agitators", but is produced by an accumulation of changes within the factory that finally pushes the workforce to strike. The "cause" of the strike maybe something quite small and incidental, a tea-break for instance, but it has become "the last straw that breaks the camel's back", to use a popular (dialectical) expression. It has become the catalyst whereby quantity changes into quality.

The same is true of a revolution, which is a product of an accumulation of discontent within society that reaches boiling point. Consciousness is normally very conservative. People cling to what they have or know. Consciousness tends to lag behind the changing objective situation. It requires great events and shocks to affect it. As a consequence, rather than a slow gradual transformation, changes in mass consciousness take place abruptly in great leaps, where it can change in 24 hours or less. Such is the characteristic of revolutionary events.

Marx stressed that the task of science is always to proceed from the immediate knowledge of appearances to the discovery of reality, of the essence, of the laws underlying the appearances. Marx's *Capital* is a fine example of this method.

> "The way of thinking of the vulgar economists," wrote Marx to Engels, "derives from the fact that it is always only the immediate form in which relationships appear which is reflected in the brain, and not their inner connections." (June 27, 1867).

The same could be said of those who in the past wrote off the Soviet Union as "state capitalist". Stalinism had nothing in common with socialism; it was a repressive regime, where workers had less rights than in the west. However, instead of a scientific analysis of the Soviet Union, they simply pronounced it state capitalist. As Trotsky explained the theorists of state capitalism looked at the USSR through the eyes of formal logic. It was either-or, black or white. The USSR was either a wonderful socialist state, as the Stalinists said, or it must be a (state) capitalist state. Such thinking is pure formalism. They never understood the possibility of a degeneration of the workers' state into a chronically deformed variant of proletarian rule, as explained by Trotsky. It is clear that the revolution, due to its isolation in a backward country, went through a process of degeneration. However, while the nationalised planned economy remained, not everything was lost. The bureaucracy was not a new ruling class with a historic mission, but a parasitic growth on the state, which usurped political power. Only a new political revolution could eliminate the bureaucracy and reintroduce soviets and workers' democracy.

As Trotsky explained just before his death: "The definition of the USSR given by comrade Burnham, 'not a workers' state and not a bourgeois state,' is purely negative, wrenched from the chain of historical development, left dangling in mid-air, void of a single particle of sociology and represents simply a theoretical capitulation of pragmatism before a contradictory historical phenomenon.

> "If Burnham were a dialectical materialist, he would have probed the following three questions: (1) What is the historical origin of the USSR? (2) What changes has this state suffered during its existence? (3) Did these changes pass from the quantitative stage to the qualitative? That is, did they create a historically necessary domination by a new exploiting class? Answering these questions

would have forced Burnham to draw the only possible conclusion – the USSR is still a degenerated workers' state." (*In Defence of Marxism*).

The supporters of state capitalism tied themselves in knots, confusing counterrevolution with revolution and vice versa. In Afghanistan, they supported the reactionary fundamentalist mujahideen as "freedom fighters" against Russian "imperialism". With the collapse of the USSR and the move to restore capitalism from 1991 onwards, they remained neutral in face of real capitalist counterrevolution.

The unity of opposites

"The contradiction, however, is the source of all movement and life; only in so far as it contains a contradiction can anything have movement, power, and effect." (Hegel).

"In brief," states Lenin, "dialectics can be defined as the doctrine of the unity of opposites. This embodies the essence of dialectics…"

The world in which we live is a unity of contradictions or a unity of opposites: cold-heat, light-darkness, Capital-Labour, birth-death, riches-poverty, positive-negative, boom-slump, thinking-being, finite-infinite, repulsion-attraction, left-right, above-below, evolution-revolution, chance-necessity, sale-purchase, and so on.

The fact that two poles of a contradictory antithesis can manage to coexist as a whole is regarded in popular wisdom as a paradox. The paradox is a recognition that two contradictory, or opposite, considerations may both be true. This is a reflection in thought of a unity of opposites in the material world.

Motion, space and time are nothing else but the mode of existence of matter. Motion, as we have explained is a contradiction, being in one place and another at the same time. It is a unity of opposites.

"Movement means to be in this place and not to be in it; this is the continuity of space and time – and it is this which first makes motion possible." (Hegel)

To understand something, its essence, it is necessary to seek out these internal contradictions. Under certain circumstances, the universal is the individual, and the individual is the universal. That things turn into their opposites –

cause can become effect and effect can become cause – is because they are merely links in the never-ending chain in the development of matter.

"The negative is to an equal extent positive," states Hegel. Dialectical thought is "comprehending the antithesis in its unity." In fact Hegel goes further:

> "Contradiction is the root of all movement and vitality, and it is only insofar as it contains a Contradiction that anything moves and has impulse and activity... Something moves, not because it is here at one point of time and there at another, but because at one and the same point of time it is here and not here, and in this here both is and is not. We must grant the old dialecticians the contradictions which they prove in motion; but what follows is not that there is no motion, but rather that motion is existent Contradiction itself." Therefore for Hegel, something is living insofar as it contains contradiction, which provides it with self-movement.

The Greek atomists first advanced the revolutionary theory that the material world was made up of atoms, considered the smallest unit of matter. The Greek word atomos means indivisible. This was a brilliant intuitive guess. Twentieth century science proved that everything was composed of atoms, although it was subsequently discovered that even smaller particles existed. Every atom contains a nucleus at its centre, composed of sub-atomic particles called protons and neutrons. Surrounding the nucleus are particles known as electrons. All protons carry a positive electrical charge, and would therefore repel each other, but they are bound together by a type of energy known as the strong nuclear force. This shows that everything that exists is based on a unity of opposites and has self-movement of "impulse and activity," to use Hegel's words.

In humans, the level of blood sugar is essential for life. Too high a level is likely to result in diabetic coma, too little and the person is incapable of eating. This safe level is regulated by the rate at which sugar is released into the bloodstream by the digestion of carbohydrates, the rate at which stored glycogen, fat or protein is converted into sugar, and the rate at which sugar is removed and utilised. If the blood sugar level rises, then the rate of utilisation is increased by the release of more insulin from the pancreas. If it falls, more sugar is released into the blood, or the person gets hungry and consumes a source of sugar. In this self-regulation of opposing forces, of positive and negative feedbacks, the blood level is kept within tolerable limits.

Lenin explains this self-movement in a note when he says:

"Dialectics is the teaching which shows how opposites can be and how they become identical – under what conditions they are identical, becoming transformed into one another – why the human mind should grasp these opposites not as dead, rigid, but living, conditional, mobile, becoming transformed into one another."

Lenin also laid great stress on the importance of contradiction as the motive force of development.

"It is common knowledge that, in any given society, the strivings of some of its members conflict with the strivings of others, that social life is full of contradictions, and that history reveals a struggle between nations and societies, as well as within nations and societies, and, besides, an alternation of periods of revolution and reaction, peace and war, stagnation and rapid progress or decline." (Lenin, *Three Sources and Three Component Parts of Marxism*).

This is best illustrated by the class struggle. Capitalism requires a capitalist class and a working class. The struggle over the surplus value created by the workers and expropriated by the capitalists leads to an irreconcilable struggle that will provide the basis for the eventual overthrow of capitalism, and the resolution of the contradiction through the abolition of classes.

The negation of the negation

The general pattern of historical development is not one of a straight line upward, but of a complex interaction in which each step forward is only achieved at the cost of a partial step backwards. These regressions, in turn, are remedied at the next stage of development.

The law of the negation of the negation explains the repetition at a higher level of certain features and properties of the lower level and the apparent return of past features. There is a constant struggle between form and content and between content and form, resulting in the eventual shattering of the old form and the transformation of the content.

This whole process can be best pictured as a spiral, where the movement comes back to the position it started, but at a higher level. In other words, historical progress is achieved through a series of contradictions. Where the previous stage is negated, this does not represent its total elimination. It does not wipe out completely the stage that it supplants.

"The capitalist method of appropriation, which springs from the capitalist method of production, and therefore capitalist private property, is the first negation of individual private property based on one's own labour. But capitalist production begets with the inevitableness of a natural process its own negation. It is the negation of the negation," remarked Marx in *Volume I* of *Capital.*

Engels explains a whole series of examples to illustrate the negation of the negation in his book *Anti-Dühring*:

"Let us take a grain of barley. Millions of such grains of barley are milled, boiled and brewed and then consumed. But if such a grain of barley meets with conditions which for it are normal, if it falls on suitable soil, then under the influence of heat and moisture a specific change takes place, it germinates; the grain as such ceases to exist, it is negated, and in its place appears the plant which has arisen from it, the negation of the grain. But what is the normal life-process of this plant? It grows, flowers, is fertilised and finally once more produces grains of barley, and, as soon as these have ripened, the stalk dies, and is in its turn negated. As a result of this negation of the negation we have once again the original grain of barley, but not as a single unit, but ten, twenty or thirty fold."

The barley lives and evolves by means of returning to its starting point – but at a higher level. One seed has produced many. Also over time, plants have evolved qualitatively as well as quantitatively. Successive generations have shown variations, and become more adapted to their environment.

Engels gives a further example from the insect world:

"Butterflies, for example, spring from the egg through a negation of the egg, they pass through certain transformations until they reach sexual maturity, they pair and are in turn negated, dying as soon as the pairing process has been completed and the female has laid its numerous eggs."

Hegel and Marx

Hegel, who had a giant intellect, illuminated a great many things. It was a debt that Marx repeatedly recognised. "The mystification which dialectic suffers in Hegel's hands, by no means prevents him from being the first to present its general form of working in a comprehensive and conscious manner," states Marx. Nevertheless, Hegel's philosophical system was a huge miscarriage. It suffered from an incurable internal contradiction. Hegel's conception of history is an evolutionary one, where there is nothing final or eternal. However, his system laid claim to being the absolute truth, in complete contradiction to the laws of dialectical thought. While Hegel defended the status quo in Germany, the dialectic embraced a revolutionary view of constant change. For Hegel, all that was real was rational. But using the Hegelian dialectic, all that is real will become irrational. All that exists deserves to perish. In this lay the revolutionary significance of the Hegelian philosophy.

The solution of this contradiction led back to materialism, but not the old mechanical materialism, but one based upon the new sciences and advances.

"Materialism rose again enriched by all the acquisitions of idealism. The most important of these acquisitions was the dialectical method, the examination of phenomena in their development, in their origin and destruction. The genius who represented this new direction of thought was Karl Marx," writes Plekhanov.

Spurred on by revolutionary developments in Europe in 1830-31, the Hegelian School split into left, right and centre.

The most prominent representative of the Hegelian Left was Ludwig Feuerbach, who challenged the old orthodoxy, especially religion, and placed materialism at the centre of things again. "Nature has no beginning and no end. Everything in it is in mutual interaction, everything at once effect and cause, everything in it is all-sided and reciprocal..." writes Feuerbach, adding that there is no place there for God. "Christians tear out the spirit, the soul, of man out of his body and make this torn-out, disembodied spirit into their God." Despite Feuerbach's limitations, Marx and Engels welcomed the new breakthrough with enthusiasm.

"But in the meantime," noted Engels, "the Revolution of 1848 thrust the whole of philosophy aside as unceremoniously as Feuerbach himself was also pushed into the background." It was left to Marx and Engels to consistently apply the dialectic to the new materialism, producing dialectical materialism. For them, the new philosophy was not an abstract philosophy, but directly linked to practice.

"Dialectics reduces itself to the science of the general laws of motion, both of the external world and of human thought – two sets of laws which are identical in substance, but differ in their expression in so far as the human mind can apply them consciously, while in nature and also up to now for the most part in human history, these laws assert themselves unconsciously, in the form of external necessity, in the midst of an endless series of seeming accidents." (Engels)

Neither Marx nor Engels left behind them a comprehensive book on dialectics as such. Marx was preoccupied with *Capital*. Engels intended to write such a book, but was overtaken by the need to complete *Capital* after Marx's death. He nevertheless wrote quite extensively on the subject, especially in *Anti-Dühring* and the *Dialectics of Nature*. Lenin commentated:

> "If Marx did not leave behind him a 'Logic' (with a capital letter), he did leave the logic of Capital, and this ought to be utilised to the full. In Capital, Marx applied to a single science logic, dialectics and the theory of knowledge of materialism (three words are not needed: it is one and the same thing) which has taken everything valuable in Hegel and developed it further."

Today, a small number of scientists, mainly from the natural sciences, have become conscious of the dialectic, which has opened their eyes to problems in their specialised fields. This relationship between science and dialectical materialism has been fully discussed in the book by Alan Woods and Ted Grant, *Reason in Revolt*. They showed, along with Engels, that nature is completely dialectical. Apart from Stephen Jay Gould and Niles Eldredge, Richard Levins and Richard Lewontin, who regard themselves as dialectical materialists, have written about the application of the dialectic to the field of biology in their book *The Dialectical Biologist*:

> "What characterises the dialectical world, in all its aspects, as we have described it is that it is constantly in motion. Constants become variables, causes become effects, and systems develop, destroying the conditions that gave rise to them. Even elements that appear to be stable are in a dynamic equilibrium of forces that can suddenly become unbalanced, as when a dull grey lump of metal of a critical size becomes a fireball brighter than a thousand suns. Yet the motion is not unconstrained and uniform. Organisms develop and differentiate, then die and disintegrate. Species arise but inevitably become extinct. Even in the simple physical world we know of no uniform motion. Even the earth rotating on its axis has slowed down in geological time. The development of systems through time, then, seems to be the consequence of opposing forces and opposing motions.

> "This appearance of opposing forces has given rise to the most debated and difficult, yet the most central, concept in dialectical thought, the principle of contradiction. For some, contradiction is an epistemic principle only. It describes how we come to understand the world by a history of antithetical theories that, in contradiction to each other and in contradiction to observed phenomena, lead to a new view of nature. Kuhn's (1962) theory of scientific revolution has

some of this flavour of continual contradiction and resolution, giving way to new contradiction. For others, contradiction becomes an ontological property at least of human social existence. For us, contradiction is not only epistemic and political, but also ontological in the broadest sense. Contradictions between forces are everywhere in nature, not only in human social institutions. This tradition of dialectics goes back to Engels (1880) who wrote, in *Dialectics of Nature*, that 'to me there could be no question of building the laws of dialectics of nature, but of discovering them in it and evolving them from it.'" (*The Dialectical Biologist*, p279)

Marxists have always stressed the unity of theory and practice. "Philosophers have only interpreted the world, in various ways; the point, however, is to change it," as Marx pointed to in his *Theses on Feuerbach*. "If the truth is abstract it must be untrue," states Hegel. All truth is concrete. We have to look at things as they exist, with a view to understanding their underlying contradictory development. This has very important conclusions, especially for those fighting to change society. Unlike the Utopian socialists who viewed socialism as a wonderful idea, Marxists see the development of socialism as arising out of the contradictions of capitalism. Capitalist society has prepared the material basis for a classless society with its highly developed productive forces and its world division of labour. It has brought into being the working class, whose very life existence brings it into conflict with capitalism. On the basis of experience, it will become fully conscious of its position in society and it will be transformed, in the words of Marx, from a "class in-itself" to a "class for-itself".

Dialectics bases itself on determinism, but this has nothing in common with fatalism which denies the existence of accident in nature, society and thought. Dialectical determinism asserts the unity of necessity and accident, and explains that necessity expresses itself through accident. All events have causes, necessary events and accidental ones alike. If there were no causal laws in nature everything would be in a state of utter chaos. It would be an impossible position where nothing could exist. So everything is dependent upon everything else, as in a continuous chain of cause and effect. Particular events always have a chance or accidental character, but these arise only as the result of a deeper necessity. In fact, necessity manifests itself through a series of accidents. Without doubt, accidents have their place, but the essential thing is to discover what laws determine this deeper necessity.

From the point of view of superficial observation, everything may appear to be accidental or open to chance. This can appear especially so when we have no knowledge of the laws that govern change and their interconnections. "Where on the surface accident holds sway, there actually it is always governed by inner, hidden laws and it is only a matter of discovering these laws," remarked Engels in *Ludwig Feuerbach*.

In nature, the evolution of matter follows a certain path, although how, when, and in what form this is realised, depends upon accidental circumstances. For example, whether life was created or not on earth depended on a whole series of accidental factors, such as the presence of water, different chemical elements, the earth's distance from the sun, an atmosphere, etc.

> "It is the nature of matter to advance to the evolution of thinking beings," states Engels, "hence, too, this always necessarily occurs whenever the conditions for it (not necessarily identical at all places and times) are present…what is maintained to be necessary is composed of sheer accidents, and the so-called accidental is the form behind which necessity hides itself."

Superficial historians have written that the First World War was "caused" by the assassination of a Crown Prince at Sarajevo. To a Marxist this event was an historical accident, in the sense that this chance event served as the pretext, or catalyst, for the world conflict which had already been made inevitable by the economic, political and military contradictions of imperialism. If the assassin had missed, or if the Crown Prince had never been born, the war would still have taken place, on some other diplomatic pretext or other. Necessity would have expressed itself through a different "accident".

In the words of Hegel, everything which exists, exists of necessity. But, equally, everything which exists is doomed to perish, to be transformed into something else. Thus what is "necessary" in one time and place becomes "unnecessary" in another. Everything begets its opposite, which is destined to overcome and negate it. This is true of individual living things as much as societies and nature generally.

Every type of human society exists because it is necessary at the given time when it arises:

> "No social order ever disappears before all the productive forces for which there is room in it have been developed: and new higher relations of production never appear before the material conditions of their existence have matured in the

womb of the old society. Therefore mankind always takes up only such problems as it can solve, since, looking at the matter more closely, we will always find that the problem itself arises only when the material conditions necessary for its solution already exist or at least are in the process of formation." (Marx, *Critique of Political Economy*).

Slavery, in its day, represented an enormous leap forward over barbarism. It was a necessary stage in the development of productive forces, culture and human society. As Hegel brilliantly explained it: "It is not so much from slavery as through slavery that man becomes free."

Similarly capitalism was originally a necessary and progressive stage in human society. However, like primitive communism, slavery, and feudalism, capitalism has long since ceased to represent a necessary and progressive social system. It has foundered upon the deep contradictions inherent in it, and is doomed to be overcome by the rising forces of the new society within the old, represented by the modem proletariat. Private ownership of the means of production and the nation state, the basic features of capitalist society, which originally marked a great step forward, now serve only to fetter and undermine the productive forces and threaten all the gains made in centuries of human development.

Capitalism is now a thoroughly degenerate social system, which must be overthrown and replaced by its opposite, socialism, if human culture is to survive. Marxism is determinist, but not fatalist. Men and women make history. The transformation of society can only be achieved by men and women consciously striving for their own emancipation. This struggle of the classes is not pre-determined. Who succeeds depends on many factors, and a rising, progressive class has many advantages over the old, decrepit force of reaction. But ultimately, the result must depend upon which side has the stronger will, the greater organisation and the most skilful and resolute leadership.

The victory of socialism will mark a new and qualitatively different stage of human history. To be more accurate, it will mark the end of the pre-history of the human race, and start a real history.

However on the other hand, socialism marks a return to the earliest form of human society – tribal communism – but on a much higher level, which stands upon all the enormous gains of thousands of years of class society. The negation of primitive communism by class society is in turn negated by socialism. The economy of superabundance will be made possible by the application of conscious planning to the industry, science and technique established by capitalism, on a world scale. This in turn will once and for all make redundant the division of labour, the difference between mental and manual labour, between town and countryside, and the wasteful and barbaric class struggle and enable the human race at last to set its resources to the conquest of nature.

The ABC of Materialist Dialectics

Leon Trotsky

The dialectic is neither fiction nor mysticism, but a science of the forms of our thinking insofar as it is not limited to the daily problems of life but attempts to arrive at an understanding of more complicated and drawn-out processes. The dialectic and formal logic bear a relationship similar to that between higher and lower mathematics.

I will here attempt to sketch the substance of the problem in a very concise form. The Aristotelian logic of the simple syllogism starts from the proposition that "A" is equal to "A" This postulate is accepted as an axiom for a multitude of practical human actions and elementary generalisations. But in reality "A" is not equal to "A".

This is easy to prove if we observe these two letters under a lens – they are quite different from each other.

But, one can object, the question is not of the size or the form of the letters, since they are only symbols for equal quantities: for instance, a pound of sugar.

The objection is beside the point; in reality a pound of sugar is never equal to a pound of sugar – a more delicate scale always discloses a difference.

Again one can object: but a pound of sugar is equal to itself. Neither is this true – all bodies change uninterruptedly in size, weight, colour, etc. They are never equal to themselves.

A sophist will respond that a pound of sugar is equal to itself "at a given moment". Aside from the extremely dubious practical value of this "axiom", it does not withstand theoretical criticism either. How should we conceive the word 'moment'? If it is an infinitesimal interval of time, then a pound of sugar is subjected during the course of that 'moment' to inevitable changes.

Or is the "moment" a purely mathematical abstraction, that is, a zero of time? But everything exists in time; and existence itself is an uninterrupted process of transformation; time is consequently a fundamental element of existence.

Thus the axiom "A" is equal to "A" signifies that a thing is equal to itself if it does not change, that is, if it does not exist.

At first glance it could seem that these "subtleties" are useless. In reality they are of decisive significance. The axiom "A" is equal to "A" appears on one hand to be the point of departure for all our knowledge, on the other hand the point of departure for all the errors in our knowledge.

To make use of the axiom "A" is equal to "A" with impunity is possible only within certain limits. When quantitative changes in A are negligible for the task at hand, then we can presume "A" is equal to "A". This is, for example, the manner in which a buyer and a seller consider a pound of sugar. We consider the temperature of the sun likewise. Until recently we considered the buying power of the dollar in the same way. But quantitative changes beyond certain limits become converted into qualitative. A pound of sugar subjected to the action of water or kerosene ceases to be a pound of sugar. A dollar in the embrace of a president ceases to be a dollar. To determine at the right moment the critical point where quantity changes into quality is one of the most important and difficult tasks in all the spheres of knowledge, including sociology.

Every worker knows that it is impossible to make two completely equal objects. In the elaboration of bearing-brass into cone bearings, a certain deviation is allowed for the cones which should not, however, go beyond certain limits (this is called tolerance). By observing the norms of tolerance, the cones are considered as being equal ("A" is equal to "A"). When the tolerance is exceeded, the quantity goes over into quality; in other words, the cone bearings become inferior or completely worthless.

Our scientific thinking is only a part of our general practice, including techniques. For concepts there also exists "tolerance" which is established not by formal logic issuing from the axiom "A" is equal to "A" but by dialectical logic issuing from the axiom that everything is always changing. "Common sense" is characterized by the fact that it systematically exceeds dialectical "tolerance".

Vulgar thought operates with such concepts as capitalism, morals, freedom, workers' state, etc., as fixed abstractions, presuming that capitalism is equal to capitalism, morals are equal to morals, etc. Dialectical thinking analyses all things and phenomena in their continuous change, while determining in the material conditions of those changes that critical limit beyond which A ceases to be A, a workers' state ceases to be a workers' state.

The fundamental flaw of vulgar thought lies in the fact that it wishes to content itself with motionless imprints of reality, which consists of eternal motion. Dialectical thinking gives to concepts, by means of closer approximations, corrections, concretisations, a richness of content and flexibility, I would even say a succulence, which to a certain extent brings them close to living phenomena. Not capitalism in general but a given capitalism at a given stage of development. Not a workers' state in general, but a given workers' state in a backward country in an Imperialist encirclement, etc.

Dialectical thinking is related to vulgar thinking in the same way that a motion picture is related to a still photograph. The motion picture does not outlaw the still photograph but combines a series of them according to the laws of motion. Dialectics does not deny the syllogism, but teaches us to combine syllogisms in such a way as to bring our understanding closer to the eternally changing reality. Hegel in his Logic established a series of laws: change of quantity into quality, development through contradictions, conflict of content and form, interruption of continuity, change of possibility into inevitability, etc., which are just as important for theoretical thought as is the simple syllogism for more elementary tasks.

Hegel wrote before Darwin and before Marx. Thanks to the powerful impulse given to thought by the French Revolution, Hegel anticipated the general movement of science. But because it was only an anticipation, although by a genius, it received from Hegel an idealistic character. Hegel operated with ideological shadows as the ultimate reality. Marx demonstrated that the movement of these ideological shadows reflected nothing but the movement of material bodies.

We call our dialectic materialist since its roots are neither in heaven nor in the depths of our "free will" but in objective reality, in nature. Consciousness grew out of the unconscious, psychology out of physiology, the organic world out of the inorganic, the solar system out of nebula. On all the rungs of this ladder of development the quantitative changes were transformed into qualitative. Our thought including dialectical thought is only one of the forms of the expression of changing matter. There is place within this system for neither God, nor Devil, nor immortal soul nor eternal norms of laws and morals. The dialectic of thinking, having grown out of the dialectic of nature, possesses consequently a thoroughly materialist character.

Darwinism, which explained the evolution of species through quantitative transformations passing into qualitative, was the highest triumph of the dialectic in the whole field of organic matter. Another great triumph was the discovery of the table of atomic weights of chemical elements and further the transformation of one element into another.

With these transformations (species, elements, etc.) is closely linked the question of classifications, just as important in the natural as in the social sciences. Linnaeus's system (eighteenth century), utilizing as its starting point the immutability of species, was limited to the description and classification of plants according to their external characteristics.

The infantile period of botany is analogous to the infantile period of logic, since the forms of our thought develop like everything that lives. Only decisive repudiation of the idea of fixed species, only the study of the history of the evolution of plants and their anatomy prepared the basis for a really scientific classification.

Marx, who in distinction from Darwin was a conscious dialectician, discovered a basis for the scientific classification of human societies in the development of their productive forces and the structure of the relations of ownership, which constitute the anatomy of society. Marxism substituted for the vulgar descriptive classification of societies and states, which even up to now still flourishes in the universities, a materialistic dialectical classification. Only through using the method of Marx is it possible correctly to determine both the concept of a workers' state and the moment of its downfall.

All this, as we see, contains nothing "metaphysical" or "scholastic", as conceited ignorance affirms. Dialectical logic expresses the laws of motion in contemporary scientific thought. The struggle against materialist dialectics on the contrary expresses a distant past conservatism of the petty bourgeoisie, the self-conceit of university routinists and . . . a spark of hope for an afterlife.

Ludwig Feuerbach and the End of Classical German Philosophy (*extract*)

Frederick Engels

Out of the dissolution of the Hegelian school, however, there developed still another tendency, the only one which has borne real fruit. And this tendency is essentially connected with the name of Marx.

The separation from Hegelian philosophy was here also the result of a return to the materialist standpoint. That means it was resolved to comprehend the real world – nature and history – just as it presents itself to everyone who approaches it free from preconceived idealist crotchets. It was decided mercilessly to sacrifice every idealist which could not be brought into harmony with the facts conceived in their own and not in a fantastic interconnection. And materialism means nothing more than this. But here the materialistic world outlook was taken really seriously for the first time and was carried through consistently – at least in its basic features – in all domains of knowledge concerned.

Hegel was not simply put aside. On the contrary, a start was made from his revolutionary side, described above, from the dialectical method. But in its Hegelian form, this method was unusable. According to Hegel, dialectics is the self-development of the concept. The absolute concept does not only exist–unknown where – from eternity, it is also the actual living soul of the whole existing world. It develops into itself through all the preliminary stages which are treated at length in the Logic and which are all included in it. Then it "alienates" itself by changing into nature, where, unconscious of itself, disguised as a natural necessity, it goes through a new development and finally returns as man's consciousness of himself. This self-consciousness then elaborates itself again in history in the crude form until finally the absolute concept again comes to itself completely in the Hegelian philosophy. According to Hegel, therefore, the dialectical development apparent in nature and history – that is, the causal interconnection of the progressive movement from the lower to the higher, which asserts itself through all zigzag movements and temporary retrogression – is only a copy [Abklatsch] of the self-movement of the concept going on from eternity, no one knows where, but at all events independently of any thinking human brain. This ideological perversion had to be done away with. We again took a materialistic view of the thoughts in our heads, regarding them as images [Abbilder] of real things instead of regarding real things as images of this or that stage of the absolute concept. Thus dialectics reduced itself to the science of the general laws of motion, both of the external world and of human thought – two sets of laws which are identical in substance, but differ in their expression in so far as the human mind can apply them consciously, while in nature and also up to now for the most part in human history, these laws assert themselves unconsciously, in the form of external necessity, in the midst of an endless series of seeming accidents. Thereby the dialectic of concepts itself became merely the conscious reflex of the dialectical motion of the real world and thus the dialectic of Hegel was turned over; or rather, turned off its head, on which it was standing, and placed upon its feet. And this materialist dialectic, which for years has been our best working tool and our sharpest weapon, was, remarkably enough, discovered not only by us but also, independently of us and even of Hegel, by a German worker, Joseph Dietzgen.

In this way, however, the revolutionary side of Hegelian philosophy was again taken up and at the same time freed from the idealist trimmings which with Hegel had prevented its consistent execution. The great basic thought that the world is not to be comprehended as a complex of readymade things, but as a complex of processes, in which the things apparently stable no less than their mind images in our heads, the concepts, go through an uninterrupted change of coming into being and passing away, in which, in spite of all seeming accidentally and of all temporary retrogression, a progressive development asserts itself in the end – this great fundamental thought has, especially since the time of Hegel, so thoroughly permeated ordinary consciousness that in this generality it is now scarcely ever contradicted. But to acknowledge this fundamental thought in words and to apply it in reality in detail to each domain of investigation are two different things. If, however, investigation always proceeds from this standpoint, the demand for final solutions and eternal truths ceases once for all; one is always conscious of the necessary limitation of all acquired knowledge, of the fact that it is conditioned by the circumstances in which it was acquired. On the other hand, one no longer permits oneself to be imposed upon by the antithesis, insuperable for the still common old metaphysics, between true and false, good and bad, identical and different, necessary and accidental. One knows that these antitheses have only a relative validity; that that which is recognized now as true has also its latent false side which will later manifest itself, just as that which is now regarded as false has also its true side by virtue of which it could previously be regarded as true. One knows that what is maintained to be necessary is composed of sheer accidents and that the so-called accidental is the form behind which necessity hides itself – and so on.

The old method of investigation and thought which Hegel calls "metaphysical", which preferred to investigate things as given, as fixed and stable, a method the relics of which still strongly haunt people's minds, had a great deal of historical justification in its day. It was necessary first to examine things before it was possible to examine processes. One had first to know what a particular thing was before one could observe the changes it was undergoing. And such was the case with natural science. The old metaphysics, which accepted things as finished objects, arose from a natural science which investigated dead and living things as finished objects. But when this investigation had progressed so far that it became possible to take the decisive step forward, that is, to pass on the systematic investigation of the changes which these things undergo in nature itself, then the last hour of the old metaphysic struck in the realm of philosophy also. And in fact, while natural science up to the end of the last century was predominantly a collecting science, a science of finished things, in our century it is essentially a systematizing science, a science of the processes, of the origin and development of these things and of the interconnection which binds all these natural processes into one great whole. Physiology, which investigates the processes occurring in plant and animal organisms; embryology, which deals with the development of individual organisms from germs to maturity; geology, which investigates the gradual formation of the Earth's surface – all these are the offspring of our century.

The Three Sources and Three Component Parts of Marxism (extract)

V I Lenin

The philosophy of Marxism is materialism. Throughout the recent history of Europe, and particularly at the end of the eighteenth century in France, which was the scene of the decisive battle against every kind of medieval rubbish, against serfdom in institutions and ideas, materialism proved to be the only consistent philosophy, true to all the teachings of natural science, hostile to superstitions, cant, etc. The enemies of democracy tried, therefore, with all their energy, to "overthrow", undermine and defame materialism, and defended various forms of philosophic idealism, which always leads, in one way or another, to the defence and support of religion.

Marx and Engels always defended philosophic materialism in the most determined manner, and repeatedly explained the profound error of every deviation from this basis. Their views are more dearly and fully expounded in the works of Engels, *Ludwig Feuerbach* and *Anti-Dühring*, which, like the *Communist Manifesto*, are household books for every conscious worker.

However, Marx did not stop at the materialism of the eighteenth century but moved philosophy forward. He enriched it by the achievements of German classical philosophy especially by Hegel's system, which in its turn had led to the materialism of Feuerbach. Of these the main achievement is dialectics, ie, the doctrine of development in its fuller, deeper form, free from one-sidedness – the doctrine, also, of the relativity of human knowledge that provides us with a reflection of eternally developing matter. The latest discoveries of natural science-radium, electrons, the transmutation of elements-are a remarkable confirmation of the dialectical materialism of Marx, despite the doctrines of bourgeois philosophers with their "new" returns to old and rotten idealism.

While deepening and developing philosophic materialism, Marx carried it to its conclusion; he extended its perception of nature to the perception of human society. The historical materialism of Marx represented the greatest conquest of scientific thought.

Chaos and arbitrariness, which reigned until then in the views on history and politics, were replaced by a strikingly consistent and harmonious scientific theory, which shows how out of one order of social life another and higher order develops, in consequence of the growth of the productive forces – how capitalism, for instance, grows out of serfdom.

Just as the cognition of man reflects nature (i.e., developing matter) which exists independently of him, so also the social cognition of man (i.e., the various views and doctrines-philosophic, religious, political, etc.) reflects the economic order of society. Political institutions are a superstructure on the economic foundation. We see, for example, that the various political forms of modern European states serve the purpose of strengthening the domination of the bourgeoisie over the proletariat.

The philosophy of Marx completes in itself philosophic materialism which has provided humanity, and especially the working class, with a powerful instrument of knowledge.

On the Question of Dialectics

V I Lenin

The splitting of a single whole and the cognition of its contradictory parts... is the essence (one of the "essentials", one of the principal, if not the principal, characteristics or features) of dialectics. That is precisely how Hegel, too, puts the matter...

The correctness of this aspect of the content of dialectics must be tested by the history of science. This aspect of dialectics (e.g. in Plekhanov) usually receives inadequate attention: the identity of opposites is taken as the sum-total of examples ["for example, a seed", "for example, primitive communism". The same is true of Engels. But it is "in the interests of popularisation ..."] and not as a law of cognition (and as a law of the objective world.)

- In mathematics: + and -. Differential and integral.

- In mechanics: action and reaction.

- In physics: positive and negative electricity.

- In chemistry: the combination and dissociation of atoms.

- In social science: the class struggle.

The identity of opposites (it would be more correct, perhaps, to say their "unity", – although the difference between the terms identity and unity is not particularly important here. In a certain sense both are correct) is the recognition (discovery) of the contradictory, mutually exclusive, opposite tendencies in all phenomena and processes of nature (including mind and society). The condition for the knowledge of all processes of the world in their "self-movement", in their spontaneous development, in their real life, is the knowledge of them as a unity of opposites. Development is the "struggle" of opposites. The two basic (or two possible? Or two historically observable?) conceptions of development (evolution) are: development as decrease and increase, as repetition, and development as a unity of opposites (the division of a unity into mutually exclusive opposites and their reciprocal relation).

In the first conception of motion, self-movement, its driving force, its source, its motive, remains in the shade (or this source is made external – God, subject, etc.). In the second conception the chief attention is directed precisely to knowledge of the source of "self"-movement.

The first conception is lifeless, pale and dry. The second is living. The second alone furnishes the key to the "self-movement" of everything existing; it alone furnishes the key to "leaps", to the "break in continuity", to the transformation into the opposite", to the destruction of the old and the emergence of the new.

The unity (coincidence, identity, equal action) of opposites is conditional, temporary, transitory, relative. The struggle of mutually exclusive opposites is absolute, just as development and motion are absolute.

NB: The distinction between subjectivism (scepticism, sophistry, etc.) and dialectics, incidentally, is that in (objective) dialectics the difference between the relative and the absolute is itself relative. For objective dialectics there is an absolute within the relative. For subjectivism and sophistry the relative is only relative and excludes the absolute...

In his Capital, Marx first analyses the simplest, most ordinary and fundamental, most common and everyday relation of bourgeois (commodity) society, a relation encountered billions of times, viz., the exchange of commodities. In this very simple phenomenon (in this "cell" of bourgeois society) analysis reveals all the contradictions (or the germs of all contradictions) of modern society. The subsequent exposition shows us the development (both growth and movement) of these contradictions and of this society in the Sum of its individual parts. From its beginning to its end.

Such must also be the method of exposition (or study) of dialectics in general (for with Marx the dialectics of bourgeois society is only a particular case of dialectics). To begin with what is the simplest, most ordinary, common, etc., with any proposition: the leaves of a tree are green; John is a man: Fido is a dog, etc. Here already we have dialectics (as Hegel's genius recognised); the individual is the universal...

Consequently, the opposites (the individual is opposed to the universal) are identical: the individual exists only in the connection that leads to the universal. The universal exists only in the individual and through the individual. Every individual is (in one way or another) a universal. Every universal is (a fragment, or an aspect, or the essence of) an individual. Every universal only approximately embraces all the individual objects. Every individual enters incompletely into the universal, etc., etc. Every individual is connected by thousands of transitions with other kinds of individuals (things, phenomena, processes) etc. Here already we have the elements, the germs, the concepts of necessity, of objective connection in nature, etc. Here already we have the contingent and the necessary, the phenomenon and the essence; for when we say: John is a man, Fido is a dog, this is a leaf of a tree, etc., we disregard a number of attributes as contingent; we separate the essence from the appearance, and counterpose the one to the other.

Thus in any proposition we can (and must) disclose as in a "nucleus" (:cell") the germs of all the elements of dialectics, and thereby show that dialectics is a property of all human knowledge in general.

And natural science shows us (and here again it must be demonstrated in any simple instance) objective nature with the same qualities, the transformation of the individual into the universal, of the contingent into the necessary, transitions, modulations, and the reciprocal connection of opposites. Dialectics is the theory of knowledge of (Hegel and) Marxism. This is the "aspect" of the matter (it is not "an aspect" but the essence of the matter) to which Plekhanov, not to speak of other Marxists, paid no attention.

* * *

Knowledge is represented in the form of a series of circles both by Hegel (see *Logic*) and by the modern epistemologists" of natural science, the eclectic and foe of Hegelianism (which he did not understand!), Paul Volkmann.

- "Circles" in philosophy: [is a chronology of persons – essential? No!]

- Ancient: from Democritus to Plato and the dialectics of Heraclitus.

- Renaissance: Descartes versus Gassendi (Spinoza?)

- Modern: Holbach-Hegel (via Berkeley, Hume, Kant).

- Hegel-Feuerbach-Marx

Dialectics as living, many-sided knowledge (with the number of sides eternally increasing), with an infinite number of shades of every approach and approximation to reality (with a philosophical system growing into a whole out of each shade) – here we have an immeasurably rich content as compared with metaphysical materialism, the fundamental misfortune of which is its inability to apply dialectics to the [Bildertheorie] theory of reflection, to the process and development of knowledge.

Philosophical idealism is only nonsense from the standpoint of crude, simple, metaphysical materialism. From the standpoint of dialectical materialism, on the other hand, philosophical idealism is a one-sided, exaggerated, development (inflation, distension) of one of the features, aspects, facets of knowledge, into an absolute, divorced from matter, from nature, apotheosised. Idealism is clerical obscurantism. True. But philosophical idealism is ("more correctly" and "in addition") a road to clerical obscurantism through one of the shades of the infinitely complex knowledge (dialectical) of man.

Human knowledge is not (or does not follow) a straight line, but a curve, which endlessly approximates a series of circles, a spiral. Any fragment, segment, section of this curve can be transformed (transformed one-sidedly) into an independent, complete, straight line, which then (if one does not see the wood for the trees) leads into the quagmire, into clerical obscurantism (where it is anchored by the class interests of the ruling classes). Rectilinearity and one-sidedness, woodenness and petrification, subjectivism and subjective blindness – voila the epistemological roots of idealism. And clerical obscurantism (= philosophical idealism), of course, has epistemological roots, it is not groundless; it is a sterile flower undoubtedly, but a sterile flower that grows on the living tree of living, fertile, genuine, powerful, omnipotent, objective, absolute human knowledge.

Summary of Dialectics
V I Lenin

1. The determination of the concept out of itself [the thing itself must be considered in its relations and in its development];

2. the contradictory nature of the thing itself (the other of itself), the contradictory forces and tendencies in each phenomenon;

3. the union of analysis and synthesis.

Such apparently are the elements of dialectics.

One could perhaps present these elements in greater detail as follows:

1. the objectivity of consideration (not examples, not divergencies, but the Thing-in-itself).

2. the entire totality of the manifold relations of this thing to others.

3. the development of this thing, (phenomenon, respectively), its own movement, its own life.

4. the internally contradictory tendencies (and sides) in this thing.

5. the thing (phenomenon, etc) as the sum and unity of opposites.

6. the struggle, respectively unfolding, of these opposites, contradictory strivings, etc.

7. the union of analysis and synthesis – the breakdown of the separate parts and the totality, the summation of these parts.

8. the relations of each thing (phenomenon, etc.) are not only manifold, but general, universal. Each thing (phenomenon, etc.) is connected with every other.

9. not only the unity of opposites, but the transitions of every determination, quality, feature, side, property into every other [into its opposite?].

10. the endless process of the discovery of new sides, relations, etc.

11. the endless process of the deepening of man's knowledge of the thing, of phenomena, processes, etc., from appearance to essence and from less profound to more profound essence.

12. from co-existence to causality and from one form of connection and reciprocal dependence to another, deeper, more general form.

13. the repetition at a higher stage of certain features, properties, etc., of the lower and

14. the apparent return to the old (negation of the negation).

15. the struggle of content with form and conversely. The throwing off of the form, the transformation of the content.

16. the transition of quantity into quality and vice versa (15 and 16 are examples of 9)

In brief, dialectics can be defined as the doctrine of the unity of opposites. This embodies the essence of dialectics, but it requires explanations and development.

Questions on Dialectical Materialism

1. Why does the working class need a philosophy?
2. Is 'common sense' a philosophy?
3. What is materialism?
4. What is idealism?
5. Is Darwin's theory of evolution correct?
6. What does 'metaphysical' mean?
7. How would you define dialectics?
8. What was wrong with the old materialism?
9. What is formal logic?
10. Does a pound of sugar equal a pound of sugar?
11. Why do workers sometimes accept major attacks on their terms and conditions, then strike over some 'small' incident?
12. Does history repeat itself?
13. Was the First World War caused by the assassination of a Crown Prince in Sarajevo? What is the role of accident in history?
14. Can you be in one place and another at the same time?
15. What was Hegel's great contribution to philosophy?
16. What was the contribution of Marx and Engels to philosophy?
17. Why can it be said that nature is the proof of dialectics?
18. What is the relevance of dialectical materialism in understanding the future?
19. Did the the universe have a beginning?
20. What is the difference between determinism and fatalism?

Suggested Reading List

- *The German Ideology*, Karl Marx & Frederick Engels
- *The Poverty of Philosophy*, Karl Marx
- *Economic and Philosophical Manuscripts*, Karl Marx
- *Ludwig Feuerbach and the End of Classical German Philosophy*, Frederick Engels
- *Anti-Dühring*, Frederick Engels
- *Dialectics of Nature*, Frederick Engels
- *Socialism Utopian and Scientific*, Frederick Engels
- *Materialism and Empirio-Criticism*, V I Lenin
- *Philosophical Notebooks*, V I Lenin
- *On Marx and Engels*, V I Lenin
- *The Three Sources and Three Component Parts of Marxism*, V I Lenin
- *In Defence of Marxism*, Leon Trotsky
- *Radio, Science, Technology and Society*, Leon Trotsky
- *The Development of the Monist View of History*, G V Plekhanov
- *The Fundamental Problems of Marxism*, G V Plekhanov
- *Introduction to the Logic of Marxism*, George Novack
- *Reason in Revolt*, Alan Woods & Ted Grant
- *Logic*, G W F Hegel

Titles listed above are available to buy from Wellred Books at:
www.wellredbooks.net
Wellred Books, PO Box 50525, London E14 6WG, United Kingdom
For further suggested reading on dialectical materialism,
see the 'Educate Yourself' section of the *In Defence of Marxism* website
(http://www.marxist.com/educate-yourself/)

2. Historical Materialism

What Is Historical Materialism?

Alan Woods

M arxists do not see history as a mere series of isolated facts but rather, they seek to discover the general processes and laws that govern nature and society. The first condition for science in general is that we are able to look beyond the particular and arrive at the general. The idea that human history is not governed by any laws is contrary to all science.

What is history?

Why should we accept that the entire universe, from the smallest particles to the most distant galaxies are determined, and the process that determine the evolution of all species, are governed by laws, and yet, for some strange reason, our own history is not. The Marxist method analyses the hidden mainsprings that underpin the development of human society from the earliest tribal societies up to the modern day. The way in which Marxism traces this winding road is called the materialist conception of history.

Those who deny the existence of any laws governing human social development invariably approach history from a subjective and moralistic standpoint. But above and beyond the isolated facts, it is necessary to discern broad tendencies, the transitions from one social system to another, and to work out the fundamental motor forces that determine these transitions.

Before Marx and Engels history was seen by most people as a series of unconnected events or, to use a philosophical term, "accidents". There was no general explanation of this, history had no inner lawfulness. By establishing the fact that, at bottom, all human development depends on the development of productive forces Marx and Engels for the first time placed the study of history on a scientific basis.

This scientific method enables us to understand history, not as a series of unconnected and unforeseen incidents, but rather as part of a clearly understood and interrelated process. It is a series of actions and reactions which cover politics, economics and the whole spectrum of social development. To lay bare the complex dialectical relationship between all these phenomena is the task of historical materialism. Humankind constantly changes nature through labour, and in so doing, changes itself.

A caricature of Marxism

Science under capitalism tends to become less and less scientific, the closer it gets to analysing society. The so-called social sciences (sociology, economics, politics), and also bourgeois philosophy, in general do not apply genuinely scientific methods at all, and therefore end up as ill-concealed attempts to justify capitalism, or at least to discredit Marxism (which boils down to the same thing).

Despite the "scientific" pretensions of bourgeois historians, the writing of history inevitably reflects a class point of view. It is a fact that the history of wars – including the class war – is written by the winners. In other words, the selection and interpretation of these events are shaped by the actual outcome of those conflicts as they affect the historian, and in turn his perception of what the reader will want to read. Moreover, in the last analysis, these perceptions will always be influenced by the interests of a class or grouping in society.

When Marxists look at society they do not pretend to be neutral, but openly espouse the cause of the exploited and oppressed classes. However, that does not at all preclude scientific objectivity. A surgeon involved in a delicate operation is also committed to saving the life of his patient. He is far from neutral about the outcome. But for that very reason, he will distinguish with extreme care between the different layers of the organism. In the same way, Marxists will strive to obtain the most scientifically exact analysis of social processes, in order to be able successfully to influence the outcome.

Very often attempts are made to discredit Marxism by resorting to a caricature of its method of historical analysis. There is nothing easier than erecting a straw man in order to knock it down again. The usual distortion is that Marx and Engels "reduced everything to economics". This mechanical caricature has nothing to do with Marxism. If that were really the case, we would be absolved from the painful necessity of fighting to change society.

Capitalism would collapse of its own accord and the new society would fall into place of its own accord, as a ripe apple falls into the lap of a man sleeping under a tree. But historical materialism has nothing in common with fatalism.

This patent absurdity was answered in the following extract of Engels' letter to Bloch:

> "According to the materialist conception of history, the ultimate determining element in history is the production and reproduction of life. More than this Marx and I have asserted. Hence, if somebody twists this into saying that the economic element is the only determining one, he transforms that proposition into a meaningless, abstract and senseless phrase." (*Engels to Bloch, 21 September 1890, Selected Correspondence*, p475)

In *The Holy Family*, written before the *Communist Manifesto*, Marx and Engels poured scorn on the idea that "History", conceived apart from individual men and women, was merely an empty abstraction:

> "History does nothing, it 'possesses no immense wealth', it 'wages no battles'. It is man, real, living man who does all that, who possesses and fights; 'history' is not, as it were, a person apart, using man as a means to achieve its own aims; history is nothing but the activity of man pursuing his aims." (Marx and Engels, *The Holy Family, Chapter VI*)

All that Marxism does is to explain the role of the individual as part of a given society, subject to certain objective laws and, ultimately, as the representative of the interests of a particular class. Ideas have no independent existence, nor their own historical development. "Life is not determined by consciousness," Marx writes in *The German Ideology*, "but consciousness by life."

Free will?

The ideas and actions of people are conditioned by social relations, the development of which does not depend on the subjective will of men and women but which take place according to definite laws. These social relations, in the last analysis, reflect the needs of development of the productive forces. The interrelations between these factors constitute a complex web that is often difficult to see. The study of these relations is the basis of the Marxist theory of history.

But if men and women are not the puppets of "blind historical forces", neither are they entirely free agents, able to shape their destiny irrespective of the existing conditions imposed by the level of economic development, science and technique, which, in the last analysis, determine whether a socio-economic system is viable or not. In *The Eighteenth Brumaire of Louis Bonaparte*, Marx explains:

> "Men make their own history, but they do not make it as they please; they do not make it under self-selected circumstances, but under circumstances existing already, given and transmitted from the past. The tradition of all dead generations weighs like an Alp on the brains of the living [...]."

Later Engels expressed the same idea in a different way:

> "Men make their own history, whatever its outcome may be, in that each person follows his own consciously desired end, and it is precisely the resultant of these many wills operating in different directions and of their manifold effects upon the outer world that constitutes history." (*Ludwig Feuerbach*).

What Marxism does assert, and it is a proposition that surely nobody can deny, is that in the last analysis, the viability of a given socio-economic system will be determined by its ability to develop the means of production, that is to say, the material foundations upon which society, culture and civilization are built.

The notion that the development of the productive forces is the basis upon which all social development depends is really such a self-evident truth that it is really surprising that some people still question it. It does not require much intelligence to understand that before men and women can develop art, science, religion or philosophy, they must first have food to eat, clothes to wear and houses to live in. All these things must be produced by someone, somehow. And it is equally obvious that the viability of any given socio-economic system will ultimately be determined by its ability to do this.

In the *Critique of Political Economy* Marx explains the relation between the productive forces and the "superstructure" as follows:

> "In the social production which men carry on they enter into definite relations that are indispensable and independent of their will; these relations of production correspond to a definite stage of development of their material powers of production... The mode of production in material life determines the general character of the social, political and spiritual processes of life. It is not the

consciousness of men that determines their existence, but, on the contrary, their social existence (which) determines their consciousness."

As Marx and Engels were at pains to point out, the participants in history may not always be aware of what motives are driving them, seeking instead to rationalise them in one way or another, but those motives exist and have a basis in the real world.

From this we can see that the flow and direction of history has been – and is – shaped by the struggles of successive social classes to mould society in their own interests and the resulting conflicts between the classes which flow from that. As the first words of the *Communist Manifesto* remind us: "The history of all hitherto existing societies is the history of class struggle." Historical materialism explains that the motor force of social development is the class struggle.

Marx and Darwin

Our species is the product of a very long period of evolution. Of course, evolution is not a kind of grand design, the aim of which was to create beings like ourselves. It is not a question of accepting some kind of preordained plan, either related to divine intervention or some kind of teleology, but it is clear that the laws of evolution inherent in nature do in fact determine the development from simple forms of life to more complex forms.

The earliest forms of life already contain within them the embryo of all future developments. It is possible to explain the development of eyes, legs and other organs without recourse to any preordained plan. At a certain stage we get the development of a central nervous system and a brain. Finally, with Homo sapiens, we arrive at human consciousness. Matter becomes conscious of itself. There has been no more important revolution since the development of organic matter (life) from inorganic matter.

Charles Darwin explained that the species are not immutable, and that they possess a past, a present and a future, changing and evolving. In the same way Marx and Engels explain that a given social system is not something eternally fixed. Evolution shows how different life forms have dominated the planet for very long periods but have been made extinct as soon as the material conditions that determined their evolutionary success changed. These previously dominant species have been replaced by other species that were seemingly insignificant and even species that seemed to have no prospect of survival.

Nowadays the idea of "evolution" has been generally accepted, at least by educated persons. The ideas of Darwin, so revolutionary in his day, are accepted almost as a truism. However, evolution is generally understood as a slow and gradual process without interruptions or violent upheavals. In politics, this kind of argument is frequently used as a justification for reformism. Unfortunately, it is based on a misunderstanding. The real mechanism of evolution even today remains a book sealed by seven seals.

This is hardly surprising since Darwin himself did not understand it. It was only as recently as the 1970s, with the new discoveries in palaeontology made by Stephen Jay Gould, who discovered the theory of punctuated equilibria, that it was demonstrated that evolution is not a gradual process. There are long periods in which no big changes are observed, but at a given moment, the line of evolution is broken by an explosion, a veritable biological revolution characterised by the mass extinction of some species and the rapid ascent of others.

We see analogous processes in the rise and fall of different socio-economic systems. The analogy between society and nature is, of course, only approximate. But even the most superficial examination of history shows that the gradualist interpretation is baseless. Society, like nature, knows long periods of slow and gradual change, but also here the line is interrupted by explosive developments – wars and revolutions, in which the process of change is enormously accelerated. In fact, it is these events that act as the main motor force of historical development. And the root cause of revolution is the fact that a particular socio-economic system has reached its limits and is unable to develop the productive forces as before.

History has more than once furnished us with examples of apparently powerful states that collapsed in a very short space of time. And it also shows how political, religious and philosophical views that were almost unanimously condemned became transformed into the accepted views of the new revolutionary power that arose to take the place of the old. The fact that the ideas of Marxism are the views of a small minority in this society is therefore no cause for concern. Every great idea in history has always started as a heresy and that applies as much to Marxism today as it did to Christianity 2,000 years ago.

The "evolutionary adaptations" that originally enabled slavery to replace barbarism, and feudalism to replace slavery in the end turned into their opposite. And now the very features that enabled capitalism to displace feudalism and emerge as the dominant socio-economic system have become the causes of its decay. Capitalism is displaying all the symptoms we associate with a socio-economic system in a state of terminal decline. In many ways it resembles the period of the decline of the Roman Empire as described in the writings of Edward Gibbon. In the period that is now unfolding before us, the capitalist system is heading for extinction.

Socialism, utopian and scientific

By applying the method of dialectical materialism to history, it is immediately obvious that human history has its own laws, and that, consequently, it is possible to understand it as a process. The rise and fall of different socio-economic formations can be explained scientifically in terms of their ability or inability to develop the means of production, and thereby to push forward the horizons of human culture, and increase the domination of humankind over nature.

But what are the laws that govern historical change? Just as the evolution of life has inherent laws that can be explained, and were explained, first by Darwin and in more recent times by the rapid advances in the study of genetics, so the evolution of human society has its own inherent laws that were explained by Marx and Engels. In *The German Ideology*, which was written before the *Communist Manifesto*, Marx wrote:

> "The first premise of all human history is, of course, the existence of living human individuals. Thus the first fact to be established is the physical organisation of these individuals and their consequent relation to the rest of nature. (…) Men can be distinguished from animals by consciousness, by religion or anything else you like. They themselves begin to distinguish themselves from animals as soon as they begin to produce their means of subsistence, a step which is conditioned by their physical organisation. By producing their means of subsistence men are indirectly producing their actual material life."

In *Socialism: Utopian and Scientific,* written much later, Engels provides us with a more developed expression of these ideas. Here we have a brilliant and concise exposition of the basic principles of historical materialism:

"The materialist conception of history starts from the proposition that the production of the means to support human life and, next to production, the exchange of things produced, is the basis of all social structure; that in every society that has appeared in history, the manner in which wealth is distributed and society divided into classes or orders is dependent upon what is produced, how it is produced, and how the products are exchanged. From this point of view, the final causes of all social changes and political revolutions are to be sought, not in men's brains, not in men's better insights into eternal truth and justice, but in changes in the modes of production and exchange."

As opposed to the utopian socialist ideas of Robert Owen, Saint-Simon and Fourier, Marxism is based upon a scientific vision of socialism. Marxism explains that the key to the development of every society is the development of the productive forces: labour power, industry, agriculture, technique and science. Each new social system – slavery, feudalism and capitalism – has served to take human society forward through its development of the productive forces.

The basic premise of historical materialism is that the ultimate source of human development is the development of the productive forces. This is a most important conclusion because this alone can permit us to arrive at a scientific conception of history. Marxism maintains that the development of human society over millions of years represents progress, in the sense that it increases humankind's power over nature and thus creates the material conditions for achieving genuine freedom for men and women. However, this has never taken place in a straight line, as the Victorians (who had a vulgar and undialectical view of evolution) wrongly imagined. History has a descending line as well as an ascending one.

Once one denies a materialist point of view, the only motor force of historical events that one is left with is the role of individuals – "great men" (or women). In other words, we are left with an idealist and subjectivist view of the historical process. This was the standpoint of the utopian socialists, who, despite their brilliant insights and penetrating criticism of the existing social order, failed to understand the fundamental laws of historical development. For them, socialism was just a "good idea", something that could therefore have been thought of a thousand years ago, or tomorrow morning. Had it been invented a thousand years ago, humankind would have been spared a lot of trouble!

It is impossible to understand history by basing oneself on the subjective interpretations of its protagonists. Let us cite one example. The early Christians, who expected the end of the world and the Second Coming of Christ at every hour, did not believe in private property. In their communities they practiced a kind of communism (although their communism was of the utopian kind, based on consumption, not production). Their early experiments in communism led nowhere, and could lead nowhere, because the development of the productive forces at that time did not permit the development of real communism.

At the time of the English Revolution, Oliver Cromwell fervently believed that he was fighting for the right of each individual to pray to God according to his conscience. But the further march of history proved that the Cromwellian Revolution was the decisive stage in the irresistible ascent of the English bourgeoisie to power. The concrete stage of development of the productive forces in 17th Century England permitted no other outcome.

The leaders of the Great French Revolution of 1789-93 fought under the banner of "Liberty, Equality and Fraternity". They believed they were fighting for a regime based on the eternal laws of Justice and Reason. However, regardless of their intentions and ideas, the Jacobins were preparing the way for the rule of the bourgeoisie in France. Again, from a scientific standpoint, no other result was possible at that point of social development.

Stages of historical development

Human society has passed through a series of stages that are clearly discernible. Each stage is based on a definite mode of production, which in turn expresses itself in a definite system of class relations. These further manifest themselves in a definite social outlook, psychology, morality, laws and religion.

The relationship between the economic base of society and the superstructure (ideology, morality, laws, art, religion, philosophy, etc.) is not simple and direct but highly complex and even contradictory. The invisible threads that connect the productive forces and class relations are reflected in the minds of men and women in a confused and distorted manner. And ideas that have their origin in the primeval past can linger on in the collective psyche for a very long time, persisting stubbornly long after the real basis from which they sprang has disappeared. Religion is a clear example of this. It is a dialectical interrelation. This was clearly explained by Marx himself:

"As to the realms of ideology which soar still higher in the air, religion, philosophy etc., these have a prehistoric stock, found already in existence and taken over in the historic period, of which we should today call bunk. These various false conceptions of nature, of man's own being, of spirits, magic forces, etc., have for the most part only a negative economic basis; but the low economic development of the prehistoric period is supplemented and also partially conditioned and even caused by the false conceptions of nature. And even though economic necessity was the main driving force of the progressive knowledge of nature and becomes ever more so, it would surely be pedantic to try and find economic causes for all this primitive nonsense.

"The history of science is the history of the gradual clearing away of this nonsense or of its replacement by fresh but already less absurd nonsense. The people who deal with this belong in their turn to special spheres in the division of labour and appear to themselves to be working in an independent field. And insofar as they form an independent group within the social division of labour, in so far do their productions, including their errors, react back as an influence upon the whole development of society, even on economic development. But all the same they themselves remain under the dominating influence of economic development." (Marx and Engels, *Selected Correspondence*, pp482-3)

And again:

"But the philosophy of every epoch, since it is a definite sphere in the division of labour, has as its presupposition certain definite intellectual material handed down to it by its predecessors, from which it takes its start. That is why economically backward countries can still play first fiddle in philosophy." (*Ibid*, p483)

Ideology, tradition, morality, religion etc., all play a powerful role in shaping people's beliefs. Marxism does not deny this self-evident fact. Contrary to what the idealists believe, human consciousness in general is very conservative. Most people do not like change, especially sudden, violent change. They will cling to the things they know and have got used to: the ideas, religion, institutions, morality, leaders and parties of the past. Routine, habit and customs all lie like a leaden weight on the shoulders of humanity. For all these reasons consciousness lags behind events.

However, at certain periods great events force men and women to question their old beliefs and assumptions. They are jolted out of the old supine, apathetic indifference and forced to come to terms with reality. In such periods consciousness can change very rapidly. That is what a revolution is. And the line of social development, which can remain fairly constant and unbroken for long periods, has been interrupted by revolutions that are the necessary motor-force of human progress.

Early human society

If we look at the entire process of human history and prehistory, the first thing that strikes us is the extraordinary slowness with which our species developed. The gradual evolution of human or humanoid creatures away from the condition of animals and towards a genuinely human condition took place over millions of years. The first decisive leap was the separation of the first humanoids from their simian ancestors.

The evolutionary process is, of course, blind – that is to say, it does not involve an objective or specific goal. However, our hominid ancestors, first by standing up right, then by using their hands to manipulate tools and finally by producing them, found a niche in a particular environment that impelled them forward.

Ten million years ago apes constituted the dominant species on the planet. They existed in a great variety – tree dwellers, ground dwellers, and a host of intermediate forms. They flourished in the prevailing climatological conditions that created a perfect tropical environment. Then all this changed. About seven or eight million years ago most of these species died out. The reason for this is not known.

For a long time the investigation of human origins was bedevilled by the idealist prejudice that stubbornly maintained that, since the main difference between humans and apes is the brain, our earliest ancestors must have been apes with a large brain. The "big brain" theory utterly dominated early anthropology. They spent many decades searching – without success – for the "missing link", which they were convinced would be a fossil skeleton with a large brain.

So convinced were they that the scientific community were completely taken in by one of the most extraordinary frauds in scientific history. On the 18th of December 1912 fragments of a fossil skull and jawbone were said to be that of the "missing link – Piltdown Man". This was hailed as a great discovery. But in 1953 a team of English scientists exposed Piltdown Man as a deliberate fraud. Instead of being almost a million years old, the skull fragments were found to be 500 years old, and the jaw in fact belonged to an orang-utan.

Why was the scientific community so easily fooled? Because they were presented with something they expected to find: an early humanoid skull with a large brain. As a matter of fact, it was the upright stance (bipedalism), and not the size of the brain, which freed the hands for labour, that was the decisive turning point in human evolution.

This was already anticipated by Engels in his brilliant work on human origins, *The Role Played by Labour in the Transition of Ape to Man*. The celebrated American palaeontologist Stephen Jay Gould wrote that it was a pity that scientists had not paid attention to what Engels wrote, as this would have spared them a hundred years of error. The discovery of Lucy, the fossilised skeleton of a young female who belonged to a new species called Australopithecus Afarensis, showed that Engels was right. The body structure of early hominids is like our own (the pelvis, leg bones etc.) thus proving bipedalism. But the size of the brain is not much bigger than a chimpanzee.

Our distant ancestors were small in size and slow-moving in comparison with other animals. They did not have powerful claws and teeth. Moreover, the human baby, which is only born once a year, is completely helpless at birth. Dolphins are born swimming, cattle and horses can walk within hours of being born and lions are able to run within 20 days of birth.

Compare this to a human baby who will require months just to be able to merely sit without support. More advanced skills like running and jumping may take years to develop in a newborn human. As a species, therefore, we were at a considerable disadvantage in comparison to our numerous competitors on the savannah of East Africa. Manual labour, together with co-operative social organisation and language, which are connected with it, was the decisive element in human evolution. The production of stone tools gave our early ancestors a vital evolutionary advantage, triggering the development of the brain.

The first period, which Marx and Engels called savagery, was characterised by an extremely low development of the means of production, the production of stone tools, and a hunter-gatherer mode of existence. Due to this the line of development remains virtually flat for a very long period. The hunter gathering mode of production originally represented at the universal condition of humankind. Those surviving remnants that, until quite recently, could be observed in certain parts of the globe provide us with important clues and insights into a long forgotten way of life.

It is not true, for example, that human beings are naturally selfish. If this were the case, our species would have been extinct over two million years ago. It was a powerful sense of cooperation that held these groups together in the face of adversity. They cared for the small babies and their mothers and respected the old members of the clan who preserved in their memory its collective knowledge and beliefs. Our early ancestors did not know what private property was, as Anthony Burnett points out:

> "The contrast between man and other species is equally clear if we compare the territorial behavior of animals with property-holding by people. Territories are maintained by formal signals, common to a whole species. Every adult or group of each species holds a territory. Man displays no such uniformity: even within a single community, vast areas may be owned by one person, while others have none. There is, even today, ownership in people. But in some countries private ownership is confined to personal property. In a few tribal groups even minor possessions are held in common. Man has, in fact, no more a 'property-owning instinct' than he has an 'instinct to steal'. Granted, it is easy to rear children to be acquisitive; yet the form of the acquisitiveness, and the extent to which it is sanctioned by society, varies greatly from one country to the next, and from one historical period to another." (Anthony Burnett, *The Human Species*, p142)

Perhaps the word "savagery" is unfortunate nowadays because of the negative connotations it has acquired. The 17th century English philosopher Thomas Hobbes famously described the lives of our early ancestors as one of "continual fear and danger of violent death, and the life of man solitary, poor, nasty, brutish, and short." No doubt their life was a hard one, but these words hardly do justice to our ancestors' way of life. The Kenyan anthropologist and archaeologist Richard Leakey writes:

> "Hobbes's view that non-agricultural people have 'no society' and are 'solitary' could hardly be more wrong. To be a hunter-gatherer is to experience a life that is intensely social. As for having 'no arts' and 'no letters', it is true that foraging people possess very little in the form of material culture, but this is simply a consequence of the need for mobility. When the !Kung move from camp to camp they, like other hunter-gatherers, take all their worldly goods with them: this usually amounts to a total of 12 kilograms (26 pounds) in weight, just over half the normal baggage allowance on most airlines. This is an inescapable conflict

between mobility and material culture, and so the !Kung carry their culture in their heads, not on their backs. Their songs, dances and stories form a culture as rich as that of any people." (Richard Leakey, *The Making of Mankind*, pp101-3)

He continues, "Richard Lee [anthropologist and author of The !Kung San: Men, Women, and Work in a Foraging Society, 1979] considers that the women do not feel themselves exploited: 'They have economic prestige and political power, a situation denied to many women in the "civilized" world'." (*Ibid*, p103)

In these societies classes in the modern sense were unknown. There was no state or organized religion and there was a deep sense of communal responsibility and sharing. Egotism and selfishness were regarded as deeply anti-social and morally offensive. The stress on equality demands that certain rituals are observed when a successful hunter returns to camp. The object of these rituals is to play down the event so as to discourage arrogance and conceit: "The correct demeanour for the successful hunter," explains Richard Lee, "is modesty and understatement."

Again:

"The !Kung have no chiefs and no leaders. Problems in their society are mostly solved long before they mature into anything that threatens social harmony. (…) People's conversations are common property, and disputes are readily defused through communal bantering. No one gives orders or takes them. Richard Lee once asked /Twi!gum whether the !Kung have headmen. 'Of course we have headmen,' he replied, much to Richard Lee's surprise. 'In fact, we are all headmen; each one of us is a headman over himself.' /Twi!gum considered the question and his witty answer to be a great joke." (*Ibid*, p107)

The basic principle that guides every aspect of life is sharing. Among the !Kung When an animal is killed, an elaborate process of sharing the raw meat begins along lines of kinship, alliances and obligations. Richard Lee emphasises the point strongly:

"Sharing deeply pervades the behaviour and values of !Kung forager', within the family and between families, and it is extended to the boundaries of the social universe. Just as the principle of profit and rationality is central to the capitalist ethic, so is sharing central to the conduct of social life in foraging societies." (*Ibid*)

Boastfulness was frowned upon and modesty encouraged, as the following extract shows:

> "A !Kung man describes it this way: 'Say that a man has been hunting. He must not come home and announce like a braggart, "I have killed a big one in the bush!" He must first sit down in silence until someone else comes up to his fire and asks, "What did you see today?" He replies quietly, "Ah, I'm no good for hunting. I saw nothing at all... Maybe just a tiny one." Then I smile to myself because I now know he has killed something big.' The bigger the kill, the more it is played down. (...) The jesting and understatement is strictly followed, again not just by the !Kung but by many foraging people, and the result is that although some men are undoubtedly more proficient hunters than others, no one accrues an unusual prestige or status because of his talents." (*Ibid*, p106-7)

This ethic is not confined to the !Kung; it is a feature of hunter-gatherers in general. Such behaviour, however, is not automatic; like most of human behaviour, it has to be taught from childhood. Every human infant is born with the capacity to share and the capacity to be selfish, Richard Lee says. "That which is nurtured and developed is that which each individual society regards as most valuable." In that sense the ethical values of these early societies are vastly superior to those of capitalism, which teach people to be greedy, selfish and antisocial.

Of course, it is impossible to say with certainty that this is an exact picture of early human society. But similar conditions tend to produce similar results, and the same tendencies can be observed in many different cultures on the same level of economic development. As Richard Lee says:

> "We mustn't imagine that this is the exact way in which our ancestors lived. But I believe that what we see in the !Kung and other foraging people are patterns of behaviour that were crucial to early human development. Of the several types of hominid that were living two to three million years ago, one of them – the line that eventually led to us – broadened its economic base by sharing food and including more meat in its diet. The development of a hunting and gathering economy was a potent force in what made us human." (Quoted in Leakey, pp108-9.)

In comparing the values of hunter-gatherer societies with those of our own times, we do not always get the better of it. For example, just compare the contemporary family, with its ghastly record of wife and child abuse, orphans, and prostitutes, with the communal child-rearing practiced by humanity during most of its history; that is, before the advent of that strange social arrangement that men are fond of calling civilization:

> "'You white people,' an American Indian said to a missionary, 'love your own children only. We love the children of the clan. They belong to all the people, and we care for them. They are bone of our bone, and flesh of our flesh. We are all father and mother to them. White people are savages; they do not love their children. If children are orphaned, people have to be paid to look after them. We know nothing of such barbarous ideas.'" (M. F. Ashley Montagu, ed, *Marriage: Past and Present: A Debate Between Robert Briffault and Bronislaw Malinowski*, Boston: Porter Sargent Publisher, 1956, p48)

However, we must not have an idealised view of the past. Life for our early ancestors remained a hard struggle, a constant battle against the forces of nature for survival. The pace of progress was extremely slow. Early humans began making stone tools at least 2.6 million years ago. The oldest stone tools, known as the Oldowan continued for about a million years until about 1.76 million years ago, when early humans began to strike really large flakes and then continue to shape them by striking smaller flakes from around the edges, resulting in a new kind of tool: the hand axe. These and other kinds of large cutting tools characterize the Acheulean culture. These basic tools, including a variety of new forms of stone core, continued to be made for an immense period of time – ending in different places by around 400,000 to 250,000 years ago.

The Neolithic Revolution

The whole of human history consists precisely in the struggle of humankind to raise itself above the animal level. This long struggle began seven million years ago, when our remote humanoid ancestors first stood upright and were able to free their hands for manual labour. The production of the first stone scrapers and hand axes was the beginning of a process whereby men and women made themselves human through labour. Ever since then, successive phases of social development have arisen on the basis of changes in the development of the productive force of labour – that is to say, of our power over nature.

For most of human history, this process has been painfully slow, as *The Economist* remarked on the eve of the new millennium:

"For nearly all of human history, economic advance has been so slow as to be imperceptible within the span of a lifetime. For century after century, the annual rate of economic growth was, to one place of decimals, zero. When growth did happen it was so slow as to be invisible to contemporaries – and even in retrospect it appears not as rising living standards (which is what growth means today), merely as a gentle rise in population. Down the millennia, progress, for all but a tiny elite, amounted to this: it slowly became possible for more people to live, at the meanest level of subsistence." (*The Economist*, December 31, 1999)

Human progress begins to accelerate as a result of the first and most important of these great revolutions which was the transition from the primitive hunter-gatherer mode of production to agriculture. This laid the basis for a settled existence and the rise of the first towns. This was the period Marxists refer to as barbarism, that is, the stage between primitive communism and early class society, when classes begin to form and with them the state.

The prolonged period of primitive communism, humankind's earliest phase of development, where classes, private property, and the state did not exist, gave way to class society as soon as people were able to produce a surplus above the needs of everyday survival. At this point, the division of society into classes became an economic feasibility. Barbarism arises out of the decay of the old commune. Here for the first time society is divided by property relations, and classes and the state are in the process of formation, although these things only emerge gradually, passing from an embryonic stage and eventually consolidating as class society. This period begins approximately 10,000 or 12,000 years ago.

On the broad scales of history, the emergence of class society was a revolutionary phenomenon, in that it freed a privileged section of the population – a ruling class – from the direct burden of labour, permitting it the necessary time to develop art, science and culture. Class society, despite its ruthless exploitation and inequality, was the road that humankind needed to travel if it was to build up the necessary material prerequisites for a future classless society.

Here is the embryo out of which grew the towns and cities (such as Jericho, which dates from about 7,000 BC), writing, industry and everything else that laid the basis for which we call civilization. The period of barbarism represents a very large slice of human history, and is divided into several more or less distinct periods. In general, it is characterised by the transition from the hunter-gathering mode of production to pastoralism and agriculture, that is, from Palaeolithic savagery, passing through Neolithic barbarism to the higher barbarism of the Bronze Age, which stands at the threshold of civilization.

This decisive turning point, which Gordon Childe called the Neolithic revolution, represented a great leap forward in the development of human productive capacity, and therefore of culture. This is what Childe has to say:

> "Our debt to preliterate barbarism is heavy. Every single cultivated food plant of any importance has been discovered by some nameless barbarian society." (G Childe, *What Happened in History*, p64)

Farming began in the Middle East around 10,000 years ago, and represents a revolution in human society and culture. The new conditions of production gave men and women more time – time for complex analytical thought. This is reflected in the new art consisting of geometrical patterns – the first example of abstract art in history. The new conditions produced a new outlook on life, social relations and the relations that bind men and women to the natural world and the universe, whose secrets were probed in a way previously undreamt of. The understanding of nature is made necessary by the demands of agriculture, and advances slowly to the degree that men and women actually learn to conquer and subdue the hostile forces of nature in practice – through collective labour on a grand scale.

The cultural and religious revolution reflects the great social revolution – the greatest in all human history till now – that brought about the dissolution of the primitive commune and established private property of the means of production. And the means of production are the means of life itself.

In agriculture, the introduction of iron tools marks a big advance. It permits a growth in population and bigger and stronger communities. Above all, it creates a bigger surplus that can be appropriated by the leading families in the community. In particular, the introduction of iron marked a qualitative change in the process of production, since iron is far more effective than copper or bronze, both for the making of tools and weapons. It was far more available than the old metals. Here for the first time weapons and warfare become democratic. The most important weapon of the times was the iron sword, which first puts in an appearance in England about 5000 BC. Every man can have an iron sword. Warfare thus loses its aristocratic chiefly character and becomes a mass affair.

The employment of iron axes and sickles transformed agriculture. The transformation is shown by the fact that one acre of cultivated land can now maintain twice as many people as before. However, there is still no money, and this remained a barter economy. The surplus produced was not reinvested, as there was no way this could be done. Part of the surplus was appropriated by the chief and his family. Part of it was used up in feasting, which occupied a central role in this society.

In a single feast as many as 2-300 people could be fed. In the remains of one such feast the bones of 12 cows and a large number of sheep, pigs and dogs were discovered. These gatherings were not only the occasion for excesses of food and drink – they played an important social and religious role. In such ceremonies people gave thanks to the gods for the surplus of food. They permitted the mingling of the clans and the settling of communal affairs. Such lavish feasts also provided the chiefs the means by which to display their wealth and power and thus boost the prestige of the tribe or clan concerned.

Out of such meeting places gradually there arose the basis of permanent settlements, markets and small towns. The importance of private property and wealth increases along with the increased productivity of labour and the growing surplus that presents a tempting target for raids. Since the Iron Age was a period of continuous wars, feuds and raids, the settlements were often fortified with huge earthworks, such as Maiden castle in Dorset and Danebury in Hampshire.

The result of warfare was a large number of prisoners of war, many of whom were sold as slaves, and these – in the latter period – were traded as merchandise with the Romans. The geographer Strabo comments that "These people will give you a slave for an amphora of wine." Exchange thus began on the periphery of these societies. Through exchange with a more advanced culture (Rome), money was gradually introduced, the earliest coins being based on Roman models.

The dominion of private property means for the first time the concentration of wealth and power into the hands of a minority. It brings about a dramatic change in the relations between men and women and their offspring. The question of inheritance now begins to assume a burning importance. As a result we see the rise of spectacular tombs. In Britain, such tombs begin to appear about 3,000 BC. They signify a statement of power of the ruling class or caste. They also provide an assertion of proprietary rights over a definite territory. The same thing can be seen in other early cultures, for example, the plains Indians of North America, for which detailed accounts exist in the 18th and 19th centuries.

Here we have the first great instance of alienation. Man's essence is alienated from him in a double or triple sense. First, private property signifies the alienation of his product, which is appropriated by another. Second, his control over his life and destiny is appropriated by the state in the person of the king or pharaoh. Last, but not least, this alienation is carried over from this life to the next – the inner being ("soul") of all men and women is appropriated by the deities of the next world, whose good will must be continually obtained through prayers and sacrifices. And just as the services to the monarch form the basis of the wealth of the upper class of mandarins and nobles, so the sacrifices to the gods form the basis of the wealth and power of the priest caste that stands between the people and the gods and goddesses. Here we have the genesis of organised religion.

With the growth in production and the productivity gains made possible by the new economies of labour, there were new changes in religious beliefs and customs. Here too, social being determines consciousness. In place of ancestor worship and stone tombs for individuals and their families, we now see a far more ambitious expression of belief. The building of stone circles of staggering proportions attest to an impressive growth in population and production, made possible by the organised use of collective labour on a grand scale. The roots of civilization are therefore to be found precisely in barbarism, and still more so, in slavery. The development of barbarism ends up in slavery or else in what Marx called the "Asiatic mode of production".

Asiatic mode of production

The really explosive growth of civilization occurs with Egypt, Mesopotamia, the Indus Valley, China and Persia. In other words, the development of class society coincides with a massive upturn in the productive forces, and as a result, of human culture, which reached unprecedented heights. It is now believed that the emergence of the city, as well as the agriculture that preceded it occurred roughly simultaneously in different locations – Mesopotamia, the Indus Valley and the Huang Ho Valley, as well as Egypt. This occurred in the fourth millennium BC. In Southern Mesopotamia the Sumerians built

Ur, Lagash, Eridu and other city states. They were a literate people who left behind thousands of clay tablets written in cuneiform script.

The main features of the Asiatic mode of production are:

1. An urban society with an agrarian base.

2. A primarily agricultural economy.

3. Public works which are frequently (but not always) identified with the need for irrigation and the upkeep and spread of intensive canal and drainage systems.

4. A despotic system of government, often with a god-king at the top.

5. A large bureaucracy.

6. A system of exploitation based on taxation.

7. Common (state) ownership of the land.

Although slavery existed (prisoners of war), these were not actually slave societies. Labour service was not free, but those who performed it were not slaves. There is an element of coercion, but the main thing is habit, tradition and religion. The community serves the god-king (or queen). It serves the temple (cf Israel). This is associated with the state, and is the state.

The origins of the state are here mixed up with religion, and this religious aura is maintained to the present. People are taught to look up to the state with feelings of awe and reverence, as a force standing above society, above ordinary men and women, who must serve it blindly.

The village commune, the basic cell of these societies, is almost entirely self-sufficient. The few luxuries accessible to a population of subsistence farmers are obtained from the bazaar or from travelling peddlers who live on the margins of society. Money is scarcely known. Taxes to the state are paid in kind. There is no connection between one village and another and internal trade is weak. The real cohesion comes from the state.

There was an almost total lack of social mobility, reinforced in some cases by the caste system. The emphasis is on the group rather than the individual. Endogamous marriage prevails – that is, people tend to marry strictly within their class or caste. Economically, they tend to follow the professions of their parents. In the Hindu caste system this is, in fact, obligatory. This lack of mobility and social rigidity helps to tie the people to the land (the village commune).

As examples of this kind of society we have the Egyptians, Babylonians and Assyrians, the Shang or Yin dynasty (traditionally dating from about 1766 to 1122 BC) was the first Chinese dynasty of which there is a record and the Indus Valley (Harappa) civilization that lasted from about 2300 to around 1700 BC in India. In an entirely separate development, the pre-Hispanic civilizations of Mexico and Peru, though with certain variations, display strikingly similar features.

The tax system, and other methods of exploitation such as obligatory labour service for the state (Corvée) is oppressive but accepted as inevitable and the natural order of things, sanctioned by tradition and religion. Corvée is unfree labour, often unpaid, that is imposed on the people, either by an aristocratic landowner, as in feudalism, or, as in this case, by the state. But whereas the corvée system is similar to that which is found in western feudalism, the system of land ownership is not at all the same. In fact, the British rulers of India had the greatest difficulty making sense of it.

Where towns and cities spring up it is usually along trade routes, on the banks of rivers, in oases or other main sources of water. The towns are the administrative and commercial centres for the villages. Here are traders and artisans: ironworkers, carpenters, weavers, dyers, shoemakers, masons, etc. Here also are the local representatives of the state power, the only ones with which the mass of the population are familiar: low grade civil servants, scribes and police or soldiers.

There are also moneylenders, charging usurious rates to the peasants who are fleeced in turn by the tax-collector, the merchant and the village usurer. Many of these ancient elements have survived until modern times in some countries of the Middle East and Asia. But the advent of colonialism destroyed the ancient Asiatic mode of production once and for all. It was, in any case, an historical dead-end from which no further development was possible.

In these societies the mental horizons of people are extremely limited. The most powerful force in peoples' lives is the family or the clan, which educates them and teaches them about their history, religion and traditions. About politics and the world at large they know little or nothing. Their only contact with the state is the village headman who is responsible for collecting taxes.

What strikes one about these early civilizations is on the one hand their longevity, on the other, the extremely slow development of the productive forces and the extremely conservative nature of their outlook. This was an essentially static model of society. The only changes were the result of periodic invasions, e.g. by the nomadic barbarians of the steppes (the Mongols etc.), or occasional peasant revolts (China) that led to a change of dynasty.

However, the substitution of one dynasty for another does not signify any real change. The social relations and the state remain untouched by all the changes at the top. The end result was always the same. The invaders were absorbed and the system continued, undisturbed as before.

Empires rose and fell. There was a continuous process of fusion and fission. But through all these political and military changes, nothing fundamental changed for the peasantry at the bottom. Life continued its seemingly eternal (and divinely ordained) routine. The Asiatic idea of a never-ending cycle in religion is a reflection of this state of affairs. At the bottom we had the ancient village commune, based on subsistence agriculture that had survived virtually unchanged for millennia. Being predominantly agricultural, the rhythm of their lives is dominated by the eternal cycle of the seasons, the annual flooding of the Nile etc.

In recent years there has been a lot of noise in certain intellectual and quasi-Marxist circles about the Asiatic mode of production. But although Marx mentioned it, he did so only rarely and usually as an aside. He never developed it, which he certainly would have done if he had considered it important. The reason he did not do so was because it was an historical dead end, comparable to the Neanderthals in human evolution. It was a form of society, which, despite its achievements, ultimately did not contain within itself the seeds of future development. These were planted elsewhere: on the soil of Greece and Rome.

Slavery

Greek society was formed under different conditions to those of the earlier civilizations. The small city states of Greece lacked the vast expanses of cultivable land, the great plains of the Nile or Indus Valley and Mesopotamia. Hemmed in by barren mountain ranges, they faced to the sea, and this fact determined their whole course of development. Ill-suited both to agriculture or industry, they were pushed in the direction of the sea, becoming a trading nation and an intermediary, as the Phoenicians had done earlier.

Ancient Greece has a different socio-economic structure, and consequently a different spirit and a different outlook to the earlier societies of Egypt and Mesopotamia. Hegel says that in the East, the ruling spirit was freedom for the One (i.e. for the ruler, the god-king). But in Greece it was freedom for the many, that is to say, freedom for the citizens of Athens who did not happen to be slaves. But the slaves who did most of the work had no rights at all. Neither did women or foreigners.

For the free citizens, Athens was a most advanced democracy. This new spirit, infused with humanity and individualism, affected Greek art, religion and philosophy, which are qualitatively different to that of Egypt and Mesopotamia. When Athens was mistress of all Greece, she had neither a treasury nor a regular system of taxation. This was completely different to the Asiatic system in Persia and other earlier civilizations. But all this was based ultimately on the labour of the slaves, who were private property.

The main division was between free men and slaves. The free citizens did not usually pay taxes, which were regarded as degrading (as was manual labour). However, there was also a bitter class struggle in Greek society, characterized by a sharp division between the classes, based on property. The slaves, as chattel that could be bought and sold, were objects of production. The Roman word for a slave was instrumentum vocale, a tool with a voice. That puts it very clearly, and despite all the changes of the last 2,000 years the real position of the modern wage slave has not fundamentally changed since then.

It may be objected, Greece and Rome stood on the basis of slavery, which is an abhorrent and inhuman institution. But Marxists cannot look at history from the point of view of morality. Apart from anything else, there is no such thing as a supra-historical morality. Every society has its own morality, religion, culture, etc. which correspond to a given level of development, and, at least in the period we call civilization, also to the interests of a particular class.

Whether a particular war was good, bad or indifferent cannot be ascertained from the point of view of the number of victims, and much less from an abstract moral standpoint. We may strongly disapprove of wars in general, but one thing cannot be denied: throughout the whole course of human history, all serious questions have ultimately been settled in this way. That goes both for the conflicts between nations (wars) and also the conflicts between classes (revolutions).

Our attitude towards a particular type of society and its culture cannot be determined by moralistic considerations. What determines whether a given socio-economic formation is historically progressive or not is first and foremost its ability to develop the productive forces – the real material basis upon which all human culture arises and develops.

Hegel, that wonderfully profound thinker, writes: "It was not so much from slavery as through slavery that humanity was emancipated." (*Lectures on the Philosophy of History*, p407) Despite its monstrously oppressive character, slavery marked a step forward inasmuch as it permitted a further development of the productive power of society. We owe all the wonderful achievements of modern science to Greece and Rome – that is, to say, ultimately, to the labour of the slaves.

The Romans utilised brute force to subjugate other peoples, sold entire cities into slavery, slaughtered thousands of prisoners of war for amusement in the public circus, and introduced such refined methods of execution as crucifixion. Yes, all that is perfectly true. To us it seems a monstrous aberration. And yet, when we come to consider where all our modern civilization, our culture, our literature, our architecture, our medicine, our science, our philosophy, even in many cases our language, comes from, the answer is – from Greece and Rome.

Decline of slave society

Slavery contains an inner contradiction that led to its destruction. Although the labour of the individual slave was not very productive (slaves must be compelled to work), the aggregate of large numbers of slaves, as in the mines and latifundia (large scale agricultural units) in Rome in the last period of the Republic and the Empire, produced a considerable surplus. At the height of the Empire, slaves were plentiful and cheap and the wars of Rome were basically slave hunts on a massive scale.

But at a certain stage this system reached its limits and then entered into a lengthy period of decline. Since slave labour is only productive when it is employed on a massive scale, the prior condition for its success is an ample supply of slaves at a low cost. But slaves breed very slowly in captivity and so the only way a sufficient supply of slaves can be guaranteed is through continuous warfare. Once the Empire had reached the limits of its expansion under Hadrian, this became increasingly difficult.

The beginnings of a crisis in Rome can already be observed in the latter period of the Republic, a period characterised by acute social and political upheavals and class war. From the earliest beginnings there was a violent struggle between rich and poor in Rome. There are detailed accounts in the writings of Livy and others of the struggles between Plebeians and Patricians, which ended in an uneasy compromise. At a later period, when Rome had already made herself mistress of the Mediterranean by the defeat of her most powerful rival Carthage, we saw what was really a struggle for the division of the spoils.

Tiberius Gracchus demanded that the wealth of Rome be divided up among its free citizens. His aim was to make Italy a republic of small farmers and not slaves, but he was defeated by the nobles and slave-holders. This was a disaster for Rome in the long run. The ruined peasantry – the backbone of the Republic and its army – drifted to Rome where they constituted a lumpen-proletariat, a non-productive class, living off dole from the state. Although resentful of the rich, they nevertheless shared a common interest in the exploitation of the slaves – the only really productive class in the period of the Republic and the Empire.

The great slave rising under Spartacus was a glorious episode in the history of antiquity. The spectacle of these most downtrodden people rising up with arms in hand and inflicting defeat after defeat on the armies of the world's greatest power is one of the most incredible events in history. Had they succeeded in overthrowing the Roman state, the course of history would have been significantly altered.

The basic reason why Spartacus failed in the end was the fact that the slaves did not link up with the proletariat in the towns. So long as the latter continued to support the state, the victory of the slaves was impossible. However, the Roman proletariat, unlike the modern proletariat, was not a productive class but purely a parasitical one, living off the labour of the slaves and dependent on their masters. The failure of the Roman revolution is rooted in this fact.

The defeat of the slaves led straight to the ruin of the Roman state. In the absence of a free peasantry, the state was obliged to rely on a mercenary army to fight its wars. The deadlock in the class struggle produced a situation similar to the more modern phenomenon of Bonapartism. The Roman equivalent is what we call Caesarism.

The Roman legionnaire was no longer loyal to the Republic but to his commander – the man who guaranteed his pay, his loot and a plot of land when he retired. The last period of the Republic is characterised by an intensification of the struggle between the classes, in which neither side is able to win a decisive victory. As a result, the state (which Lenin described as "armed bodies of men") began to acquire increasing independence, to raise itself above society and to appear as the final arbiter in the continuing power struggles in Rome.

A whole series of military adventurers appear: Marius, Crassus, Pompey, and lastly Julius Caesar, a general of brilliance, a clever politician and a shrewd businessman, who in effect put an end to the Republic whilst paying lip-service to it. His prestige boosted by his military triumphs in Gaul, Spain and Britain, he began to concentrate all power in his hands. Although he was assassinated by a conservative faction who wished to preserve the Republic, the old regime was doomed.

After Brutus and the others were defeated by the triumvirate, the Republic was formally recognised, and this pretence was kept up by the first Emperor, Augustus. The very title "Emperor" (*imperator* in Latin) is a military title, invented to avoid the title of king that was so offensive to republican ears. But a king he was, in all but name.

The forms of the old Republic survived for a long time after that. But they were just that – hollow forms with no real content, an empty husk that in the end could be blown away by the wind. The Senate was devoid of all real power and authority. Julius Caesar had shocked respectable public opinion by making a Gaul a member of the senate. Caligula considerably improved upon this by making his horse a senator. Nobody saw anything wrong with this, or if they did they kept their mouths firmly shut.

It often happens in history that outworn institutions can survive long after their reason to exist has disappeared. They drag out a miserable existence like a decrepit old man who clings onto life, until they are swept away by a revolution. The decline of the Roman Empire lasted for nearly four centuries. This was not an uninterrupted process. There were periods of recovery and even brilliance, but the general line was downwards.

In periods like this, there is a general sense of malaise. The predominant mood is one of scepticism, lack of faith and pessimism in the future. The old traditions, morality and religion – things that act as a powerful cement holding society together – lose their credibility. In place of the old religion, people seek out new gods. In its period of decline, Rome was inundated with a plague of religious sects from the east. Christianity was only one of these, and although ultimately successful, had to contend with numerous rivals, such as the cult of Mithras.

When people feel that the world in which they live is tottering, that they have lost all control over their existence and that their lives and destinies are determined by unseen forces, then mystical and irrational tendencies get the upper hand. People believe that the end of the world is nigh. The early Christians believed this fervently, but many others suspected it. In point of fact what was coming to an end was not the world but only a particular form of society – slave society. The success of Christianity was rooted in the fact that it connected with this general mood. The world was evil and sinful. It was necessary to turn one's back on the world and all its works and look forward to another life after death.

Why the barbarians triumphed

By the time the barbarians invaded, the whole structure of the Roman Empire was on the verge of collapse, not only economically, but morally and spiritually. No wonder the barbarians were welcomed as liberators by the slaves and poorer sections of society. They merely completed a job that had been well prepared in advance. The barbarian attacks were a historical accident that served to express a historical necessity.

Once the Empire reached its limits and the contradictions inherent in slavery began to assert themselves, Rome entered into a long period of decline that lasted for centuries, until it was eventually overrun by the barbarians. The mass migrations that brought about the collapse of the Empire were a common phenomenon among nomadic pastoral peoples in antiquity and occurred for a variety of reasons – pressure on pasture land as a result of population growth, climate changes, etc.

Successive waves of barbarians swept out of the east: Goths, Visigoths, Ostrogoths, Alans, Lombards, Suevi, Alemanni, Burgundians, Franks, Thuringians, Frisians, Heruli, Gepidae, Angles, Saxons, Jutes, Huns and

Magyars, pushed their way into Europe. The all-powerful and eternal Empire was reduced to ashes. With remarkable swiftness the Empire collapsed under the hammer blows of the barbarians.

The decay of the slave economy, the monstrously oppressive nature of the Empire with its bloated bureaucracy and predatory tax farmers, was already undermining the whole system. There was a steady drift to the countryside where the basis was already being laid for the development of a different mode of production – feudalism. The barbarians merely delivered the coup de grâce to a rotten and moribund system. The whole edifice was tottering, and they merely gave it a last and violent push.

In the *Communist Manifesto* Marx and Engels wrote:

"Freeman and slave, patrician and plebeian, lord and serf, guild-master and journeyman, in a word, oppressor and oppressed, stood in constant opposition to one another, carried on an uninterrupted, now hidden, now open fight, a fight that each time ended, either in a revolutionary reconstitution of society at large, or in the common ruin of the contending classes." (My emphasis, AW)

What happened to the Roman Empire is a striking illustration of the last-named variant. The failure of the oppressed classes of Roman society to unite to overthrow the brutally exploitative slave-state led to an inner exhaustion and a long and painful period of social, economic and cultural decay, which prepared the way for the barbarians.

The immediate effect of the barbarian onslaught was to wipe out civilization and throw society and human thought back for a thousand years. The productive forces suffered a violent interruption. The cities were destroyed or abandoned. The invaders were an agricultural people and knew nothing of towns and cities. The barbarians in general were hostile to the towns and their inhabitants (a psychology that is quite common among peasants in all periods). This process of devastation, rape and pillage was to continue for centuries, leaving behind a terrible heritage of backwardness, which we call the Dark Ages.

Yet although the barbarians succeeded in conquering the Romans, they themselves were fairly quickly absorbed, and even lost their own language and ended up speaking a dialect of Latin. Thus, the Franks, who gave their name to modern France, were a Germanic tribe speaking a language related to modern German. The same thing happened to the Germanic tribes that invaded

Spain and Italy. This is what normally happens when a more economically and culturally backward people conquers a more advanced nation. Exactly the same thing happened later to the Mongol hoards that conquered India. They were absorbed by the more advanced Hindu culture and ended up founding a new Indian dynasty – the Moguls.

Feudalism

The rise of the feudal system following the collapse of Rome was accompanied by a long period of cultural stagnation in all of Europe north of the Pyrenees. With the exception of two inventions: the water wheel and windmills, there were no real inventions for about over a thousand years. One thousand years after the fall of Rome the only decent roads in Europe were Roman roads. In other words, there was a complete eclipse of culture. This was a result of the collapse of the productive forces, upon which culture ultimately depends. That is what we mean by a descending line in history. And let nobody imagine that such a thing cannot recur.

The barbarian invasions, wars and plagues meant that progress was punctuated with periods of retrogression. But eventually the chaotic conditions that coincided with the fall of Rome were replaced by a new equilibrium: feudalism. The decline of the Roman Empire caused a sharp falling off of urban life throughout most of Europe. The barbarian invaders were gradually absorbed and by the tenth century Europe entered slowly into a new period of ascent.

Of course, this statement is relative in character. Culture did not regain comparable levels to those of antiquity until the beginning of the renaissance in the late 14th and 15th centuries. Learning and science were strictly subordinated to the authority of the Church. Men's energies were absorbed either in constant warfare or monastic dreams, but gradually the downward spiral came to an end and was replaced by a long upward slope.

The closing of avenues of communication led to a collapse of trade. The money economy was undermined and increasingly replaced by barter. In place of the integrated international economy of the slave system under the Empire, we had the proliferation of small isolated agricultural communities.

The basis of feudalism was already laid in Roman society, when the slaves were freed and turned into colons, tied to the land, who later became serfs. This process, which occurred at different times, assuming different forms in different countries, was accelerated by the barbarian conquests. The Germanic warlords became the lords of the conquered lands and their inhabitants, offering military protection and a degree of security in exchange for expropriation of the labour of the serfs.

In the early period of feudalism the atomization of the nobility allowed relatively strong monarchies but later the royal power found itself confronted with strong estates capable of challenging it and overthrowing it. The barons had their own feudal armies which they frequently led into the field against each other and also against the king.

The feudal system in Europe was mainly a decentralized system. The power of the monarchy was limited by the aristocracy. The central power was usually weak. The centre of gravity of the feudal lord, his power base, was his manor and estate. The state power was weak and the bureaucracy non-existent. This weakness of the centre was what later permitted the independence of the towns (royal charters) and the emergence of the bourgeoisie as a separate class.

The romantic idealisation of the Middle Ages is based on a myth. This was a bloody and convulsive period, characterised by great cruelty and barbarism and what Marx and Engels called a brutal display of energy. The Crusades were characterised by unusual viciousness and inhumanity. The German invasions of Italy were exercises in futility.

The last period of the Middle Ages was a troubled time, characterised by continuous convulsions, wars and civil wars – just like our own times. To all intents and purposes the old order was already dead. Although it still remained defiantly on its feet, its existence was no longer regarded as something normal – something that had to be accepted as inevitable.

For a hundred years England and France were engaged in a bloody war that reduced large parts of France to ruin. The battle of Agincourt was the last and bloodiest battle of the Middle Ages. Here, in essence, two rival systems were pitted against each other on the battlefield: the old feudal military order, based on the nobility and the idea of chivalry and service, clashed with a new mercenary army based on wage labour.

The French nobility was decimated, defeated shamefully by an army of mercenary commoners. In the first 90 minutes 8,000 of the flower of the French aristocracy was butchered and 1,200 taken prisoner. At the end of the day not only the whole of the French nobility lay dead and bleeding on the battlefield, but the feudal order itself.

This had important social and political consequences. From this moment, the French nobility's grip on power began to weaken. When the English were driven from France it was by an uprising of the people led by a peasant girl, Joan of Arc. Amidst the wreckage of their lives, the chaos and bloodshed, the French people became conscious of their national identity and acted accordingly. The bourgeois began to demand their rights and charters and a new central monarchical power, leaning on the bourgeoisie and the people, began to seize the reins of power, forging a national state out of which modern France finally emerged.

The Black Death

When a given socio-economic system enters into crisis and decline, this is reflected not only in stagnation of the productive forces, but at every level. The decline of feudalism was an epoch when intellectual life was dead or dying. The dead hand of the Church paralysed all cultural and scientific initiatives.

The feudal structure was based on a pyramid in which God and the King stood at the top of a complex hierarchy, each segment of which was linked to the others by so-called duties. In theory, the feudal lords "protected" the peasants, who in return put food on their table and clothes on their backs, fed and enabled them to live a life of luxury and idleness; the priests prayed for their soul, the knights defended them and so on.

This system lasted a very long time. In Europe it lasted approximately one thousand years: from about the middle of the fifth to the middle of the fifteenth centuries. But by the 13th century feudalism in England and other countries was already reaching its limits. The growth in population put the whole system under colossal strain. Marginal lands had to be brought under cultivation, and much of the population merely eked out a bare living at the level of subsistence on small plots of land.

It was an "edge-of-chaos" situation, where the whole unsound edifice could be brought crashing down by a sufficiently powerful external shock. And what shock could be more powerful than this? The ravages of the Black Death, which killed off between one third and half the population of Europe, served to throw into sharp relief the injustice and misery, ignorance and intellectual and spiritual darkness of the fourteenth century.

It is now generally accepted that the Black Death played an important role in undermining feudalism. This was particularly clear in the case of England.

Having already killed half the population of Europe, the plague spread to England in the summer of 1348. As the plague spread inland to the villages of rural England, the population was decimated. Whole families, sometimes, whole villages, were wiped out. As on the European mainland, about half the population perished. However, those who managed to survive frequently found themselves in possession of quite large amounts of land. A new class of rich peasants was being created.

The colossal loss of life led to an extreme shortage of labour. There were simply not enough labourers to gather in the harvest or artisans to perform all the other necessary functions. This laid the basis for a profound social transformation. Feeling their strength, the peasants demanded, and got, higher wages and lower rents. If the lord refused to meet their demands, they could always leave and go to another master who was willing to do so. Some villages were abandoned altogether.

The old bonds were first loosened and then broken. As the peasants threw off the yoke of feudal obligations, many flocked to the towns to seek their fortune. This, in turn, led to a further development of the towns and therefore furthered the rise of the bourgeoisie. In 1349 King Edward III passed what was possibly the first wages policy in history: the Statute of Labourers. This decreed that wages must be held at the old levels. But the law was a dead letter from the start. The laws of supply and demand were already stronger than any royal decree.

Everywhere there was a new spirit of rebelliousness. The old authority was already undermined and discredited. The whole rotten edifice was tottering for a fall. One good push, it seemed, would finish it. In France there were a whole series of peasant uprisings known as jacqueries. Even more serious was the Peasants Rising in England (1381), when the rebels occupied London and for a time had the king in their power. But ultimately these risings could not succeed.

These uprisings were just premature anticipations of the bourgeois revolution at a time when the conditions for this had not completely matured. They expressed the dead end of feudalism and the deep discontent of the masses. But they could not show a way out. As a result the feudal system, although substantially modified, survived for a period, manifesting all the symptoms of a diseased and declining social order. The last period of the

Middle Ages was a troubled time, characterised by continuous convulsions, wars and civil wars – just like our own times.

The feeling that the end of the world is nigh is common to every historical period when a particular socio-economic system had entered into irreversible decline. This was the period when large numbers of men took to the roads, barefoot and dressed in penitential rags, flogging themselves till they bled. The flagellant sects awaited the end of the world, which they anxiously expected from one hour to the next.

In the end, what occurred was not the end of the world but only the end of feudalism, and what arrived was not the new Millennium but only the capitalist system. But they could not be expected to understand this. One thing was clear to all. The old world was in a state of rapid and irremediable decay. Men and women were torn by contradictory tendencies. Their beliefs were shattered and they were cut adrift in a cold, inhuman, hostile and incomprehensible world.

The rise of the bourgeoisie

When all the old certainties were overthrown. It was as if the lynchpin of the world had been removed. The result was terrifying turbulence and uncertainty. By the middle of the 15th century, the old system of beliefs began to unravel. People no longer looked to the Church to provide salvation, comfort and solace. Instead religious dissent arose in many different forms, and served as a guise for social and political opposition.

Peasants were defying the old laws and restrictions, demanding freedom of movement and asserting it by migrating to the towns without a licence. Contemporary chronicles express the irritation of the lords at the unwillingness of the labourers to take orders. There were even some strikes.

Amidst all this darkness new forces were stirring, announcing the birth of a new power and a new civilization that was gradually growing up inside the womb of the old society. The rise of trade and the towns brought with it a new aspiring class, the bourgeoisie, which began to jostle for position and power with the feudal ruling classes, the nobility and the Church. The birth of a new society was announced in art and literature, where new trends began to emerge in the course of the next hundred years.

To all intents and purposes the old order was already dead. Although it still remained defiantly on its feet, its existence was no longer regarded as something normal – something that had to be accepted as inevitable. The general perception (or rather feeling) that the end of the world was approaching was not entirely wrong. Only it was not the end of the world but the end of the feudal system.

The rise of the towns, those islands of capitalism in a sea of feudalism, was gradually undermining the old order. The new money economy, appearing at the margins of society, was gnawing at the foundations of feudal economy. The old feudal restrictions were now unbearable impositions, intolerable barriers to progress. They had to be shattered, and they were shattered. But the victory of the bourgeoisie did not come all at once. A long period was required for it to gain a final victory over the old order. Only gradually did a new spark of life reappear in the towns.

The slow recovery of trade led to the rise of the bourgeoisie and a revival of the towns, notably in Flanders, Holland and northern Italy. New ideas began to appear. After the fall of Constantinople to the Turks (1453) there was a new interest in the ideas and art of classical antiquity. New forms of art appeared in Italy and the Netherlands. Boccaccio's Decameron may be considered as the first modern novel. In England the writings of Chaucer are full of life and colour, reflecting a new spirit in art. The Renaissance was taking its first hesitant steps. Gradually, out of chaos a new order was arising.

The Reformation

By the 14th century capitalism was well established in Europe. The Netherlands became the factory of Europe, and trade flourished along the river Rhine. The cities of Northern Italy were a powerful locomotive of economic growth and commerce, opening up trade with Byzantium and the East. From about the 5th to the 12th centuries, Europe consisted of largely isolated economies. No longer! The discovery of America, the rounding of the Cape and the general expansion of trade gave a fresh impetus not only to the creation of wealth but to the development of men's minds.

Under such conditions, the old intellectual stagnation was no longer possible. The ground was cut from under the feet of the conservatives and reactionaries, as Marx and Engels explained in the *Communist Manifesto*:

"The discovery of America, the rounding of the Cape, opened up fresh ground for the rising bourgeoisie. The East-Indian and Chinese markets, the colonisation of America, trade with the colonies, the increase in the means of exchange and in commodities generally, gave to commerce, to navigation, to industry, an impulse never before known, and thereby, to the revolutionary element in the tottering feudal society, a rapid development."

It is no coincidence that the rise of the bourgeoisie in Italy, Holland, England and later in France was accompanied by an extraordinary flourishing of culture, art and science. Revolution, as Trotsky once said, has always been the driving force of history. In countries where the bourgeois revolution triumphed in the 17th and 18th centuries, the development of the productive forces and technology was complemented by a parallel development of science and philosophy, which undermined the ideological dominion of the Church forever.

In the epoch of the rise of the bourgeoisie, when capitalism still represented a progressive force in history, the first ideologists of that class had to fight a hard battle against the ideological bastions of feudalism, starting with the Catholic Church. Long before destroying the power of feudal landlords, the bourgeoisie had to break down the philosophical and religious defences mounted to protect the feudal system around the Church and its militant arm, the Inquisition. This revolution was anticipated by the revolt of Martin Luther against the authority of the Church.

During the fourteenth and fifteenth centuries Germany saw a move from an entirely agrarian economy and the rise of new social classes that clashed with the traditional feudal hierarchy. Luther's attacks on the Roman Catholic Church acted as the spark that ignited revolution. The burghers and lesser nobility sought to break the power of the clergy, escape the clutches of Rome, and, last but not least, enrich themselves through the confiscation of church property.

But in the depths of feudal society, other more elemental forces were stirring. When Luther's appeals against the clergy and ideas about Christian freedom reached the ears of the German peasants, they acted as a powerful stimulus to the repressed rage of the masses who had long suffered in silence the oppression of the feudal lords. Now they rose up to extract a terrible vengeance upon all their oppressors.

Beginning in 1524, the Peasants' War spread across the Germanic regions of the Holy Roman Empire during 1525 until its suppression in 1526. What happened after this has been repeated frequently in subsequent history. When confronted with the consequences of his revolutionary ideas, Luther had to choose a side, and he joined with the burghers, nobility, and princes in crushing the peasants.

The peasants found a better leader in the person of Thomas Müntzer. While Luther preached peaceful resistance, Thomas Müntzer attacked the priesthood in violent sermons, calling for the people to rise up in arms. Like Luther he cited biblical references to justify his actions: "Does not Christ say, 'I came not to send peace, but a sword'?"

The most radical wing of the movement were the Anabaptists, who were already beginning to question private property, taking as their model the primitive communism of the early Christians described in The Acts of the Apostles. Müntzer maintained that the Bible was not infallible, that the Holy Spirit had ways of communicating directly through the gift of reason.

Luther was horrified and wrote the notorious pamphlet Against the Murderous, Thieving Hoards of Peasants. The revolt was crushed with unspeakable barbarity, which set Germany back for centuries. But the tide of bourgeois revolt that was reflected in the rise of Protestantism was now unstoppable.

Those lands where the reactionary feudal forces quelled the embryo of the new society before birth, were sentenced to the nightmare of a long and inglorious period of degeneration, decline and decay. The example of Spain is the most graphic in this regard.

The bourgeois revolution

The first bourgeois revolution took the form of a national revolt of the Netherlands against the oppressive rule of Catholic Spain. In order to succeed, the wealthy Dutch burgers leaned on the men of no property: those courageous desperados drawn mainly from the poorest layers of society. The shock troops of the Dutch Revolution were known contemptuously by their enemies as the Sea Beggars.

This description was not altogether inaccurate. They were poor artisans, labourers, fishermen, homeless and dispossessed people – all those regarded as the dregs of society, but fired up with Calvinist fanaticism, they inflicted one defeat after another on the forces of mighty Spain. It was this that laid the basis for the rise of the Dutch Republic and a modern prosperous bourgeois Holland.

The next episode in the bourgeois revolution was even more significant and far-reaching in its implications. The English revolution of the seventeenth century assumed the form of civil war. It expressed itself as dual power, the royal power, resting upon the privileged classes or the upper circles of these classes – the aristocrats and bishops, based in Oxford – was confronted by the bourgeoisie and the small landowners and plebeian masses, based around London.

The English Revolution only succeeded when Oliver Cromwell, basing himself on the most radical elements, that is, the armed plebeians, swept the bourgeoisie to one side and waged a revolutionary war against the Royalists. As a result, the king was captured and executed. The conflict ended with a purging of the Parliament and the dictatorship of Cromwell.

The lower ranks of the army, under the leadership of the Levellers – the extreme left wing of the revolution – tried to carry the Revolution further, questioning private property, but were crushed by Cromwell. The reason for this defeat must be found in the objective conditions of the period. Industry had not yet developed to the point where it could provide the basis for socialism.

The proletariat itself remained at an embryonic stage of development. The Levellers themselves represented the lower levels of the petty bourgeoisie, and therefore, despite all their heroism, were unable to have their own, individual historic path. After Cromwell's death the bourgeoisie reached a compromise with Charles II that enabled it to hold real power while maintaining the Monarchy as a bulwark against any future revolutions against private property.

The American Revolution, which took the form of a war of national independence only succeeded to the degree that it involved the mass of poor farmers who waged a successful guerrilla war against the armies of King George of England.

The French Revolution of 1789-93 was on a far higher level than the English Revolution. This was one of the greatest events in human history. Even today it is an endless source of inspiration. And whereas Cromwell fought under the banner of religion, the French bourgeoisie raised the banner of Reason. Even before it brought down the formidable walls of the Bastille, it had brought down the invisible, but no less formidable, walls of the Church and religion.

At every stage the motor force that drove the French Revolution forward, sweeping aside all obstacles, was the active participation of the masses. And when this active participation of the masses ebbed, the Revolution came to a full stop and went into reverse. That was what led directly to reaction, firstly of the Thermidorian and later of the Bonapartist variety.

The enemies of the French Revolution always try to blacken its image with the accusation of violence and bloodshed. As a matter of fact the violence of the masses is inevitably a reaction against the violence of the old ruling class. The origins of the Terror must be sought in the reaction of the revolution to the threat of violent overthrow from both internal and external enemies. The revolutionary dictatorship was the result of revolutionary war and was only an expression of the latter.

Under the rule of Robespierre and the Jacobins, the semi-proletarian Sans-culottes carried the Revolution to a successful conclusion. In fact, the masses pushed the leaders to go far further than they had intended. Objectively, the Revolution was bourgeois-democratic in character, since the development of the productive forces and the proletariat had not yet reached a point where the question of socialism could be posed.

At a certain point, the process, having reached its limits, had to go into reverse. Robespierre and his faction struck down the Left wing and were then cut down themselves. The Thermidorian reactionaries in France hunted and oppressed the Jacobins, while the masses, worn out by years of exertion and sacrifice, had begun to fall into passivity and indifference. The pendulum now swung sharply to the right. But it did not restore the Ancien Regime. The fundamental socio-economic gains of the Revolution remained. The power of the landed aristocracy was broken.

The rotten and corrupt Directory was followed by the equally rotten and corrupt personal dictatorship of Bonaparte. The French bourgeoisie was terrified of the Jacobins and the Sans-culottes with their egalitarian and levelling tendencies. But it was even more terrified by the threat of royalist counterrevolution, which would drive it from power and put the clock back to pre-1789. The wars continued and there were still internal revolts by reactionaries. The only way out was to reintroduce dictatorship, but in the form of military rule. The bourgeoisie was looking for a Saviour and found one in the person of Napoleon Bonaparte.

With the defeat of Napoleon in the Battle of Waterloo, the last flickering embers of the fires lit by revolutionary France were extinguished. A long, grey period settled down on Europe like a thick coat of suffocating dust. The forces of triumphant reaction seemed firmly in the saddle. But that was only in appearance. Beneath the surface, the Mole of Revolution was busy digging the foundations for a new revolution.

The victory of capitalism in Europe laid the basis for a colossal upswing of industry, and with it, the strengthening of that class that is destined to overthrow capitalism and usher in a new and higher stage of social development – socialism. Marx and Engels wrote in the *Communist Manifesto*:

> "A spectre is haunting Europe – the spectre of communism. All the powers of old Europe have entered into a holy alliance to exorcise this spectre: Pope and Tsar, Metternich and Guizot, French Radicals and German police-spies."

These words describe the reactionary system that was established by the Congress of Vienna following the defeat of Napoleon in 1815. It was intended to eliminate the risk of revolution forever, to exorcise the spectre of the French Revolution forever. The brutal dictatorship of the "powers of old Europe" seemed as if it would last forever. But sooner or later things would turn into their opposite. Beneath the surface of reaction, new forces were gradually maturing and a new revolutionary class – the proletariat – was stretching its limbs.

The counter-revolution was overthrown by a new revolutionary wave that swept over Europe in 1848. These revolutions were fought under the banner of democracy – the same banner that was raised over the barricades of Paris in 1789. But everywhere the leading force in the revolution was not the cowardly, reactionary bourgeoisie but the lineal descendants of the French Sans-culottes – the working class, which inscribed on its banner a new kind of revolutionary ideal, the ideal of Communism.

The revolutions of 1848-9 were defeated through the cowardice and treachery of the bourgeoisie and its Liberal representatives. Reaction ruled once more until 1871, when the heroic proletariat of France stormed heaven in the Paris Commune, the first time in history that the working class overthrew the old bourgeois state and began to create a new kind of state – a workers' state. That glorious episode only lasted a few months and was finally drowned in blood. But it left a lasting heritage and laid the basis for the Russian Revolution of 1917.

The Russian Revolution

For Marxists, the Bolshevik Revolution was the greatest single event in human history. Under the leadership of the Bolshevik Party of Lenin and Trotsky, the working class succeeded in overthrowing its oppressors and at least begin the task of the socialist transformation of society.

However, the Revolution took place, not in an advanced capitalist country as Marx had expected, but on the basis of the most frightful backwardness. To give an approximate idea of the conditions that confronted the Bolsheviks, in just one year, 1920, six million people starved to death in Soviet Russia.

Marx and Engels explained long ago that socialism – a classless society – requires the right material conditions in order to exist. The starting point of socialism must be a higher point of development of the productive forces than the most advanced capitalist society (the USA for instance). Only on the basis of a highly developed industry, agriculture, science and technology, is it possible to guarantee the conditions for the free development of human beings, starting with a drastic reduction in the working day. The prior condition for this is the participation of the working class in the democratic control and administration of society.

Engels long ago explained that in any society in which art, science and government is the monopoly of a minority, that minority will use and abuse its position in its own interests. Lenin was quick to see the danger of the bureaucratic degeneration of the Revolution in conditions of general backwardness. In *The State and Revolution*, written in 1917, he worked out a programme on the basis of the experience of the Paris Commune. Here he explains the basic conditions – not for socialism or communism – but for the first period after the Revolution, the transitional period between capitalism and socialism. These were:

1. Free and democratic elections and the right of recall for all officials.

2. No official to receive a wage higher than a skilled worker.

3. No standing army but the armed people.

4. Gradually, all the tasks of running the state to be carried out in turn by the workers: when everybody is a "bureaucrat" in turn, nobody is a bureaucrat.

This is a finished programme for workers' democracy. It is directly aimed against the danger of bureaucracy. This in turn formed the basis of the 1919 Bolshevik Party Programme. In other words, contrary to the calumnies of the enemies of socialism, Soviet Russia in the time of Lenin and Trotsky was the most democratic regime in history.

However, the regime of soviet workers' democracy established by the October Revolution did not survive. By the early 1930s, all the above points had been abolished. Under Stalin, the workers' state suffered a process of bureaucratic degeneration which ended in the establishment of a monstrous totalitarian regime and the physical annihilation of the Leninist Party. The decisive factor in the Stalinist political counter-revolution in Russia was the isolation of the Revolution in a backward country. The way in which this political counter-revolution took place was explained by Trotsky in *The Revolution Betrayed*.

It is not feasible for society to jump straight from capitalism to a classless society. The material and cultural inheritance of capitalist society is far too inadequate for that. There is too much scarcity and inequality that cannot be immediately overcome. After the socialist revolution, there must be a transitional period that will prepare the necessary ground for superabundance and a classless society.

Marx called this first stage of the new society "the lowest stage of communism" as opposed to "the highest stage of communism", where the last residue of material inequality would disappear. In that sense, socialism and communism have been contrasted to the "lower" and "higher" stages of the new society.

In describing the lower stage of communism Marx writes:

"What we are dealing with here is a communist society, not as it has developed on its own foundations, but, on the contrary, just as it emerges from capitalist society; which is thus in every respect, economically, morally and intellectually, still stamped with the birth marks of the old society from whose womb it emerges." (Marx and Engels, *Selected Works*, *Critique of the Gotha Programme*, by Marx, *Vol 3*, p17 From here on referred to as *MESW*)

"Between capitalist and communist society," states Marx, "lies the period of the revolutionary transformation of the one into the other. Corresponding to this is also a political transition period in which the state can be nothing but the revolutionary dictatorship of the proletariat."

As all the greatest Marxist theoreticians explained, the task of the socialist revolution is to bring the working class to power by smashing the old capitalist state machine. The latter was the repressive organ designed to keep the working class in subjection. Marx explained that this capitalist state, together with its state bureaucracy, cannot serve the interests of the new power. It has to be done away with. However, the new state created by the working class would be different from all previous states in history. Engels described it as a semi-state, a state designed in such a way that it was destined to disappear.

However, for Marx – and this is a crucial point – this lower stage of communism from its very beginning would be on a higher level in terms of its economic development than the most developed and advanced capitalism. And why was this so important? Because without a massive development of the productive forces, scarcity would prevail and with it the struggle for existence.

As Marx explained, such a state of affairs would pose the danger of degeneration:

"This development of the productive forces is an absolutely necessary practical premise [of communism], because without it want is generalised, and with want the struggle for necessities begins again, and that means that all the old crap must revive." (*MESW, The German Ideology, Vol 1*, p37, my emphasis, AW)

These prophetic words of Marx explain why the Russian Revolution, so full of promise, ended in bureaucratic degeneration and the monstrous totalitarian caricature of Stalinism, which in turn prepared the way for capitalist restoration and a further regression. "All the old crap" revived because the Russian Revolution was isolated in conditions of frightful material and cultural backwardness. But today with the tremendous advance in science and technique, the conditions have been prepared whereby this would no longer be the case.

Unprecedented advance

Every phase of human development has its roots in all previous development. This is true both of human evolution and social development. We have evolved from lower species and are genetically related to even the most primitive life forms, as the human genome has conclusively proved. We are separated from our nearest living relatives the chimpanzees by a genetic difference of less than 2%. But that very small percentage represents a tremendous qualitative leap.

We have emerged from savagery, barbarism, slavery and feudalism, and each of these stages represented a definite stage in the development of the productive forces and culture. Hegel expressed this idea in a beautiful passage in the Phenomenology of Mind:

> "The bud disappears when the blossom breaks through, and we might say that the former is refuted by the latter; in the same way when the fruit comes, the blossom may be explained to be a false form of the plant's existence, for the fruit appears as its true nature in place of the blossom. The ceaseless activity of their own inherent nature makes these stages moments of an organic unity, where they not merely do not contradict one another, but where one is as necessary as the other; and constitutes thereby the life of the whole."

Every stage in the development of society is rooted in necessity and emerges out of the preceding stages. History can only be understood if these stages are taken in their unity. Each had its raison d'être in the development of the productive forces, and each entered into contradiction with their further development at a certain stage, when a revolution was necessary to cast off the old forms and allow new forms to emerge.

As we have seen, the victory of the bourgeoisie was achieved by revolutionary means, although nowadays the defenders of capitalism do not like to be reminded of the fact. And as Marx explained, the bourgeoisie, historically, has played a most revolutionary role:

> "The bourgeoisie cannot exist without constantly revolutionising the instruments of production, and thereby the relations of production, and with them the whole relations of society. Conservation of the old modes of production in unaltered form, was, on the contrary, the first condition of existence for all earlier industrial classes. Constant revolutionising of production, uninterrupted disturbance of all social conditions, everlasting uncertainty and agitation distinguish the bourgeois epoch from all earlier ones." (*Communist Manifesto*)

Under capitalism the productive forces have experienced spectacular development, unprecedented in the history of mankind: despite the fact that capitalism is the most exploitative and oppressive system that has ever existed; despite the fact that, in Marx's words, "Capital came onto the stage of history dripping blood from every pore," it nevertheless represented a colossal leap forward in the development of the productive forces – and therefore of our power over nature.

During the last two centuries the development of technology and science has proceeded at a far faster rate than in all previous history. The curve of human development, which was virtually flat for most of our history, suddenly experienced a steep ascent. The dizzying progress of technology is the precondition for the final emancipation of humankind, the abolition of poverty and illiteracy, ignorance, disease and the domination of nature by man through conscious planning of the economy. The road is open to conquest, not only on Earth, but in space.

Capitalism in decline

It is the illusion of every epoch that it will last forever. Every social system believes that it represents the only possible form of existence for human beings; that its institutions, its religion, its morality are the last word that can be spoken. That is what the cannibals, the Egyptian priests, Marie Antoinette and Tsar Nicholas all fervently believed. And that is what the bourgeoisie and its apologists today wish to demonstrate when they assure us, without the slightest basis, that the so-called system of "free enterprise" is the only possible system – just when it is beginning to show all the signs of senile decay.

The capitalist system today resembles the Sorcerer's Apprentice who conjured up powerful forces which he could not control. The fundamental contradiction of capitalist society is the antagonism between the social nature of production and the private form of appropriation. From this central contradiction many others arise. This contradiction is expressed by periodic crises, as Marx explains:

> "In these crises, a great part not only of the existing products, but also of the previously created productive forces, are periodically destroyed. In these crises, there breaks out an epidemic that, in all earlier epochs, would have seemed an absurdity – the epidemic of over-production. Society suddenly finds itself put back into a state of momentary barbarism; it appears as if a famine, a universal

war of devastation, had cut off the supply of every means of subsistence; industry and commerce seem to be destroyed; and why? Because there is too much civilisation, too much means of subsistence, too much industry, too much commerce. The productive forces at the disposal of society no longer tend to further the development of the conditions of bourgeois property; on the contrary, they have become too powerful for these conditions, by which they are fettered, and so soon as they overcome these fetters, they bring disorder into the whole of bourgeois society, endanger the existence of bourgeois property. The conditions of bourgeois society are too narrow to comprise the wealth created by them. And how does the bourgeoisie get over these crises? On the one hand by enforced destruction of a mass of productive forces; on the other, by the conquest of new markets, and by the more thorough exploitation of the old ones. That is to say, by paving the way for more extensive and more destructive crises, and by diminishing the means whereby crises are prevented." (*Communist Manifesto*)

This is an exact description of the present situation. It is a terrible paradox that the more humanity develops its productive capacity, the more spectacular the advances of science and technology, the greater the suffering, starvation, oppression and misery of the majority of the world's population. The sickness of capitalism on a world scale manifested itself in the collapse of 2008. This was the beginning of the biggest crisis in the entire 200 year existence of capitalism, and it is far from being resolved. This is an expression of the impasse of capitalism, which in the last analysis is a result of the revolt of the productive forces against the straitjacket of private property and the nation state.

Socialism or barbarism

For thousands of years culture has been the monopoly of a privileged minority, while the great majority of humanity was excluded from knowledge, science, art and government. Even now, this remains the case. Despite all our pretensions, we are not really civilized. The world we live in now certainly does not merit the name. It is a barbaric world, inhabited by people who have yet to overcome a barbarous past. Life remains a harsh and unrelenting struggle to exist for the great majority of the planet, not only in the underdeveloped world but in the developed capitalist countries as well.

Marx pointed out that there were two possibilities before the human race: socialism or barbarism. The question is therefore posed in the starkest terms: in the coming period, either the working class will take into its hands the running of society, replacing the decrepit capitalist system with a new social order based on the harmonious and rational planning of the productive forces and the conscious control of men and women over their own lives and destinies, or else we will be faced with a most frightful spectacle of social, economic and cultural collapse.

The crisis of capitalism represents not just an economic crisis that threatens the jobs and living standards of millions of people throughout the world. It also threatens the very basis of a civilised existence – insofar as this exists. It threatens to throw humankind back on all fronts. If the proletariat – the only genuinely revolutionary class – does not succeed in overthrowing the rule of the banks and monopolies, the stage will be set for a collapse of culture and even a return to barbarism.

Consciousness

Dialectics teaches us that sooner or later, things change into their opposite. It is possible to draw parallels between geology and society. Just as the tectonic plates, having moved too slowly, compensate the delay by a violent earthquake, so the lagging of consciousness behind events is compensated by sudden changes in the psychology of the masses. The most striking manifestation of dialectics is the crisis of capitalism itself. Dialectics are taking their revenge on the bourgeoisie who have understood nothing, predicted nothing and are capable of solving nothing.

The collapse of the Soviet Union created a mood of pessimism and despair amongst the working class. The defenders of capitalism launched a ferocious ideological counteroffensive against the ideas of socialism and Marxism. They promised us a future of peace, prosperity and democracy thanks to the wonders of the free market economy. Two decades have passed since then and a decade is not such a long time in the grand scheme of history. Not one stone upon another now remains of these comforting illusions.

Everywhere there are wars, unemployment, poverty and hunger. And everywhere a new spirit of revolt is arising and people are looking for ideas that can explain what is happening in the world. The old, stable, peaceful, prosperous capitalism is dead, and with it the old peaceful, harmonious relations between the classes. The future will be one of years and decades of austerity, unemployment and falling living standards. That is a finished recipe for a revival of the class struggle everywhere.

The embryo of a new society is already maturing within the womb of the old. The elements of a workers' democracy already exist in the form of the workers' organisations, the shop stewards committees, the trade unions, the cooperatives etc. In the period that opens up, there will be a life and death struggle – a struggle of those elements of the new society to be born, and an equally fierce resistance on the part of the old order to prevent this from happening.

It is true that the consciousness of the masses has been lagging far behind events. But that also will change into its opposite. Great events are forcing men and women to question their old beliefs and assumptions. They are being jolted out of the old supine, apathetic indifference and forced to come to terms with reality. We can already see this in outline with the events in Greece. In such periods consciousness can change very rapidly. And that is just what a revolution is.

The rise of modern capitalism and of its gravedigger, the working class, has made much clearer what is at the heart of the materialist conception of history. Our task is not merely to understand but bring to a successful conclusion the historic struggle of the classes by means of the victory of the proletariat and the socialist transformation of society. Capitalism has failed after all to "end" history. The task of Marxists is to work actively to hasten the overthrow of the old, decrepit system and help to bring about the birth of a new and better world.

From necessity to freedom

The scientific approach to history that historical materialism gives us does not incline us to draw pessimistic conclusions from the horrific symptoms of decline that confront us on all sides. On the contrary, the general tendency of human history has been in the direction of ever greater development of our productive and cultural potential.

The relation between the development of human culture and the productive forces was already clear to that great genius of antiquity, Aristotle, who explained in his book *Metaphysics* that "man begins to philosophise when the means of life are provided," and added that the reason why astronomy and mathematics were discovered in Egypt is that the priest caste did not have to work. This is a purely materialist understanding of history.

The great achievements of the last hundred years have for the first time created a situation where all the problems facing humankind can easily be solved. The potential for a classless society already exists on a world scale. What is necessary is to bring about a rational and harmonious planning of the productive forces in order that this immense, practically infinite, potential can be realised.

Once the productive forces are freed from the straitjacket of capitalism, the potential exists to produce a great number of geniuses: artists, writers, composers, philosophers, scientists and architects. Art, science and culture would flower as never before. This rich, beautiful and wonderfully diverse world would at last become a place fit for human beings to live in.

In a certain sense socialist society is a return to primitive tribal communism but on a vastly higher productive level. Before one can envisage a classless society, all the hallmarks of class society, especially inequality and scarcity, would have to be abolished. It would be absurd to talk of the abolition of classes where inequality, scarcity and the struggle for existence prevailed. It would be a contradiction in terms. Socialism can only appear at a certain stage in the evolution of human society, at a certain level of development of the productive forces.

On the basis of a real revolution in production, it would be possible to achieve such a level of abundance that men and women would no longer have to worry about their everyday necessities. The humiliating concerns and fears that fill every thinking hour of men and women now will disappear. For the first time, free human beings will be masters of their destinies. For the first time they will be really human. Only then will the real history of the human race begin.

On the basis of a harmonious planned economy in which the tremendous productive power of science and technology will be harnessed for the satisfaction of human needs, not the profits of a few, culture will reach new and undreamed-of levels of development. The Romans described slaves as "tools with voices". Nowadays we do not need to enslave people to do the work. We already have the technology to create robots that can not only play chess and perform elementary tasks on production lines but drive vehicles more safely than humans and even carry out quite complex tasks.

On the basis of capitalism, this technology threatens to displace millions of workers: not only lorry drivers and unskilled workers but people like accountants and computer programmers are threatened with losing their livelihoods. Millions will be thrown on the scrapheap while those who retain their jobs will be working longer hours than before.

In a socialist planned economy, the same technology would be used to reduce the working day. We could immediately introduce a thirty hour week, followed by a twenty hour week, a ten hour week or even less, while increasing production and expanding the wealth of society far more than what is conceivable under capitalism.

This would represent a fundamental change in people's lives. For the first time, men and women would be freed from the drudgery of labour. They would be free to develop themselves physically, mentally and one might even add spiritually. Men and women will be free to lift their eyes to the heavens and contemplate the stars.

Trotsky once wrote: "How many Aristoteles are herding swine? And how many swineherds are sitting on thrones?" Class society impoverishes people, not just materially but psychologically. The lives of millions of human beings are confined to the narrowest limits. Their mental horizons are stunted. Socialism would release all the colossal potential that is being wasted by capitalism.

It is true that people have different characters and aptitudes. Not everyone can be an Aristotle, a Beethoven or an Einstein. But everybody has the potential to do great things in one field or another, to become a great scientist, artist, musician, dancer or footballer. Communism will provide all the conditions needed to develop those potentials to the fullest extent.

This would be the greatest revolution of all time. It would carry human civilization to a new and qualitatively superior level. In the words of Engels it would be Humankind's leap from the realm of necessity to the realm of true freedom.

London 8th July, 2015

Letter to J Bloch, London, 21ˢᵗ September 1890

Frederick Engels

According to the materialist conception of history, the ultimately determining element in history is the production and reproduction of real life. Other than this neither Marx nor I have ever asserted. Hence if somebody twists this into saying that the economic element is the only determining one, he transforms that proposition into a meaningless, abstract, senseless phrase. The economic situation is the basis, but the various elements of the superstructure – political forms of the class struggle and its results, to wit: constitutions established by the victorious class after a successful battle, etc., juridical forms, and even the reflexes of all these actual struggles in the brains of the participants, political, juristic, philosophical theories, religious views and their further development into systems of dogmas – also exercise their influence upon the course of the historical struggles and in many cases preponderate in determining their form. There is an interaction of all these elements in which, amid all the endless host of accidents (that is, of things and events whose inner interconnection is so remote or so impossible of proof that we can regard it as non-existent, as negligible), the economic movement finally asserts itself as necessary. Otherwise the application of the theory to any period of history would be easier than the solution of a simple equation of the first degree.

We make our history ourselves, but, in the first place, under very definite assumptions and conditions. Among these the economic ones are ultimately decisive. But the political ones, etc., and indeed even the traditions which haunt human minds also play a part, although not the decisive one. The Prussian state also arose and developed from historical, ultimately economic, causes. But it could scarcely be maintained without pedantry that among

99

the many small states of North Germany, Brandenburg was specifically determined by economic necessity to become the great power embodying the economic, linguistic and, after the Reformation, also the religious difference between North and South, and not by other elements as well (above all by its entanglement with Poland, owing to the possession of Prussia, and hence with international political relations – which were indeed also decisive in the formation of the Austrian dynastic power). Without making oneself ridiculous it would be a difficult thing to explain in terms of economics the existence of every small state in Germany, past and present, or the origin of the High German consonant permutations, which widened the geographic partition wall formed by the mountains from the Sudetic range to the Taunus to form a regular fissure across all Germany.

In the second place, however, history is made in such a way that the final result always arises from conflicts between many individual wills, of which each in turn has been made what it is by a host of particular conditions of life. Thus there are innumerable intersecting force, an infinite series of parallelograms of forces which give rise to one resultant – the historical event. This may again itself be viewed as the product of a power which works as a whole unconsciously and without volition. For what each individual wills is obstructed by everyone else, and what emerges is something that no one willed. Thus history has proceeded hitherto in the manner of a natural process and is essentially subject to the same laws of motion. But from the fact that the wills of individuals – each of whom desires what he is impelled to by his physical constitution and external, in the last resort economic, circumstances (either his own personal circumstances or those of society in general) – do not attain what they want, but are merged into an aggregate mean, a common resultant, it must not be concluded that they are equal to zero. On the contrary, each contributes to the resultant and is to this extent included in it.

I would furthermore ask you to study this theory from its original sources and not at second-hand; it is really much easier. Marx hardly wrote anything in which it did not play a part. But especially The Eighteenth Brumaire of Louis Bonaparte is a most excellent example of its application. There are also many allusion to it in Capital. Then may I also direct you to my writings: Herr Eugen Dühring's Revolution in Science and *Ludwig Feuerbach and the end of Classical German Philosophy* in which I have given the most detailed account of historical material which, as far as I know, exists. [*The German Ideology* was not published in Marx or Engels lifetime]

Marx and I are ourselves partly to blame for the fact that the younger people sometimes lay more stress on the economic side than is due to it. We had to emphasise the main principle vis-á-vis our adversaries, who denied it, and we had not always the time, the place or the opportunity to give their due to the other elements involved in the interaction. But when it came to presenting a section of history, that is, to making a practical application, it was a different matter and there no error was permissible. Unfortunately, however, it happens only too often that people think they have fully understood a new theory and can apply it without more ado from the moment they have assimilated its main principles, and even those not always correctly. And I cannot exempt many of the more recent "Marxists" from this reproach, for the most amazing rubbish has been produced in this quarter, too...

Ludwig Feuerbach and the end of Classical German Philosophy *(extract)*

Frederick Engels

Men make their own history, whatever its outcome may be, in that each person follows his own consciously desired end, and it is precisely the resultant of these many wills operating in different directions, and of their manifold effects upon the outer world, that constitutes history. Thus it is also a question of what the many individuals desire. The will is determined by passion or deliberation. But the levers which immediately determine passion or deliberation are of very different kinds. Partly they may be external objects, partly ideal motives, ambition, "enthusiasm for truth and justice", personal hatred, or even purely individual whims of all kinds. But, on the one hand, we have seen that the many individual wills active in history for the most part produce results quite other than those intended – often quite the opposite; that their motives, therefore, in relation to the total result are likewise of only secondary importance. On the other hand, the further question arises: What driving forces in turn stand behind these motives? What are the historical forces which transform themselves into these motives in the brains of the actors?

The old materialism never put this question to itself. Its conception of history, in so far as it has one at all, is therefore essentially pragmatic; it divides men who act in history into noble and ignoble and then finds that as a rule the noble are defrauded and the ignoble are victorious. hence, it follows for the old materialism that nothing very edifying is to be got from the study of history, and for us that in the realm of history the old materialism becomes untrue to itself because it takes the ideal driving forces which operate there as ultimate causes, instead of investigating what is behind them, what are the driving forces of these driving forces. This inconsistency does not lie in the fact that ideal driving forces are recognized, but in the investigation not being carried further back behind these into their motive causes. On the other hand, the philosophy of history, particularly as represented by Hegel, recognizes that the ostensible and also the really operating motives of men who act in history are by no means the ultimate causes of historical events; that behind these motives are other motive powers, which have to be discovered. But it does not seek these powers in history itself, it imports them rather from outside, from philosophical ideology, into history. Hegel, for example, instead of explaining the history of ancient Greece out of its own inner interconnections, simply maintains that it is nothing more than the working out of "forms of beautiful individuality", the realization of a "work of art" as such. He says much in this connection about the old Greeks that is fine and profound, but that does not prevent us today from refusing to be put off with such an explanation, which is a mere manner of speech.

When, therefore, it is a question of investigating the driving powers which – consciously or unconsciously, and indeed very often unconsciously – lie behind the motives of men who act in history and which constitute the real ultimate driving forces of history, then it is not a question so much of the motives of single individuals, however eminent, as of those motives which set in motion great masses, whole people, and again whole classes of the people in each people; and this, too, not merely for an instant, like the transient flaring up of a straw-fire which quickly dies down, but as a lasting action resulting in a great historical transformation. To ascertain the driving causes which here in the minds of acting masses and their leaders – to so-called great men – are reflected as conscious motives, clearly or unclearly, directly or in an ideological, even glorified, form – is the only path which can put us on the track of the laws holding sway both in history as a whole, and at particular periods and in particular lands. Everything which sets men in motion must go through their minds; but what form it will take in the mind will depend very much upon the circumstances. The workers have by no means become reconciled to capitalist machine industry, even though they no longer simply break the machines to pieces, as they still did in 1848 on the Rhine.

Preface to a Contribution to the Critique of Political Economy

Karl Marx

In the social production of their life, men enter into definite relations that are indispensable and independent of their will, relations of production which correspond to a definite stage of development of their material productive forces. The sum total of these relations of production constitutes the economic structure of society, the real foundation, on which rises a legal and political superstructure and to which correspond definite forms of social consciousness.

The mode of production of material life conditions the social, political and intellectual life process in general. It is not the consciousness of men that determines their being, but, on the contrary, their social being that determines their consciousness.

At a certain stage of their development, the material productive forces of society come in conflict with the existing relations of production, or – what is but a legal expression for the same thing – with the property relations within which they have been at work hitherto. From forms of development of the productive forces these relations turn into their fetters.

Then begins an epoch of social revolution. With the change of the economic foundation the entire immense superstructure is more or less rapidly transformed. In considering such transformations a distinction should always be made between the material transformation of the economic conditions of production, which can be determined with the precision of natural science, and the legal, political, religious, aesthetic or philosophic – in short, ideological forms in which men become conscious of this conflict and fight it out. Just as our opinion of an individual is not based on what he thinks of himself, so can we not judge of such a period of transformation by its own consciousness; on the contrary, this consciousness must be explained rather from the contradictions of material life, from the existing conflict between the social productive forces and the relations of production.

No social order ever perishes before all the productive forces for which there is room in it have developed; and new, higher relations of production never appear before the material conditions of their existence have matured in the womb of the old society itself. Therefore mankind always sets itself only such tasks as it can solve; since, looking at the matter more closely, it will always be found that the tasks itself arises only when the material conditions of its solution already exist or are at least in the process of formation.

In broad outlines Asiatic, ancient, feudal, and modern bourgeois modes of production can be designated as progressive epochs in the economic formation of society. The bourgeois relations of production are the last antagonistic form of the social process of production – antagonistic not in the sense of individual antagonisms, but of one arising from the social conditions of life of the individuals; at the same time the productive forces developing in the womb of bourgeois society create the material conditions for the solution of that antagonism. This social formation brings, therefore, the prehistory of society to a close.

Questions on Historical Materialism

1. What separates human beings from the rest of nature?
2. Do we have free will?
3. What role do Marxists explain is played by individuals in history?
4. What do we mean by 'class'?
5. How did humankind arise as a species?
6. Are we naturally selfish beings?
7. What was the neolithic revolution?
8. What was the Asiatic mode of production and why was it not a focus of Marx's writings?
9. How did slave society help civilisation to develop?
10. Why did the 'Dark Ages' happen?
11. What ultimately undermined the class struggle of the peasantry against the landlords during feudal times?
12. Of what was the 'Black Death' a symptom?
13. What were the tasks of the bourgeois revolutions?
14. How does the exploitation of the wage worker differ from that of the serf?
15. What part did the 'revolutionising of the means of production' play in the development of capitalism?
16. Describe some modern-day exmaples of this process.
17. How does the proletarian revolution differ from bourgeois revolutions?
18. Why did Marx described the working class as the 'gravediggers' of capitalism?
19. How does human consciousness change?
20. In what ways would socialism take society forward?

Suggested reading

- *The Communist Manifesto*, Karl Marx & Frederick Engels
- *The German Ideology*, Karl Marx & Frederick Engels
- *Revolution and Counter-Revolution in Germany*, Karl Marx and Frederick Engels
- *The Poverty of Philosophy*, Karl Marx
- *The Eighteenth Brumaire of Louis Bonaparte*, Karl Marx
- *The Civil War in France*, Karl Marx
- *The Class Struggles in France*, Karl Marx
- *The Holy Family*, Karl Marx
- *Capital Volume I*, chapters on the *Primitive Accumulation of Capital*, Karl Marx
- Preface and Introduction of *a Contribution to the Critique of Political Economy*, Karl Marx
- *Grundrisse*, Karl Marx
- *The Critique of the Gotha Programme*, Karl Marx
- *The Origin of the Family, Private Property and the State*, Frederick Engels
- *Socialism: Utopian and Scientific*, Frederick Engels
- *Ludwig Feuerbach and the End of Classical German Philosophy*, Frederick Engels
- *The Part Played by Labour in the Transition from Ape to Man*, Frederick Engels
- *The Peasant War in Germany*, Frederick Engels
- *The Three Sources and Three Component Parts of Marxism*, V I Lenin
- *The State and Revolution*, V I Lenin
- *Imperialism: The Highest Stage of Capitalism*, V I Lenin

- *On Marx and Engels,* V I Lenin
- *The Permanent Revolution,* Leon Trotsky
- *The History of the Russian Revolution Volumes One, Two and Three,* Leon Trotsky
- *The Living Thoughts of Karl Marx,* Leon Trotsky
- *The Role of the Individual in History,* G V Plekhanov
- *The Development of the Monist View of History,* G V Plekhanov
- *The Foundations of Christianity,* Karl Kautsky
- *Behind the Myths,* John Pickard

Titles listed above are available to buy from Wellred Books at:
www.wellredbooks.net
Wellred Books, PO Box 50525, London E14 6WG, United Kingdom
For further suggested reading on historical materialism,
see the 'Educate Yourself' section of the *In Defence of Marxism* website
(http://www.marxist.com/educate-yourself/)

3. Marxist Economics

What Is Marxist Economics?

Rob Sewell

The capitalist system is experiencing its worst crisis in living memory, possibly in its history. As a result, there is a renewed interest in understanding the way in which the system works and, above all, in Marxist economics.

At first glance, Marxist economics may seem quite difficult to understand. To begin with, the language appears difficult. That is the case with all sciences, which require their own shorthand. However, once you understand the basic principles it becomes quite straight forward, and the effort is certainly worth it. In fact, the rewards are truly amazing. Marxism will provide answers to many questions that are shrouded in mystery, not least, how workers are exploited and why the capitalist system experiences devastating periodic crises.

Marx never looked on the economic system from a subjective point of view, but from an objective one. It is the same approach as a natural scientist who examines the workings of a beehive. When you look at the society we live in, everything appears to be dominated by money and the buying and selling of things. Making money is the driving force behind almost everything. Money relations have become burned deep into everyday life and consciousness. Money even becomes personified, while people are viewed in cash terms. "The pound is doing a bit better today on financial markets," says the financial news, as if referring to the health of a sick individual. On the other hand, the millionaire landowner Duke of Westminster is said to be "worth" so many millions. What is the reason for this strange state of affairs, which Marx describes as a "commodity fetish"?

Put simply, this bizarre concept is a product of the market economy, where social relations are distorted and reduced to a series of cash payments. As we live in a world dominated by such relationships, they permeate our thinking and view of things. This outlook mystifies, for example, our view of economic activities, of which we are a part. Our daily lives are dominated by mysterious forces. Such things operate behind our backs and we do not fully understand them. Like primitive peoples that worshipped inanimate objects, our world is dominated by money and commodities, which acquire seemingly extraordinary powers. No one has control over the market. And yet it dominates everyone.

This situation did not always exist. Under feudal society, for instance, social relations were starker and more transparent. They were based on social obligations, which in turn were based on a hierarchy of land ownership. Everyone had and knew their place. Society was socially static.

But the capitalists ruthlessly put an end to feudalism and its ways and established their own rule.

> "The bourgeoisie, wherever it got the upper hand, has put an end to all feudal, patriarchal, idyllic relations," state Marx and Engels in the *Communist Manifesto*. "It has pitilessly torn asunder the motley feudal ties that bound man to his 'natural superiors', and has left remaining no other nexus between man and man than naked self-interest, than callous 'cash payment'."

Capitalism revolutionises the productive forces in comparison to past societies, but brings with it its own laws and contradictions. The rising capitalist class dispossessed the peasants of their land and their independent means of living and turned them into wage labourers. They monopolised the means of production and forced the former serfs, the propertyless workers, to work for the new men of property. This new class division was the outcome of the new social order. This is what Marx described as the period of "primitive accumulation", whereby capitalism came into being "dripping with blood from every pore". Through this brutal process emerged the working class and the newly-enriched capitalist class, with their own separate class interests. The capitalists, the dominant class, ruthlessly exploited the workers, from which they derived surplus value, their wealth and economic power.

Every class society developed its own exploiting classes, namely, slave owners, feudal landlords and capitalists. Under slave society, the producers were the property of slave owners. Under feudalism, the land, to which the serfs were tied, the most important factor in an agricultural society, is owned by the feudal lords. Under capitalism, the machines and factories, the means of production, are privately owned by the capitalists, while the propertyless workers are forced to sell themselves – or, more correctly, their labour power – in order to survive.

Where production for exchange has developed and a wide range of goods are produced, a division of labour arises. Although production is common to all forms of society, production for exchange is not. In peasant societies, people live off the crops they produce, and exchange plays no role. Under feudalism, the lords simply expropriated the surplus production of the serfs who worked on their lands. Under capitalism, production for exchange becomes the dominant form.

To underline the difference between production in general and production for exchange, Marx uses the distinctive terms of use-value and exchange-value. The expression value has two senses. One is a use-value, which is something that satisfies a human want. It has the quality of being useful. A mobile phone is a use-value in that it is a device that allows us to talk to other phone users. However, a use-value need not be a physical thing. Singing has a use-value, providing someone with enjoyment; but when finished, nothing tangible remains. Again, not all use-values are products of human labour. Air is a use-value, as if it cannot be inhaled then people will die; but no labour is involved in its production. However, almost all products of human labour are nevertheless use-values.

Second is an exchange-value, which reflects the value of a commodity when one commodity is exchanged for another. So many pairs of shoes can be exchanged for so many pairs of trousers. A commodity is a thing that is produced for sale. It is a use-value that also has an exchange-value, namely something that can be sold on the market. The seller of commodities is only interested in exchange-value. They are interested in the price it will fetch and nothing more. The buyer, on the other hand, is interested in the use-value (what use something has) and also how much it costs. The exchange-value of a commodity is determined by its value.

These dual characteristics of a commodity – use-value and exchange-value – are intertwined. If a commodity that has been produced has no use to anyone, then nobody will buy it and it cannot be exchanged. In such a situation, exchange-value becomes meaningless. The commodity, therefore, contains useless labour.

It was the job of Marx to understand these relationships. Through this understanding he was able to reveal how the exploitation of the working class under capitalism occurs. He was able to do this by developing the labour theory of value, which became the cornerstone not only of early bourgeois political economists, such as Adam Smith and David Ricardo, but also of Marxist economics.

The basis of this theory is straight forward enough. The primary argument is that labour is the source of all value. Human beings can only live and satisfy their basic needs through labour, the production of use-values. We need to work in order to survive. Of course, this can also take the form of an exploiting class living off the labour of others, as under capitalism. Therefore, without labour we would all perish. "Every child knows that any nation that stopped working, not for a year, but let us say, just for a few weeks, would perish," wrote Marx.

Prior to the development of capitalism, the majority of production was for personal consumption. Peasants tended their crops and made the things they needed. Any small surpluses were sold at the local market. But this was a secondary thing. However, as the market becomes dominant, most producers create commodities not for themselves but for others, namely for exchange. Here then lies the embryo of modern capitalist economic relations. Everyone becomes dependent on everyone else due to the social division of labour, i.e., because everyone needs the products produced by others. Exchange is the social tie between persons. This is the basis of generalised commodity production. It means the mass production of exchange-values.

The exchange of commodities is based on an exchange of equivalents. One thing is exchanged for something else of equal value. While some merchants buy cheap and sell dear, this is only a form of swings and roundabouts. One seller's gain is another buyer's loss, and vice versa. Society as a whole does not benefit from this; it merely distributes what is. Nevertheless, from barter onwards, there is a striving to exchange a certain quantity of a product for a certain quantity of another, but based on an exchange of equivalents.

Commodities, as we explained, are things that are produced for exchange. The question arises: what is being exchanged exactly? Things are so different and have different uses, so what have they all in common? What allows them to be compared, one with another?

This common feature is clearly not weight, colour, size, or any other physical quality, which all vary considerably between one commodity and another. A pair of shoes is very different from a pair of trousers. In exchange, what they have in common is that they are all products of human labour.

"Nature builds no machines, no locomotives, railways, electric telegraphs, self-acting mules, etc. These are products of human industry," explained Marx. Nature provides the materials, but it is labour that fashions them into use-values and values. Nature provides us with materials for free, without any value. It is human labour, through the expenditure of time and effort that serves to create values.

As a consequence, through exchange, so much generalised labour in one commodity can be compared with so much generalised labour in another. In exchange, so many watches are traded for so many pairs of shoes, depending on the quantity of labour-time involved in their production. Commodities can therefore be regarded in exchange as a certain quantity of condensed labour-time. The expenditure of human effort is the real cost involved in production.

Even the early bourgeois economists accepted this principle. It was in *The Wealth of Nations* by Adam Smith that Marx first came across the classical definition of value which he copied down word for word in his notebook: "It was not by gold or by silver, but by labour, that all the wealth of the world was originally purchased; and its value, to those who possess it, is precisely equal to the quantity of labour which it can enable them to purchase or command."

Marx discovered however an important truth in that value is a relationship between persons, a social relationship. However, under capitalism this appears in a "fantastic form" as a relation between things. It is people alone, with their own interests, who engage in this exchange, using inanimate objects for sale, not the other way round. Commodities do not take themselves to market.

We must see beyond the appearance of things to understand the real relationships that exist below the surface. The laws that govern capitalism operate behind the backs of society. It is the aim of Marxism, a genuine science, to discover these underlying relationships and laws.

Socially necessary labour time

Value, in the Marxist sense, appears a rather strange thing. It is neither a natural nor physical quality of the commodity. As such, value cannot be seen even with a powerful microscope. Neither can it be touched or smelled, as it has no physical presence. But exchange-value (or just "value") certainly exists, just like gravity, and is not an arbitrary thing.

As Marx explained, value is a definite social quality and only appears when exchange takes place between commodities. In exchange, a certain quantity of generalised labour changes hands through the exchange of values. In exchange, the work of say the tailor or builder are made equivalent. The respective forms of labour are disregarded and their products are all reduced to generalised simple labour. All labour, whether it is simple, unskilled, semi-skilled or skilled labour is reduced in exchange to quantities of average labour, where skilled labour becomes simply a multiple of unskilled labour. As a social relation, value is expressed as a relationship between the labour of the different producers. Value is therefore the result not of a particular form of labour, but of abstract human labour, or labour in general.

Capitalists will not sell things at their cost value. They are looking for profit. In the process of production labour alone produces value. Machines do not create value but simply transfer their own value bit by bit to the new commodities through wear and tear or depreciation. Machines, in any case, have to be put to use by workers, otherwise standing alone they produce nothing. Raw materials, likewise, are used up in the process and simply transfer their value to the new products. In other words, a tailor adds value to that value transferred from the materials on which he is working by applying labour through cutting and sewing.

The cost of a house, for example, will be made up from the cost of materials needed to build it: bricks, cement, wood, plaster, etc., and the labour of the workers involved. What determines their price? The bricks, wood, cement, etc., were all produced by human labour. Therefore costs can be reduced to quantities of labour-time involved in their production. Therefore, prices are determined by production costs, namely the labour-time required to produce them. This is a combination of past and present labour (dead and living labour, as Marx called it).

More correctly, the value of a commodity is measured not by labour-time as such, but by the amount of socially necessary labour-time invested in its production. Marx made this vital distinction between "labour-time" and "socially necessary labour-time". Value is not simply equal to the amount of labour involve in production, as a lazy or inefficient worker would then be the source of much greater values, having spent more time in producing things.

Clearly this is false. Value is produced by "socially necessary" labour, namely the average labour used to produce goods under average social conditions and under the existing level of technique. Whether a commodity contains socially necessary labour or not will be revealed in exchange as commodities are sold or rejected in the market place.

If it takes longer to produce a certain commodity than the average time, then this excess labour-time is useless labour. In the market, such "high value" (over-priced) commodities will not find a buyer. All those commodities made at a cost higher than the social average will remain unsold or will have to be sold at a loss by the capitalist. Our capitalists employing unproductive (wasted) labour will soon find themselves driven out of business, unable to sell their goods at the "going rate". Prices will tend to reflect the "socially-necessary" time spent on production.

Profits and Productivity

The drive of the capitalists is to make money. When a capitalist introduces new production techniques and produces commodities below the costs of production, then he will be able to sell more goods more cheaply and make super profits -- that is until everyone else follows suit and also introduces the new technique. Once this happens, and the new level of technique becomes the average, the price falls to a new level to correspond with the new "socially necessary" labour-time. Each commodity now takes less time to produce and therefore contains less value than before, thereby effectively reducing its cost and its price. Of course, socially necessary labour-time is always changing with the constant changes in technique. However, there exists a general average standard at any one point, which is in turn superseded in a never-ending process of technical advance.

Capitalism is an anarchic system. There is no planning whatsoever once the goods enter the market. Here the blind forces of the market dominate. If a capitalist produces 1,000 beds for sale at £100 each but finds other capitalists, more than usual, have done the same, he will fear that not all his beds will be sold. He then reduces his price to undermine his competitors, but the others follow suit. With prices falling, people who did not intend to buy, now become interested. As the price falls, demand increases. In this case, either some beds will remain unsold or the price of each bed will be lower than usual. Instead of making £100,000, as expected, he has to settle for say £70,000.

However, the capitalists making wardrobes have fared better. There were fewer sellers, but many people who were interested in buying wardrobes. The wardrobes that were normally selling for £200 were being lapped up. The capitalists then raised their prices. As this happens, fewer people buy the wardrobes. There is a limit to which the prices can be raised if they are all to be sold. The price rose to £300. At the end of the day, our capitalist sold all this wares and made £150,000 from the sales.

The capitalists making beds saw the profits being made by those making wardrobes. In the end, more and more began to switch their production to more profitable wardrobe production, rather than making beds.

In other words, capital flows to those sectors of the economy that offers the highest rates of return. But as new capacity comes on stream the production of wardrobes increases and the price of wardrobes falls (as well as the profits). As a consequence, capital then seeks out other areas of higher rates of profit, possibly in bed production, which now experiences shortages and thus a rise in the price of beds. As one opportunity opens up, another one closes. This results in a new division of labour in society, reflecting the changes in demand and prices.

While the value of a commodity, based upon the socially necessary labour-time needed for its production, is not immediately visible, prices certainly are. Walk into any shop and all the goods have price tags. While commodities of equal value tend to have equal exchange-values and prices, this is not always the case. In fact, in most cases they don't. Indeed, the law of value would not operate unless prices did not differ from values. A new division of labour and allocation of resources arises from prices rising above or falling below values in response to changes in the supply and demand for particular goods.

So prices do not on all occasions reflect values, but tend to orbit around the value of a commodity. This fluctuation of prices can be compared to sea-levels. While the tide ebbs and flows, it nevertheless has a certain reference point, a certain average level, around which the sea rises and falls. The variation arises from the fact that the sea is in constant motion, and affected by gravitational pull. Nevertheless, there is a certain level, the sea-level, around which these ebbs and flows take place.

In regard to the economy, whatever the degree of divergence individually, the sum of all prices is equal to the sum of all values, "for in the final reckoning only the values that have been created by human labour are at the disposal of society," explained Trotsky, "and prices cannot break through this limitation, including even the monopoly prices of trusts; where labour has created no new value, there even Rockefeller can get nothing."

Through this means, the law of value determines the ratios of commodities that need to be produced and the distribution of labour power throughout the various sectors of the economy. This demonstrates how the law of value operates, through price signals and market forces, as the basic regulator of the capitalist system.

It is worthwhile underlining the difference, which is often muddled, between material wealth and value. Value is a social and historical category, which is only valid as long as commodity production exists. When commodity production disappears and we have production for need, value will also disappear. This takes place under socialist society. Wealth, on the other hand, is something material, and consists of use-values, irrespective of the form of society.

All things being equal, a rise in the productivity of labour will generate a rise in the material wealth of society: more clothes, cars, TV sets, houses, etc., etc. However, the total amount of existing values may at the same time remain unchanged, provided that the quantity of labour expended is the same. If a car worker produces 100 car engines instead of 50 in the space of 8 hours, still 8 hours labour would be spent in their production. One car would now incorporate half the value or labour-time as before. Again, a favourable harvest increases the wealth of a country, but the total values represented by the harvest would remain the same if the amount of socially-necessary labour expended remained unaltered.

The bourgeois critics take delight in pointing to such apparent "contradictions" in Marx, without understanding Marx's scientific method of analysis. Incapable of answering him, they instead prefer to distort and twist everything he says. All they are interested in is the market and market relations, which constitute the surface appearances of capitalist economic relations.

The constant drive of the capitalists to keep up with "socially necessary" labour-time also explains why capitalism cannot exist without continually revolutionising the mode of production. In its turn, the introduction of machinery, together with an expansion of capital, means an increase in the productivity of labour.

"The development of capitalist production," states Marx, "makes it constantly necessary to keep increasing the amount of capital laid out in a given industrial undertaking, and competition makes the immanent laws of capitalist production to be felt by each individual capitalist, as external laws. It compels him to keep constantly extending his capital, in order to preserve it, but extend it he cannot, except by means of progressive accumulation."

Prices and Values

Marx never said that exchange-value was the only thing that determined price. He never denied the effects of supply and demand on price. Neither did he deny the existence of monopoly prices. He drew the distinction between value and price and recognised that a price tag can be applied to anything, including things that have no value whatsoever. Things, such as virgin land, can be priced and sold for enormous amounts of money. Rare works of art are sold for millions, far beyond the original intrinsic "value", due to the frenzied speculation of those with money, keen to "invest" in these unique artefacts. With supply limited to a single object, individual Rembrandt paintings can be sold for a fortune. The only thing that determines their price is the amount that the super-rich are prepared to pay. Works of art cannot be produced or reproduced, except as inferior imitations, and therefore such things are unique, one-off things. This monopoly situation has a direct bearing on their price or what people are prepared to pay. If the item is one of a kind, the restricted supply means it can attract an astronomical price.

Such examples, despite the rational explanations, have been used to attack the labour theory of value. However, these attacks are groundless.

In practice, such unique things, such as original classical paintings, lie beyond the realm of the labour theory of value, which deals with commodities that can be reproduced without limitations or restrictions. Otherwise, what we are dealing with here are monopoly prices.

Economic textbooks will tell you that all prices are determined by supply and demand. But this is only partly true. Of course, a corner shop can charge customers more for things at midnight, as either you buy or you go home empty handed. While the price of beans can rise very high for reasons of scarcity, it can only rise within limits. But whatever the cost of bread or baked beans, they will always be less than a tractor. While prices may vary due to supply and demand, they will always hover around an axis, namely the value of a commodity. That is why certain commodities, like a tin of baked beans, will always be cheaper than commodities that contain a higher labour-time expended on their production, whether it is a motor car or tractor. Increased prices will, as explained, cause capital to flow into this sector, attracted by high profits, and will increase the future production of baked beans, thereby reducing their price. Such a process takes place across the entire economy.

This demonstrates the fluctuation of market prices, but still leaves the question of what it is that lies behind these prices. For Marx, the answer is the labour theory of value. As for bourgeois economists, they simply ignore this question, as they do not want to be seen to justify such heretical ideas.

Utility theory

The Austrian School of economists was the chief artillery of the bourgeois counter-offensive against Marxism. For them, wages were simply regarded as a part of the national income, along with rent, interest and profit. Labour had no special place in production and surplus value for them did not exist. Their concept of value was not based on any objective criteria, but simply expressed a subjective choice or wishful thinking. In the words of the Reverend Archbishop Whately, "It is not that pearls fetch a high price because men have dived for them, but on the contrary, men dive for them because they fetch a high price."

In fact, the high price of pearls arises from the difficult labour involved in retrieving them, and their high value spurs people to engage in this activity. Our Archbishop is blind to the essential question: what is the value of a pearl and how is it determined? Marx explains the reason in regard to diamonds:

> "Diamonds are of very rare occurrence on the world's surface, and hence their discovery costs, on average, a great deal of labour-time. Consequently, much labour is represented in a small volume."

The same can be said of pearls.

While Marx regards value as an objective thing, the advocates of marginal utility theory regard it as a subjective question. They place the whole business on its head in an idealist fashion. This was then taken up by later economists and became the basis of modern bourgeois economics. At this point, bourgeois economics ceased to be a science. Its whole purpose was simply to justify the capitalist system.

According to them, if someone wants something badly, it has considerable utility for that person; the more he wants it, the more he is willing to pay for it. It depends on your point of view, namely how much satisfaction a person gets from consuming a certain commodity. Oddly, while it is possible to see that the same commodity has different amounts of utility for different people, it nevertheless sells in a supermarket at the same price. This means that price cannot be subjective, but must be based upon a real foundation of value. If utility is supposed to measure value, how is it that different amounts of utility are sold for the same price? They attempt to get around this contradiction by reference to the "margin", and in economic textbooks to "marginal utility". But we will leave this realm of idealist fantasy.

Labour Power and Wages

Under feudal society, the existence of exploitation is very clear for all to see. The serfs work on their own land to grow the crops for themselves and their families. They then work on the lord's land to produce a surplus that is appropriated by the lord. Both are separated by both time and place. Under slavery, surplus labour is not performed in this way. The illusion is created that the slave-owner takes everything. In fact, the slave has to eat in order to work. The slave owner must provide this. Therefore some slave labour is necessary labour (to cover their keep) while the remainder is surplus labour taken by the owner. Under capitalism, exploitation is hidden, as necessary and surplus labour are not separated in time and space. The whole process is shrouded in a veil.

But Marx shows how surplus value under capitalism is produced. He explains that the capitalist finds in the market place a particular commodity, which, unlike all other commodities, is the source of values greater than its own value. This commodity is called labour power. This labour power is the ability to work using brain and muscle. Marx defined it as the "aggregate of those mental and physical capabilities existing in a human being". The purchase and use of these "mental and physical capabilities", all the effort and strain that goes into the labouring process, when put to work by the capitalist, constitutes the exploitation of the working class. The capitalists squeeze every ounce of energy from the worker during every minute of the working day.

What is the price of labour power, or the value of wages, paid to workers? Human labour power is a commodity like any other. Like all commodities, this value is determined by the labour-time socially necessary for its production. Labour power is directly linked to the wellbeing of working people. They need food, clothing, housing, etc., to survive and be fit for work the following day. This must also include the upkeep of the family, the next generation of workers. Workers also need to be educated and trained. Therefore the value of labour power is determined by the value of the means of subsistence, namely the means by which labour power is reproduced. There is also a historical element in addition, dependent on time and place. Wages, the price of labour power, are regarded as the "going rate" for the job. However, the capitalist is interested in keeping wages as low as possible. The workers have the opposite need. Wages – the price of labour power – can therefore fluctuate to a certain extent according to the struggle of living forces, i.e., the class struggle.

After purchasing labour power for a certain wage, the capitalist proceeds to put his "hired hands" to work. While the worker has a contract to work for, say, 8 hours, he/she covers the value of their wage in perhaps only 4 hours. This initial period Marx describes as necessary labour-time. This is where the worker produces values equivalent to the value of the means of subsistence necessary for the reproduction of his/her labour power. But once having covered the value of their wage, the worker does not stop work, but continues until the end of their 8-hour shift. This extra period beyond the necessary part is called surplus labour-time and is where the worker produces surplus value for the capitalist. This 4 hour period is unpaid labour and is where capitalists' profits come from.

The value of the raw materials and the tools, etc., used up in the production of the commodity do not create new value, but simply transfer their existing value to the new product. This includes the wear and tear of the machines, which only gradually transfer their value, known as depreciation. Labour (combined with nature) is the source of all new value, including surplus value. A machine simply increases the productivity of human labour, which allows the effort of the workers to produce more in a given time. However, it is not the machine that creates the new values, but the labour of the workers.

All the existing value (from past labour) contained in the raw materials, the wear and tear, etc., is transferred to the new commodities created by the worker. This transferred value is referred to by Marx as "dead labour", as opposed to the new value that has been added, which Marx describes as "living labour". He compares it to a blood-sucking vampire. "Capital is dead labour," explains Marx, "that vampire-like, only lives by sucking living labour, and lives the more, the more labour it sucks."

The overriding driving force of capitalism is the production of surplus value. The capitalist is determined to squeeze the last drop of profit from the unpaid labour of the working class. He does this through a combination of ways: lengthening the working day; speeding up the machines; introducing labour-saving machines; rationalisation; productivity deals; new shifts; time and motion studies; lean production techniques, etc. There is a whole host of these things which workers have become very familiar with, especially over the past period of years.

The total capital invested by the capitalist was divided by Marx into two parts. The capital made up of means of production, raw materials, power, etc., is deemed constant capital, as it simply transfers its value to the new commodities. The value they impart is fixed. However, the capital represented by labour power (the cost of wages) is regarded as variable capital, as it is the source of all new additional value. The amount of value it imparts is not fixed, but expanding, thus the name variable.

Therefore, total capital can be presented as c + v, where c is the constant part and v is the variable. It follows that the total value of all commodities is made up of c + v + s, where s represents the surplus value. During the production process surplus value (s) is created. As the surplus value is "locked up" inside the commodity, the capitalist can only obtain or realise this surplus value when the commodities are sold on the market. Thus, whilst surplus value is created in production, it can only be realised in exchange, in the market place. If a commodity cannot be sold it cannot realise its surplus value and is worthless.

The capitalist class forces the working class to perform more labour than required to cover their means of subsistence, thus producing surplus value. The capitalists are constantly seeking to increase the rate of surplus value – that is, the amount of surplus value that can be produced for a given quantity of purchased labour-power. This rate of surplus value can be expressed in terms of the ratio of surplus labour to necessary labour, or s/v. In simple terms, it is the rate of exploitation of labour by capital; of the worker by the capitalist.

The capitalists squeeze increases this rate of exploitation by lengthening the working day through over-time and shift work. Many industries work on a 24 hour basis, forcing its workers to follow suit. While labour is the source of value, there are physical limits to its exploitation. A worker may be able to work 8, 10 or 12 hours a day, but they have to eat and sleep in order to be revived for the next working day. Workers also have to travel to work, which make take two hours or more on top of this. So despite the demands of capitalism for 24 hour production, there is nevertheless a barrier to the amount of surplus value that can be physically extracted in a 24-hour period. Nevertheless, the struggle to lengthen the working day is an on-going battle. Such exploitation produces, according to Marx, absolute surplus value.

Since there are limits to lengthening the working day, the capitalists revert to measures to increase the intensification of labour. New machines are introduced to speed up the production process. The continuous increase in the intensity of labour becomes the means of reproducing the value of machinery (constant capital) in the shortest possible time. Workers are forced to work harder in a shorter space of time. Marx called this the production of relative surplus value.

"There cannot be the slightest doubt that the tendency that urges capital, so soon as a prolongation of the hours of labour is once and for all forbidden, to compensate itself, by a systematic heightening of the intensity of labour, and to convert every improvement in machinery into a more perfect means of exhausting the workman, must soon lead to a state of things in which a reduction of the hours of labour will again be inevitable," states Marx.

The capitalists, however, will never shorten the working day of their own account, for they will never voluntarily renounce their surplus value. Only the struggle of the working class can hope to bring this about. It is the class struggle that decides.

Of course, the capitalists seek to conceal this system of exploitation. They maintain that they buy the workers' labour rather than the workers' labour power. But this is not the case. The capitalists would not employ workers unless they could make a profit from them, and the unpaid labour of the workers is the source of this profit. They therefore pay in wages less than the worker produces in value.

The circulation of money as capital may be described as M-C-M', where money capital is turned into commodities, which are then in turn sold for more money. This Marx calls the "general formula for capital", where M' exceeds M. The difference between M' and M, the value gained by the capitalist, is surplus value. While exploitation is transparent under feudalism, as the serf labours on the lord's land for free for so many days, under capitalism, surplus and necessary labour performed by the worker are not separated in time and space and therefore the exploitation of workers is not so obvious. The exploitation is the same, but the mode of exploitation is different.

> "The essential difference between the various economic forms of society, between, for instance, a society based on slave labour, and one based on wage labour," explained Marx, "lies only in the mode in which this surplus labour is in each case extracted from the actual producer, the labourer."

Productive and Unproductive Labour

As we can see, the production of surplus value takes place in production and not in circulation. It is through the exploitation of the working class during the production process that profit is produced. What kind of work is performed is irrelevant. Marx explains that the capitalist is not interested whatsoever in the particular use-values created in the production process. Whether they produce pencils, shoes, motor cars or luxury yachts is irrelevant. These are simply a means to an end for the capitalist and nothing more. The capitalists are interested only in the exchange-value, and thereby the surplus value, which they will realise once the commodity has been sold. The whole basis of capitalist production is the production of surplus value. Marx therefore concludes that under the profit system: "Only labour which produces surplus value is productive labour."

Whether workers produce tangible things or not is also unimportant, as long as by their labour they produce surplus value. "A writer is a productive labourer not in so far as he produces ideas, but in so far as he enriches the publisher who publishes his works, or if he is a wage labourer for a capitalist," explains Marx.

Surplus value can arise from a service of some kind, depending on how it is exploited. A doctor or nurse working for a profit-making private clinic, which does not produce a material thing as such, but a service, nevertheless produces surplus value. The opera singer will produce surplus value for the theatre owner assuming the singer is only paid the value of their labour power. The earnings taken from ticket sales to watch the performance will be greater than the wages to the performers. In this case, the singer will be deemed "productive" by capitalism. It makes no difference whether the product lasts for a few seconds or not.

Money and Credit

With the development of exchange and trade, a special commodity emerges, namely money, to facilitate this process. At any given time, a certain quantity of money is required to circulate the commodities produced. Here we see the importance of money, which Marx calls the "universal equivalent". Although the value of commodities is determined by their labour-time, we price them in terms of money. Price is simply exchange-value expressed in monetary terms.

Money arises historically and has taken many forms: slaves, cattle, precious metals. Money is clearly far superior to barter, which is a primitive form of exchange. The universal equivalent – money – can easily be used to exchange one commodity for another. In the past, gold and silver were used as money. Of course, gold and silver also have value, which, like all commodities, is determined by the amount of labour socially necessary for their production. Money (or currency) became increasingly expressed in terms of precious metals: copper, bronze, silver and gold. It makes possible the exchange or circulation of commodities. When money was gold coin, the British government issued gold sovereigns with a nominal value of one pound sterling.

Money is a measure of value, where commodities are expressed in terms of a quantity or certain weight of the precious metal. It becomes a universal means of payment. It can be accumulated, an index of the wealth of individuals, as well as being a reserve or store of value. Gold has historically stood out as the universal commodity – far easier to handle, carry and store, as well as being divisible and durable.

In more recent times, money has been represented by paper currencies, namely promises by the central bank to pay the amount stated on its bank notes. "I promise to pay the bearer," states the currency of the Bank of England, although it has long ceased to do this. This currency is no longer backed by gold in the banks. Today, we have fiat money, which has no intrinsic value but is backed by the authority of the state. These worthless pieces of paper are only valuable as long as the state acts as guarantor. They become legal tender.

These tokens allow the owner a certain share of the wealth of society. If 10 tokens are issued equal to the size of the national cake, then you are entitled to a 10% share. Clearly, if you issue more tokens, but do not increase the size of the cake, you debase the currency.

Paper money becomes a far easier way of manipulating the currency. If two bank notes are placed in circulation where only one existed previously, then (all other things being equal) prices will double. This represents a devaluation. Governments attempted to guard against this by granting a central back the sole authority to print money. The state in the past regulated a fiduciary currency, where circulating bank notes were only covered by a proportion of bank reserves. If this is exceeded, there is a loss of value of the currency. Ultimately, gold remains the only universal equivalent on the world market. After the Second World War, the dollar was used as an international reserve currency, as this was backed by the huge gold reserves in Fort Knox. While still important, it has been undermined by the weakening of the American economy and the "floating" exchange rates introduced after the 1971 financial crisis.

Alongside money came credit. Instead of shipping large quantities of gold from one country to another in payment of goods, a credit system came into being to make such laborious and dangerous transactions unnecessary. As the 18th century economist Richard Cantillon explained: "If England owes France 100,000 ounces of silver for the balance of trade, if France owes 100,000 ounces to Holland, and Holland 100,000 to England, all these three amounts may be set off by bills of exchange between the respective Bankers of these States without any heed of sending silver on either side."

Credit becomes a very important lubricant for the development of capitalism. Without credit, the capitalists would need to keep a fund of money to fund their transactions; otherwise factories would become idle, waiting for payment at every stage of production, distribution or retail. No capitalist wants their money tied up in stock. The banks provide this credit by charging interest. This process reflects the merger of finance capital with industrial capital.

Banks hold deposits, but lend out in excess of these and only keep enough in the bank to cover normal withdrawals. For them, the less idle money in their vaults, the better it is. Their profits are simply a section of the surplus value, creamed off from production by financiers and bankers. The task of the banks and finance houses is to redistribute the surplus value created in production into their coffers. In many ways, they act like the tollgate owners of old, who were very busy making money by charging for the opening and closing of gates, but who were socially completely unproductive. This was revealed in the financial crash of 2007, when the banks over extended themselves, with lending in some cases reaching 50 times their entire reserves. While banking liquidity is subject to certain rules which require banks to keep a fixed proportion of their cash in reserves, they are able to get around this by "off balance accounting" and other methods. Shadow banking was built up to circumvent these restrictions. But as soon as there is a loss of confidence and a bank run, the whole thing collapsed and banks go bankrupt. The state has to step in to bail them out, as in the recent period.

Money in modern society is not simply notes and coin, but credit card payments and online sales, which has become a book keeping exercise.

Credit allows capitalism to go beyond its limits. This can have colossal benefits, but it can also introduce colossal dangers. Banks do not have to print money physically, but simply allocate more overdrafts. Quantitative Easing is the creation of electronic money by central banks. Speculative bubbles can be created, which produce volatility and eventually collapse. The Tulip Bubble and the South Sea Bubble are examples of such speculation. Today, we have derivatives, SIVs and CDOs and other strange creations, described by Warren Buffet as financial "weapons of mass destruction". Marx described these things as "fictitious capital", which have no real value and express no real assets. Fictitious capital nevertheless allows its owner a share of the surplus value produced by society; but unlike a factory, it exists only on paper. Marx simply explained that the capitalists were attempting to make profit less and less from real production, and instead were turning increasingly to speculation, namely the desire to make money from money, without the trouble of producing anything. Speculation, however, does not produce surplus value, but only redistributes the surplus value created in real production.

Competition and Accumulation

The economic categories used by Marx are, of course, rejected wholesale by today's bourgeois economists, whose role it is to disguise and cover up the exploitation that exists. The concepts of Marx are an anathema to them.

Through competition, the capitalist is forced to invest to produce commodities more cheaply than his rivals. In the hands of capitalists, money is accumulated to beget more money. That is its purpose. Capital is therefore a self-expanding value. Accumulation is a compelling law under capitalism. Capitalism had become "accumulation for accumulation's sake," explained Marx. Or put another way, "Production for production's sake." Those industries where the productivity of labour lags behind the average are driven out of business by those using the most up-to-date methods. In this way, the introduction of machinery increases the productivity of labour, and reduces the necessary labour-time (thereby increasing surplus labour-time). It allows those who introduce new techniques to sell their products above their individual value (the labour-time it costs to produce them) but less than the average cost, thereby gaining super profits.

The level of industry determines the proportion of the means of production used and the workers employed. In other words, the capital of a firm will correspond to a certain ratio of constant and variable capital. With increased investment, the productivity of labour grows, so that the worker produces more than before in the same space of time. This means more machinery at the elbow of the workers, and hence the more constant capital grows in relation to variable capital. This is an inevitable development of the accumulation of capital. Marx describes this as a rising organic composition of capital, defined as c/v – the ratio between the constant capital and variable capital employed by the capitalist in the productive process.

Through competition, large capitals destroy smaller capitals, leading to a greater concentration and centralisation of wealth and industry. This process results in the development of giant corporations, with the most modern equipment and technique. Whereas in the past the chemical giant ICI would spend £2m for a plant, these days it would pay around £600m. This accumulation of capital constitutes the historic mission of capitalism to develop the productive forces. In the United States, where the process has gone furthest, 500 giant monopolies account for 73.5% of total GDP output in 2010. If these 500 corporations formed an independent country, it would be the world's second largest economy. In 2011, these 500 firms generated an all-time record of $4,824.5 billion in profits – a 16% jump from 2010. On a world scale, the 2,000 biggest companies had an income of $32 trillion: $2.4 trillion in profits, $138 trillion in assets and $38 trillion in market value, with profits rising an astonishing 67% between 2010 and 2011. The driving force of capitalist production is not the satisfaction of human need but the production of surplus value at an ever-increasing rate, a large part of which must be accumulated and incorporated into new means of production.

This drive to ever-increasing monopolisation leads, however, to a relative decrease in variable capital (labour power) to constant capital (means of production, raw materials, etc.), which results in more investment being placed at the elbow of every worker employed. This has certain adverse consequences.

Ultimately, the amount of surplus value obtained by the capitalists depends upon two things: the rate of surplus value and the number of workers employed. Clearly, the introduction of machinery tends to reduce the number of workers and therefore changes the ratio between variable and constant capital; the relationship between dead and living labour. Machinery serves to expel workers from the factories. This inevitably leads, all things being equal, to a declining rate of profit. "Hence, the application of machinery for the production of surplus value," explains Marx, "implies a contradiction which is immanent in it."

The Rate of Profit

As explained, profit comes from the variable part of capital, labour power, as the constant part of capital simply transfers its own value to the end product. With the development of capitalism, the capitalists invest greater and greater amounts of capital. But with increasing technological advance, the greater proportion goes into constant capital, and the proportion going to variable capital decreases. But as it is from the variable capital that profit is made, the result is a falling rate of profit.

While the rate of surplus value measures the ratio between the surplus value created and variable capital paid for, the rate of profit measures the ratio between the capitalist's profit and the total capital the capitalist has to pay out for production. This is considered the capitalist's rate of return.

If we take the example of an economy where the total income in a year is £50 million, this is made up of c + v + s (constant capital, variable capital and surplus value). In figure terms, this might be: c = £10 million; v = £20 million; s = £20 million. The rate of exploitation in this economy is therefore s/v or 20/20 = 100%.

However, the rate of profit is the ratio between the surplus value and the entire capital outlay: s/(c + v), 20/30, or just under 67%. This measures profitability of the capitalist's investment.

If the capitalist invests £10 million in new machines and equipment, it means that constant capital (c) has now doubled to £20 million per year. We take the rate of exploitation as constant. The rate of profit then falls: 20/40 = 50%. There has been an increase in the organic composition of capital, which brings about a fall in the rate of profit. This is a general tendency under capitalism, as the system expands and the productivity of labour grows.

At one point, Marx describes this tendency for the rate of profit to fall as "in every respect the most important law of modern political economy." He later modified this view to a law of "great importance". The emphasis clearly changed. In any case, Marx never considered this law or tendency an absolute phenomenon.

Every capitalist is striving to increase the productivity of his workforce, namely the amount produced in a given period of time. If this is so, why is there not a permanent fall in the rate of profit? How was capitalism able to get round this inherent obstacle?

> "There must be some counteracting influences at work, which cross and annul the effect of the general law, and which give it merely the characteristic of a tendency, for which reason we have referred to the fall of the general rate of profit as a tendency to fall," states Marx. (*Capital Volume III*, p227)

Marx explains that this "double-edged law" is more of a tendency, which produces its own counteracting tendencies, and under certain conditions, can even result in the rate of profit to rise.

He deals with these counteracting factors in *Chapter 14* of *Volume III* of *Capital*, where he outlines an array of factors which serves to modify this law.

These counteracting factors outlined in *Capital* include:

- The increasing intensity of exploitation

- Depression of wages below the value of labour power

- Cheapening of the elements of constant capital

- Relative over-population

- Foreign trade

- The increase of stock capital, which theoretically "may be introduced into the calculation"

Marx pointed out that the intensification of exploitation ("relative surplus value") can restore the rate of profit. We have clearly witnessed this effect in the employers' offensive over the last three decades, as all workers can testify. The capitalists have sought to increase their profit margins by squeezing every atom of surplus value from the sweat and nervous strain of the working class. Globalisation and the use of migrant labour has also been a means of driving down wage rates, which in many cases are below the value of labour power. This can also be seen in the various sweatshops that exist around the world, which produce all kinds of commodities, from shoe wear to clothing, for multinational companies. Sweated labour has been used where workers have been stripped of all rights, paid below the minimum and treated like cattle. These methods have worked hand in hand with the existence of mass unemployment, which acts as a downward pressure on wage rates.

The opening up of the former Soviet Union and China to capitalism has provided a massive boost to capitalism in the form of ever-cheapening supply of commodities, including machinery. The price of computers and its components has fallen dramatically, as well as mobile phones and other electronic equipment. Their cost of production has fallen due to the less labour-time needed for their production. This cheapening of the different elements of constant capital has again been a feature of the current period, and has helped drive up the rate of profit from historically low levels. This process has benefited from globalisation and the opening up of new markets and the increased exploitation of the old. Privatisation of state companies and utilities has again meant a bonanza for the multinational corporations and the financial giants which stride the world, squeezing out surplus value from every quarter.

Labour's share in national income has been in decline across the main capitalist economies (OECD) since 1980. The gap has been especially wide in the USA, where productivity rose by 83% between 1973 and 2007, but male median real wages increased by just 5%. The share of the US national income that goes to wages has fallen to its lowest level since records began after the Second World War. The production of relative surplus value is a process of progressively cheapening commodities, with the new commodities containing less value than before. A larger mass of use-values will be expressed in a smaller total value.

Therefore, what we are dealing with in regards to the tendency of the rate of profit to fall is only a tendency which manifests itself over the whole history of capitalist development. "The law operates therefore simply as a tendency, whose effect is decisive only under certain particular circumstances and over long periods," explains Marx. Thus, there can be long periods, even decades, where the tendency of the rate of profit to fall is cancelled out by the above counteracting tendencies. These can cut across the process and even reverse it, but not indefinitely.

In his book The Current Crisis written in 1987, Mark Glick publishes the following figures for the long-term rate of profit in the United States:

- 1899 – 22%

- 1914-18 – 18%

- 1921 – 12%

- 1929 – 17%

- 1932 – 2%

- 1939 – 7%

- 1945 – 23%

- 1948 – 17%

- 1965 – 18%

- 1983 – 10%

These figures reveal that from a broad historical point of view, while leaving aside the inevitable cyclical fluctuations, the rate of profit now is lower than it was a hundred years ago. And yet for whole periods this tendency has been reversed.

Eventually, this downward tendency will inevitably reassert itself and act as a further barrier to the development of capitalism. But the crisis of capitalism cannot be explained simply by the tendency of the rate of profit to decline. Attributing the cause of capitalist crisis to a declining rate of profit does not correspond to the theory or the facts. Rosa Luxemburg ridiculed those who believed that capitalism would collapse as soon as the rate of profit fell to zero. She poked fun at how long it would take before capitalism would collapse as a result of a falling rate of profit: "roughly until the sun burns out!"

However, the capitalists can put up with a falling rate of profit for a long time, as we have seen. What they cannot afford is when the mass of profit falls. This took place towards the end of 2008, which precipitated the biggest slump since the 1930s.

Crisis and Overproduction

In this epoch of monopoly capitalism, the laws governing the system become increasingly twisted and distorted. Monopoly does not abolish competition, but twists and mangles it. The power of the monopolies colossally distorts the market by restricting supply, as well through price fixing. While capitalism appears to be chaotic, it is not complete chaos. In fact, as Engels explained, its laws operate in and through the anarchy of production.

The capitalist system experiences periodic crises – booms and slumps. These have always been present under the capitalist system, and such crises are in fact unique to capitalism. The idea that capitalism is a system of equilibrium (and not periodic crisis), first put forward by Jean Baptiste Say ("Say's Law") and more recently connected to the "efficient market hypothesis", has been demonstrated to be utterly false. The idea that "supply creates its own demand" was – and is – simply not true. The market economy is not a self-adjusting system, as once thought. This is evident today with the existence of mass unemployment and deep-seated crisis. All attempts to abolish the boom/slump cycle have utterly failed.

Capitalism's periodic crises are crises of over-production of both consumer and capital goods for the purposes of capitalist production. This is not simply the over-production of capital, but also the over-production of commodities. One goes hand in hand with the other. Over-production arises from the contradictions of the market economy and the division of society into mutually conflicting classes. In the final analysis, the working class, the producer of all values, cannot buy back the values it produces, which at a certain point becomes a barrier to further economic development and leads to a crisis of over-production.

As Engels explained in *Anti-Dühring*:

"The enormous expansive force of modern industry, compared with what of gases is mere child's play, appears to us now as a necessity for expansion, both qualitative and quantitative, that laughs at all resistance. Such resistance is offered by consumption, by sales, by the markets for the products of modern industry. But the capacity for expansion, extensive and intensive, of the markets is primarily governed by quite different laws that work much less energetically. The extension of the markets cannot keep pace with the extension of production. The collision becomes inevitable, and as this cannot produce any real resolution as it does not break in pieces the capitalist mode of production, the collisions become periodic. Capitalist production has begotten another 'vicious circle'."

He goes on to describe a crisis, where all the laws of production and circulation are turned upside down. Money, the means of circulation, becomes now a hindrance to circulation. The factors that served to promote the boom now turned into their opposite.

"Commerce is at a standstill, the markets are glutted, products accumulate, as multitudinous as they are unsaleable, hard cash disappears, credit vanishes, factories are closed, the mass of the workers are in want of the means of subsistence, because they have produced too much of the means of subsistence; bankruptcy follows bankruptcy, execution upon execution. The stagnation lasts for years; productive forces and products are wasted and destroyed wholesale, until the accumulated mass of commodities finally filter off, more or less depreciated in value, until production and exchange gradually begin to move again… And over and over again."

The productive forces have outgrown the narrow limits of private ownership and the nation state.

"And how does the bourgeoisie get over these crisis?" ask the authors of the *Communist Manifesto*. "On the one hand by enforced destruction of a mass of productive forces; on the other, by the conquest of new markets, and by the more through exploitation of the old ones. That is to say, by paving the way for more extensive and more destructive crises and by diminishing the means whereby crises are prevented."

These lines are as fresh and relevant today as when they were first written, over 160 years ago. The ultimate cause of capitalist crisis is over-production. The working class can never buy back the total product of its labour.

The capitalists cannot simply increase wages to the level where the surplus value is eliminated, since the justification of capitalism is the maximum extraction of surplus value. Other things being equal, if the wages of the working class increase, the capitalists' profits will fall and this will cause a fall in investment. The system, however, is clearly not in a permanent state of crisis, and functions temporarily through the interaction between the two main "departments" of the economy: the production of consumer goods and the production of capital goods (the means of production). The capitalists are able to overcome the contradictions they face through investment, namely by reinvesting the surplus value extracted from the labour of the working class into new means of production and thereby creating new markets. In other words, capitalism creates its own market through investment, temporarily overcoming its contradictions.

However, there are limits to everything. This investment in turn creates greater productive capacity overall and serves to exacerbate the new crisis of over-production when it finally arrives. At a certain point, the market cannot absorb the commodities that are produced and overproduction ensues. Markets become saturated and the surplus value held within commodities cannot be realised. Factories are closed and workers are thrown out of work. There is no escape from this. In other words, this re-investment and expansion of the market only serves to create the conditions for an even deeper slump in the future.

As Marx explained:

"The ultimate reason for all real crises always remains the poverty and restricted consumption of the masses, in the face of the drive of capitalist production to develop the productive forces as if only the absolute consumption capacity of society set a limit to them."

"The conditions for immediate exploitation and for the realisation of that exploitation are not identical," explained Marx. "Not only are they separate in time and space, they are also separate in theory. The former is restricted only by the society's productive forces, the latter by the proportionality between the different branches of production and by the society's power of consumption."

We are not taking about peoples' needs in regards to consumption, but their "ability to pay". This is determined "by the power of consumption within a given framework of antagonistic conditions of distribution, which reduce the consumption of the vast majority of society to a minimum level," explains

Marx. "But the more productivity develops, the more it comes into conflict with the narrow basis on which the relations of consumption rests."

Marxism and Keynesianism

Theories of "under-consumption" are often confused with Marx's ideas. But these are not the same. While under-consumption certainly exists for the masses, as any worker can testify, it is not the direct cause of capitalist crisis. If that was the case, there would be permanent crisis from the first day of capitalism's existence. Modern "under-consumption" theory is closely identified with John Maynard Keynes, who believed that the problem of the lack of "effective" demand could be resolved by the intervention of the state. The state, through deficit financing, would plug the gap. In effect, the state would pay people to dig holes and fill them in again. These workers would then spend their wages and create new demand further down the line, thus solving the problem. But there is an inherent snag. The theory of under-consumption overlooks the basic fact that capitalist production is production for profit, and not for consumption. If there is no profit, there will be no production. The disparity between the productive capacity in the economy and the purchasing power of the masses will continue so long as there is production for profit.

Marx answered this Keynesian argument long ago.

"It is a sheer tautology to say that crises are caused by the scarcity of effective consumption, or effective consumers. The capitalist system does not know [of] any other modes of consumption than effective ones. That commodities are unsaleable means only that no effective purchasers have been found for them...

"But if one were to attempt to give this tautology the semblance of a profounder justification by saying that the working class receives too small a portion of its own product and the evil would be remedied as soon as it receives a larger share of it and its wages increase in consequence, one could only remark that crises are always prepared by precisely a period in which wages rise generally and the working class actually gets a larger share of that part of the annual product which is intended for consumption. From the point of view of these advocates of sound and 'simple' (!) common sense, such a period should rather remove the crisis."

In other words, wages tend to rise at the peak of a boom, where labour tends to be in short supply, shortly before a slump in the economy. Therefore, the immediate lack of demand, one element, cannot be considered the real cause of the crisis of over-production, as the Keynesians believe.

The whole fallacy of Keynesianism rests on the inability to understand that crisis is not something incidental or external to the workings of capitalism but springs from the inherent contradictions of capitalist production itself. While the capitalists attempt to keep wages as low as possible, they also produce as much as possible for an unknown market. This is especially the case at the height of a boom, just before the crash.

Of course, while we fight for higher wages, the idea that this will solve the crisis of capitalism is utterly false. In fact, on a capitalist basis, increased wages will simply eat into profits and push the capitalists to cut back on investment and production, thereby exacerbating the capitalist crisis. It is impossible to create demand from thin air. The laws of capitalism are based upon a system of commodity production, which includes labour power.

The illusion of "demand" management has of course a grain of truth in it, but it is entirely one-sided. It is clear that the "demand" side of capitalism in a crisis is lacking; but this is only the other side of the fact that the working class receives in wages only a part of the value that it produces. Therefore, as already underlined, it cannot afford to buy back the goods which are produced. As Marx pointed out, the problem is not why there is a crisis, but why this is not a permanent crisis. The answer to this is, as explained above, the division between two sectors: the production of consumer goods and the production of the means of production. So long as the surplus extracted from the labour of the working class is reinvested into industry, machinery and infrastructure, the system can develop, albeit preparing the way for a new, deeper crises in the future. Workers cannot buy back all of the goods they produce, and therefore re-investment of the surplus in society is the key to the continual development of capitalist economy. However, this process cannot last forever, and instead only produces further contradictions.

To call for the state to "create" demand or "reflate" the economy as a solution to capitalist crisis is also utopian. The attempt to use the printing press to "create" money, not backed by the production of more commodities, will only serve to fuel inflation and reduce workers' income. The only other way for the state to increase spending is to take in more through increased taxation. But taxation can only come from the capitalists or the working class. To tax the capitalists will mean cutting into profits, which will discourage them from investing. To tax the working class will cut into their consumption, thereby reducing demand still further. If the state resorts to borrowing, this will sooner or later need to be paid back – with interest. At the end of the day, such "solutions" simply intensify the contradictions of capitalism, not resolve them. It is a catch 22 situation for capitalism, from which there is no way out and no escape.

The abandonment of Keynesianism and the return to orthodox economics is simply moving from the frying pan into the fire. The capitalists have gone back to "sound" budgets and the unfettered rule of the market, at least in words. This has only prepared an even bigger disaster. The turn towards laissez-faire economics is a product of the impasse of capitalism and is no solution to the contradictions the ruling class faces.

The Marxist theory of crisis is based upon an analysis of insoluble contradictions: the unlimited drive to produce, which is unique to the capitalist mode of production, combined with the limited consumption of the masses arising from their social position. As a consequence, capitalism is like a man sawing away the branch on which he is sitting. Crises are endemic to the capitalist system. It simultaneously creates and destroys the market at the same time, by squeezing more and more surplus-value out of the working class, while attempting to hold down wages to the bare minimum. This in turn becomes a barrier to the expansion of the market and therefore the realisation of surplus value, as we are witnessing in this present period of permanent austerity.

Capitalism and Socialism

Capitalism is a crisis-ridden system, where the law of value asserts itself by way of crises. The contradictions, which have reached their limits, are a product of the capitalist system. Nevertheless, the system will not fall of its own volition. It will need to be overthrown by the conscious movement of the working class, the revolutionary class created in the womb of capitalism.

Capitalism, in developing the productive forces, creates the basis for a new higher form of society. This is the historical justification for class society. Private ownership and the nation state have now become a colossal barrier to the further development of the productive forces. The capitalist system has exhausted itself, as graphically illustrated in the present crisis of deepening austerity and mass unemployment.

Instead of capitalist anarchy, private ownership of the means of production will need to be abolished and replaced by a rationally planned economy. Of course, we are not in favour of taking over the small shops and small businesses, but of the giant economic levers that dominate the economy.

In order to create a unified system of credit and investment, together with the introduction of a rational plan based on our needs, it will be necessary to take over the banks and finance houses and merge them into a national credit and banking system. This is a prerequisite for democratic economic planning. This will not mean the seizure of ordinary people's bank deposits. On the contrary, a publicly-owned state bank will create much more favourable terms for small depositors than the profit-greedy private banks. In the same way, it will be able to provide cheap credit for small businesses presently crushed by the big monopolies.

The giant companies that dominate the economy will be taken over, without compensation, and run democratically under workers' control and management. The task is to reorganise the whole system of production and distribution on a more dignified and workable basis. Such resources, bequeathed by capitalism, can then be used to abolish unemployment and drastically reduced the working week. This will be accompanied by a substantial rise in living standards and will provide the means for working people to be involved in the running of society.

Under capitalism, the capitalists plan production within their factories and corporations. They would not dream of allowing blind market forces to operate within their factories. They themselves decide how best to combine workers and machines to generate the optimum results. If they allowed the market to do this, they would be driven out of business. The capitalists devise their own planning arrangements. The conscious control over economic life which will takes place under socialism begins to develop, albeit in a hierarchical and coercive form, in the capitalist factory. How different things are once you leave the factory, where nothing is planned or foreseen and everything is left to the "invisible hand"! What a contrast to the anarchy of production in relation to the capitalist economy as a whole. This alone shows how the market economy is an unnatural way to run our lives and needs to be replaced.

A nationalised economy, run under democratic workers' control and management, would mean that conscious planning and control, not market forces and the law of value, would decide the most efficient use of resources.

Given the technology that now exists, a collective, democratically and rationally planned society is entirely possible. The fact that today the mobile phone and the computer have become ubiquitous opens up possibilities for popular, democratic participation that could not have been dreamed of 50 years ago.

With new technology and automation in production, almost any job that involves sitting in front of a screen and manipulating information is either disappearing, or will do soon. Offshore workers in India are just as vulnerable as their counterparts in the west. Blue collar and white collar workers face the same bleak future under capitalism. China is the fastest growing market for robots. No human can compete with the relentless falling costs of automation. But as labour becomes "uneconomic" relative to machines, purchasing power diminishes. The capitalist system finds itself in a massive contradiction. It cannot utilise the technological, scientific, and productive potential it has brought into being.

A future of prosperity faces the human race, providing it can harness this potential. Soul-destroying work can be abolished. A vast social and cultural transformation is within our grasp. But on a capitalist basis, a nightmare is opening up. It will be a merciless race to the bottom. The task facing us is to sweep away the capitalist system. That is the only alternative.

Towards the end of the nineteenth century, Paul Lafargue, a French Marxist, wrote a pamphlet called The Right to be Lazy. It put forward the virtues of ending the drudgery of work and the need for leisure time. The ruling class have always had a monopoly over art, science, culture and government. It is time that ordinary working people had genuine access to and control over these things.

Socialism would abolish the waste, duplication and inefficiency of capitalism and do away with the anarchic free-for-all of the market. Resources, including the allocation of social labour, will take place rationally and according to social requirements. It would transform our lives and transform world in which we live in the most wondrous ways. Economic value, which is a category that belongs to commodity production, will disappears with this mode of production. As Engels correctly commented, "people will arrange everything very simply without the intervention of the much-famed 'value'." For the first time, humanity would control its own destiny.

The Living Thoughts of Karl Marx *(extract)*

By *Trotsky*

Certain of Marx's argumentations, especially in the first, the most difficult chapter, may seem to the uninitiated reader far too discursory, hair-splitting, or "metaphysical". As a matter of fact, this impression arises in consequence of the want of habit to approach overly habitual phenomena scientifically. The commodity has become such an all-pervasive, customary and familiar part of our daily existence that we, lulled to sleep, do not even attempt to consider why men relinquish important objects, needed to sustain life, in exchange for tiny discs of gold or silver that are of no earthly use whatever. The matter is not limited to the commodity. One and all of the categories (the basic concepts) of market economy seem to be accepted without analysis, as self-evident, as if they were the natural basis of human relations. Yet, while the realities of the economic process are human labour, raw materials, tools, machines, division of labour, the necessity to distribute finished products among the participants of the labour process, and the like, such categories as "commodity", "money", "wages", "capital", "profit", "tax", and the like are only semi-mystical reflections in men's heads of the various aspects of a process of economy which they do not understand and which is not under their control. To decipher them, a thoroughgoing scientific analysis is indispensable.

In the United States, where a man who owns a million is referred to as being "worth" a million, market concepts have sunk in deeper than anywhere else. Until quite recently Americans gave very little thought to the nature of economic relations. In the land of the most powerful economic system economic theory continued to be exceedingly barren. Only the present deep-going crisis of American economy has bluntly confronted public opinion with the fundamental problems of capitalist society. In any event, whoever has not overcome the habit of uncritically accepting the ready-made ideological reflections of economic development, whoever has not reasoned out, in the footsteps of Marx, the essential nature of the commodity as the basic cell of the capitalist organism, will prove to be forever incapable of scientifically comprehending the most important and the most acute manifestations of our epoch.

Marx's Method

Having established science as cognition of the objective recurrences of nature, man has tried stubbornly and persistently to exclude himself from science, reserving for himself special privileges in the shape of alleged intercourse with supersensory forces (religion), or with timeless moral precepts (idealism). Marx deprived man of these odious privileges definitely and forever, looking upon him as a natural link in the evolutionary process of material nature; upon human society as the organisation of production and distribution; upon capitalism as a stage in the development of human society.

It was not Marx's aim to discover the "eternal laws" of economy. He denied the existence of such laws. The history of the development of human society is the history of the succession of various systems of economy, each operating in accordance with its own laws. The transition from one system to another was always determined by the growth of the productive forces, i.e., of technique and the organisation of labour. Up to a certain point, social changes are quantitative in character and do not alter the foundations of society, i.e., the prevalent forms of property. But a point is reached when the matured productive forces can no longer contain themselves within the old forms of property; then follows a radical change in the social order, accompanied by shocks. The primitive commune was either superseded or supplemented by slavery; slavery was succeeded by serfdom with its feudal superstructure; the commercial development of cities brought Europe in the sixteenth century to the capitalist order, which thereupon passed through several stages. In his *Capital*, Marx does not study economy in general, but capitalist economy, which has its own specific laws. Only in passing does he refer to the other economic systems to elucidate the characteristics of capitalism.

The self-sufficient economy of the primitive peasant family has no need of a "political economy", for it is dominated on the one hand by the forces of nature and on the other by the forces of tradition. The self-contained natural economy of the Greeks or the Romans, founded on slave labour, was ruled by the will of the slave-owner, whose "plan" in turn was directly determined by the laws of nature and routine. The same might also be said about the mediaeval estate with its peasant serfs. In all these instances economic relations were clear and transparent in their primitive crudity. But the case of contemporary society is altogether different. It destroyed the old self-contained connections and the inherited modes of labour. The new economic relations have linked cities and villages, provinces and nations. Division of labour has encompassed the planet, having shattered tradition and routine, these bonds have not composed themselves to some definite plan, but rather apart from human consciousness and foresight, and it would seem as if behind the very backs of men. The interdependence of men, groups, classes, nations, which follows from division of labour, is not directed or managed by anyone. People work for each other without knowing each other, without inquiring about one another's needs, in the hope, and even with the assurance, that their relations will somehow regulate themselves. And by and large they do, or rather were wont to.

It is utterly impossible to seek the causes for the recurrences of capitalist society in the subjective consciousness – in the intentions or plans – of its members. The objective recurrences of capitalism were formulated before science began to think about them seriously. To this day the preponderant majority of men know nothing about the laws that govern capitalist economy. The whole strength of Marx's method was in his approach to economic phenomena, not from the subjective point of view of certain persons, but from the objective point of view of society as a whole, just as an experimental natural scientist approaches a beehive or an anthill.

For economic science the decisive significance is what and how people do, not what they themselves think about their actions. At the base of society is not religion and morality, but nature and labour. Marx's method is materialistic, because it proceeds from existence to consciousness, not the other way around. Marx's method is dialectic, because it regards both nature and society as they evolve, and evolution itself as the constant struggle of conflicting forces.

Marxism and Official Science

Marx had his predecessors. Classical political economy – Adam Smith, David Ricardo – reached its full bloom before capitalism had grown old, before it began to fear the morrow. Marx paid to both great classicists the perfect tribute of profound gratitude. Nevertheless the basic error of classical economics was its view of capitalism as humanity's normal existence for all time instead of merely as one historical stage in the development of society. Marx began with a criticism of that political economy, exposed its errors, as well as the contradictions of capitalism itself, and demonstrated the inevitability of its collapse. As Rosa Luxemburg has very aptly observed, Marx's economic teaching is a child of classical economics, a child whose birth cost its mother her life.

Science does not reach its goal in the hermetically sealed study of the scholar, but in flesh-and-blood society. All the interests and passions that rend society asunder, exert their influence on the development of science – especially of political economy, the science of wealth and poverty. The struggle of workers against capitalists forced the theoreticians of the bourgeoisie to turn their backs upon a scientific analysis of the system of exploitation and to busy themselves with a bare description of economic facts, a study of the economic past and, what is immeasurably worse, a downright falsification of things as they are for the purpose of justifying the capitalist regime. The economic doctrine which is nowadays taught in official institutions of learning and preached in the bourgeois press offers no dearth of important factual material, yet it is utterly incapable of encompassing the economic process as a whole and discovering its laws and perspectives, nor has it any desire to do so. Official political economy is dead. Real knowledge of capitalist society can be obtained only through Marx's *Capital*.

The Three Sources and Three Component Parts of Marxism (extract)

V I Lenin

Having recognised that the economic system is the foundation on which the political superstructure is erected, Marx devoted his greatest attention to the study of this economic system. Marx's principal work, *Capital*, is devoted to a study of the economic system of modern, i.e., capitalist, society.

Classical political economy, before Marx, evolved in England, the most developed of the capitalist countries. Adam Smith and David Ricardo, by their investigations of the economic system, laid the foundations of the labour theory of value. Marx continued their work; he provided a proof of the theory and developed it consistently. He showed that the value of every commodity is determined by the quantity of socially necessary labour time spent on its production.

Where the bourgeois economists saw a relation between things (the exchange of one commodity for another) Marx revealed a relation between people. The exchange of commodities expresses the connection between individual producers through the market. Money signifies that the connection is becoming closer and closer, inseparably uniting the entire economic life of the individual producers into one whole. Capital signifies a further development of this connection: man's labour-power becomes a commodity. The wage-worker sells his labour-power to the owner of land, factories and instruments of labour. The worker spends one part of the day covering the cost of maintaining himself and his family (wages), while the other part of the day he works without remuneration, creating for the capitalist surplus-value, the source of profit, the source of the wealth of the capitalist class.

The doctrine of surplus-value is the corner-stone of Marx's economic theory.

Capital, created by the labour of the worker, crushes the worker, ruining small proprietors and creating an army of unemployed. In industry, the victory of large-scale production is immediately apparent, but the same phenomenon is also to be observed in agriculture, where the superiority of large-scale capitalist agriculture is enhanced, the use of machinery increases and the peasant economy, trapped by money-capital, declines and falls into ruin under the burden of its backward technique. The decline of small-scale production assumes different forms in agriculture, but the decline itself is an indisputable fact.

By destroying small-scale production, capital leads to an increase in productivity of labour and to the creation of a monopoly position for the associations of big capitalists. Production itself becomes more and more social – hundreds of thousands and millions of workers become bound together in a regular economic organism – but the product of this collective labour is appropriated by a handful of capitalists. Anarchy of production, crises, the furious chase after markets and the insecurity of existence of the mass of the population are intensified.

By increasing the dependence of the workers on capital, the capitalist system creates the great power of united labour.

Marx traced the development of capitalism from embryonic commodity economy, from simple exchange, to its highest forms, to large-scale production.

And the experience of all capitalist countries, old and new, year by year demonstrates clearly the truth of this Marxian doctrine to increasing numbers of workers.

Capitalism has triumphed all over the world, but this triumph is only the prelude to the triumph of labour over capital.

Questions on Marxist economics

1. What is primitive accumulation?
2. Explain the difference between use-value and exchange-value.
3. What is a commodity?
4. Describe the labour theory of value.
5. How did Marx develop upon it?
6. What is socially necessary labour time?
7. What governs the price of commodities?
8. What is the 'utility theory of value' and how is it flawed?
9. How do labour-power and wages correlate?
10. How can we define productive and unproductive labour?
11. What is constant and variable capital?
12. What is money and what is its function?
13. What is the tendency of capitalist accumulation?
14. Why is credit created?
15. How is 'under-consumption' really caused?
16. Where does surplus value come from, and why can't it arise from the circulation of capital?
17. What are absolute and relative surplus value?
18. What is the fundamental cause of capitalist crisis?
19. How does the class struggle relate to Marxist economics?
20. How would a socialist planned economy function?

Suggested reading

- *Wage Labour and Capital*, Karl Marx
- *Value, Price and Profit*, Karl Marx
- *Capital Volumes I-III*, Karl Marx
- *Theories of Surplus Value Volume I-III*, Karl Marx
- *Grundrisse*, Karl Marx
- *Critique of Political Economy*, Karl Marx
- *On Capital*, Frederick Engels
- *Anti-Dühring*, Frederick Engels
- *The Three Sources and Three Component Parts of Marxism*, V I Lenin
- *Will there be a Slump?* Ted Grant
- *A Companion to Marx's Capital Volumes 1-2*, David Harvey

Titles listed above are available to buy from Wellred Books at:
www.wellredbooks.net
Wellred Books, PO Box 50525, London E14 6WG, United Kingdom
For further suggested reading on Marxist economics,
see the 'Educate Yourself' section of the *In Defence of Marxism* website
(http://www.marxist.com/educate-yourself/)

Glossary

The following glossary compiles brief definitions of the central theoretical terms employed in this work's introductory pieces on dialectical materialism; by Marx and Engels in *The Communist Manifesto* (historical materialism); and by Marx in *Capital Volume I* (**Marxist economics**). Many of these terms are used in various senses and with diverse shades of meaning. We hope, therefore, that the reader will both find this glossary useful and be aware of its limitations.

Dialectical Materialism

Dialectics: The dynamic interrelations between things that give rise to a philosophical worldview which considers everything not in static isolation from anything else but in interconnected motion, as part of a developing process.

Formal logic: A linear set of laws useful in everyday life: the law of identity; the law of non-contradiction; and the law of excluded middle. 'Lower mathematics' to the 'higher mathematics' of dialectics.

Idealism: A mode of thought which takes the subjective reality of the human mind as its starting point.

Materialism: A mode of thought which takes the objective reality of the physical world as its starting point.

Metaphysics: The sphere of concepts or objects as treated in abstraction, singularity or with isolated formulae, by the philosophical worldview which takes its name.

Negation of the negation: One of Hegel's three laws of dialectics, which expresses the direction, form and result of a dialectical process. The law determines that the "double negation", ie the overcoming of two prior stages, leads to the restoration of some elements of the first negated stage.

Punctuated equilibrium: The scientific theory of evolutionary development pioneered by Stephen Jay Gould, which suggests that rather than a linear process natural evolution is characterised dialectically by long periods of stability and sudden periods of massive transformation.

Transformation of quantity into quality: One of Hegel's three laws dialectics, which corresponds to the mechanism of a dialectical process. The law posits that with a critical quantitave accumulation comes a transformative "qualitative leap".

Unity of opposites: One of Hegel's three laws dialectics, which explains the source of a dialectical development. The law demands that it is the coming together of two counterposing objects or forces which causes a development to take place.

Historical Materialism

Absolutism: A historical phenomenon before the advance of capitalism in which the ruling monarch had absolute sovreignty over the land that they governed. Typically associated with feudal societies.

Asiatic mode of production: The economic base of the earliest-developed human societies in Egypt, Mesopotamia, the Indus Valley, China and Persia. Whilst these societies were ruled by despots and had cities inhabited by swollen bureaucratic castes, the collective ownership of the land and emphasis on agricultural production meant that they were never able to develop the productive forces to the extent of classical civilisations to the west.

Barbarism: The name given to human societies which preceded fully-formed class structures but were more advanced than primitive communist societies.

Bonapartism: Marx's term for the phenomenon of a historical figure standing above mutually antagonistic class forces during a revolutionary period, and balancing power between them. Named after Napoleon Bonaparte and his nephew, because of their respective roles in counter-revolutionary periods in France.

Bourgeoisie: The capitalist class which has historically revolutionised the means of production, which stands counterposed to and makes its wealth from the labour of the working class, or proletariat.

Bourgeois revolution: The historical event in which the capitalist class takes power from the feudal monarch and nobility, most notably in Holland, England and France.

Bureaucracy: Typically a caste within societies of various modes and levels of production, which has a privileged position of power and wealth by virtue of its role in the runnning of society.

Burgher: A member of the bourgeoisie within feudal society who could be assigned admininstrative roles in a city.

Capitalism: The system of production primarily for commodity exchange, in which workers exchange their labour-power for a wage.

Communism: A system of production without class antagonisms.

Feudalism: The system of production in which the lands of an absolute monarch are kept by landlords who force serfs to work their land.

Neolithic revolution: The historical period which saw a qualitative shift in human social development from nomadic hunter-gatherer societies to ones which became permanently settled on the basis of agricultural production.

Peasant: An agricultural labourer tied to the land on which they subsist in order to produce for a landlord.

Petite-bourgeoisie: A social class between the bourgeoisie and the working class, comprised of small-scale merchants and semi-autonomous peasantry.

Proletarian revolution: The historical event in which the working class of society overthrows capitalism and takes power into its hands.

Proletariat: The working class under capitalism, which sells its labour power for a wage in order to subsist.

Reform: A change in policy from the ruling class of a given economic system which doesn't fundamentally change the system as a whole.

Reformation: A historic revolt by the nascent bourgeoisie in Germany, leading the peasantry behind them, against the feudal tyranny of the Church.

Revolution: A historical event in which masses of people actively engage in a struggle for power over the productive forces of an economy.

Serf: A peasant necessarily bound by the feudal system.

Slavery: The system of production in which the people who produce the surplus value for society are themselves commodities to be exchanged (slaves).

Socialism: A system of production which is run and planned democratically by those who produce the wealth in society and any surplus is re-invested on the basis of need.

Marxist Economics

Absolute surplus-value: Surplus-value produced by extending the length of the working day beyond necessary labour time and thus directly augmenting surplus labour time.

Abstract labour: labour in its general or quantitative aspect as a producer of value, abstracted from its particular qualities as labour productive of a certain kind of use-values.

Capital: Value capable of self-expansion through the purchase and use of labour-power (a social relation) and the consequent production of surplus-value.

Capital accumulation: the reinvestment (or capitalization) of a portion of surplus-value in new elements of constant and variable capital, thereby increasing the scale of production; also termed 'extended reproduction' and 'concentration of capital.'

Centralisation of capital: Combination of individual capitals to form larger capitals. as in mergers and takeovers.

Collective labourer: A cooperative combination of workers, e.g., made necessary by capitalism's socialization of the labour process; under capitalism, the collective labourer includes all those agents who perform productive labour for capital including intellectual workers in the sphere of production.

Commodity: A product of human labour which is produced in order to be exchanged.

Composition of capital: The division of capital into that part which purchases material means of production (constant capital) and that part which purchases labour-power (variable capital); in terms of use-values: the 'technical composition of capital'; in value terms: the 'value composition of capital, the term 'organic composition of capital' expresses the dependence of the value composition on the technical composition.

Concrete labour: Labour as work of particular kind; labour as a creator of use-values; labour in its qualitative aspect.

Constant capital: That part of capital which purchases material means of production (raw materials, auxiliary materials, and instruments of labour); that part of advanced capital which does not expand its value in production.

exchange-value: the relative proportions in which commodities ex-change for each other on the market; an expression of their value or the form in which value is manifested.

Fetishism of commodities: The mistaken idea that the value of a commodity is an intrinsic property of the commodity as an object; the failure to understand how exchange relations are determined by social relations.

Forces of production: Include the technical division of labour, the means of production, and the knowledge and skills available to the producers; the forces of production combine with the relations of production to provide the basis for a mode of production.

Intensity of labour: The degree of effort expended in work; labour more intense than average creates more use-values, and hence more value than average in a given time.

Labour-power: Literally, the capacity for work; the commodity the labourer sells to the capitalist in exchange for wages; the use-value of labour-power is labour; its value is the value of the commodities comprising the worker's subsistence.

Labour process: The process of creating use-values; its factors include the activity of the worker, the instruments of labour, and the subject of labour.

Manufacture: That mode of production based upon a detailed division of handicraft labour within the workplace; entails the 'formal subjection' (social subordination) of labour to capital without fundamentally altering the technical basis of production.

Means of production: The material factors of the labour process, including raw materials, auxiliary materials, and instruments of labour.

mode of production: literally, 'a way of producing,' used by Marx in several senses; the strongest sense is the one that combines forces and relations of production; each mode of production (e.g., the capitalist mode of production) represents a combination of a fundamental class relation, labour process, and form of extraction of surplus labour.

Modern industry: That mode of production, specific to capitalism, which affects not only the social organization of production, but revolutionizes as well, its technical basis and, in so doing, results in the 'real subjection' of labour to capital.

Money: A commodity (typically, gold or other precious metal) which serves as a universal value equivalent and consequently as the measure of value and the medium of commodity circulation.

Necessary labour: That part of the working day during which the labourer produces value equal to the value of his labour-power, value that he realizes in his wage.

Price: The expression of value in money; sometimes the actual ex-change proportions of commodities which may depart from their values (e.g., because of supply and demand).

Primitive accumulation: The historical process of separating the independent commodity producer from the means of production; this separation ensures the existence of wage labour and therefore is a fundamental condition of capitalist production; additionally, all accumulation from outside the capitalist mode of production may be seen as primitive accumulation.

Productive labour: Under capitalism, labour which produces surplus-value for capital.

Productivity (productiveness): The quantity of use-values of a particular sort produced in a certain amount of labour time; thus the value of commodities varies inversely with the average social productivity of the labour which creates them.

Relations of production: The class relations necessitated by a particular mode of production; every mode of production combines forces and social relations of production; in the capitalist mode of production, the fundamental relation of production is the wage relation between the capitalist class and the working class.

Relative surplus population: Working-class population in excess of the needs of capital; serves to regulate wages through the supply of and demand for labour.

Relative surplus-value: Surplus-value produced as a consequence of shortening necessary labour time, for example, by decreasing the value of subsistence goods

Revenue: That portion of surplus-value which the capitalist spends for his personal consumption.

Simple commodity production: The unity of the labour process and the process of creating value; differentiated from capitalist production of commodities in that it is undertaken by independent commodity producers who exchange the products of their labour rather than their labour-power – the basis for the development of surplus-value, wage labour, is absent.

Simple reproduction: The expenditure of all of surplus-value as revenue so that there is no capital accumulation.

Socially necessary labour time: The average amount of labour expended in the production of a commodity under current conditions (including, for example, the average productivity and intensity of labour).

surplus labour: that part of the working day extending beyond necessary labour; the time during which the worker produces surplus-value for the capitalist.

Surplus-value: Value accruing to the capitalist as a consequence of the working day extending beyond necessary labour time; the rate of surplus-value, the ratio of surplus-value to variable capital (wages) or of surplus to necessary labour time, expresses the degree of exploitation of labour by capital.

use-value: the use(s) to which a commodity may be put; its utility based upon its concrete properties as an object.

Value: The amount of socially necessary labour time for the production of a commodity incorporated in that commodity.

Variable capital: That portion of capital expended (in wages) for the purchase of labour-power; that part of advanced capi tal which expands its value in production.

Wage: The value of labour-power in money expressed on the surface of society as the price of labour; in real terms, the sum of commodities comprising the worker's subsistence.

For Beginners from Wellred Books

THE CLASSICS OF MARXISM
VOLUME ONE
Marx, Engels, Lenin and Trotsky

Published 2013
Paperback
225 Pages
ISBN: 978 1 900 007 49 8

Now for the first time, *The Communist Manifesto*, *Socialism: Utopian and Scientific*, *The State and Revolution*, and *The Transitional Programa*re available in a single, compact volume.

LENIN AND TROTSKY: WHAT THEY REALLY STOOD FOR
Alan Woods and Ted Grant

Published 2000
Paperback
224 Pages
ISBN: 978 8 492 183 26 5

The ideas of Lenin and Trotsky are among the most slandered and distorted in history. Originally written as a reply to Monty Johnstone, a leading theoretician of the British Communist Party, this book uncovers their real legacy.

ANTI-DÜHRING
Frederick Engels

Publication Date: 2011 Paperback
370 Pages
ISBN: 978 1 900 007 39 9

This book was highly recommended by Lenin as a "text book" of scientific socialism. It polemicises against a German revisionist Eugen Dühring and in doing so explains in the clearest fashion the revolutionary theories of Marxism

**Order online at www.wellredbooks.net
or send orders to PO Box 50525, London E14 6WG,
United Kingdom.**

Latest Titles from Wellred Books

THE REVOLUTION BETRAYED
Leon Trotsky

Publication Date: 2015
Paperback
252 Pages
ISBN: 978 1 900 007 54 2

The Revolution Betrayed is one of the most important Marxist texts of all time. It is the only serious Marxist analysis of what happened to the Russian Revolution after the death of Lenin. In this book, Trotsky provided a brilliant and profound analysis of Stalinism, which has never been improved upon, let alone superseded. With a delay of 60 years, it was completely vindicated by history.

MARXISM AND ANARCHISM
Engels, Lenin, Plekhanov and others

Publication Date: 2015
Paperback
372 Pages
ISBN: 978 1 900 007 53 5

This collection of classic and contemporary writings helps to clarify the Marxist perspective on Anarchist theory and practice, and the need for a revolutionary party.

GERMANY: FROM REVOLUTION TO COUNTER-REVOLUTION
Rob Sewell

Published 2014
Paperback
142 Pages
ISBN: 978 1 900 007 51 1

From 1918 to 1933 revolution and counter-revolution followed hot on each others' heels. The barbarity of the Nazis is well-documented. Rob Sewell gives a picture of the less well-known, tumultuous events that preceded Hitler's rise to power.

More Titles

Bolshevism: The Road to Revolution

by Alan Woods

Ted Grant Writings: Volumes 1-2

by Ted Grant

Reason in Revolt

by Alan Woods and Ted Grant

Reformism and Revolution

by Alan Woods

Kashmir's Ordeal

by Lal Khan

Dialectics of Nature

by Frederick Engels

Coming Soon

Ted Grant Writings: Volume Three

by Ted Grant

The Classics of Marxism Volume Two

by Marx, Engels, Lenin and Trotsky

Trotsky, Mao and the Permanent Revolution in China

by John Peter Roberts

Stalin: An Appraisal of the Man and His Influence

by Leon Trotsky

Ireland: Republicanism and Revolution

by Alan Woods